Primary
Teaching Assistants:
Curriculum in Context

Edited by Carrie Cable and Ian Eyres

 David Fulton Publishers in association with  The Open University

David Fulton Publishers Ltd
The Chiswick Centre, 414 Chiswick High Road, London W4 5TF

www.fultonpublishers.co.uk
www.onestopeducation.co.uk

First Published in Great Britain by David Fulton Publishers 2005
Reprinted 2006

10 9 8 7 6 5 4 3 2

David Fulton Publishers is a division of Granada Learning Limited,
part of ITV plc.

British Library Cataloguing in Publication Data
A catalogue record for this book is available from the British Library.

ISBN 1 85346 9785

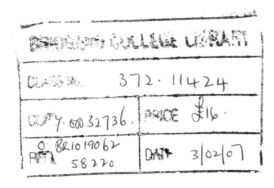

Typeset by Refinecatch, Suffolk
Printed and bound in Great Britain

Contents

Acknowledgements

We wish to thank those who have written chapters for this Reader or who have given their permission for us to edit and reprint writing from other publications. Special thanks to Katy Thomas and Liz May for their preparation of the final manuscript for handover to the publishers and to Kathy Simms for her invaluable secretarial and administrative support. Thanks to Roger Hancock for his advice, encouragement and involvement with some of the selected pieces. Grateful acknowledgement is made to the following sources for permission to reproduce material in this book. Every attempt has been made to contact the copyright holders of all articles reproduced in this book. If any requirements for the reproduction of these works remain unfulfilled, please contact the publisher. Those chapters not listed have been specially commissioned.

Chapter 1: Northen, S. (2003) 'Play', *Times Education Supplement*, 2nd May. Reproduced by kind permission of the author.

Chapter 2: Mercer, N., Fernandez, M., Dawes, L., Wegerif, R., and Sams, C. (2003) 'Talk about texts at the computer: using ICT to develop children's oral and literate abilities', *Reading: literacy and language*, July. Reproduced by kind permission of the UK Literacy Association.

Chapter 3: Ralston, J. (2004) 'ICT, learning and primary mathematics', *Education 3–13*. *Education 3–13* is the official journal of the Association of Primary Education – ASPE.

Chapter 4: Hall, K. (2004) 'National literacy strategy in England', *Literacy*. Article first appeared in *Literacy* journal and is reproduced with the kind permission of the UK Literacy Association.

Chapter 5: Bills, C. (2003) 'What can teachers learn from the language that children use?', *Education 3–13*, **31** (1), Stoke-on-Trent: Trentham Books.

Chapter 6: Nutbrown, C. (2001) 'Watching and learning: the tools of assessment' from *Contemporary Issues in the Early Years* by Gillian Pugh. Reproduced by kind permission of Sage Publications.

Chapter 7: Watson, J. (2001) 'Social constructivism in the classroom' in *Support for Learning: British Journal of Learning Support*, **16** (3) (August).

Chapter 8: Murphy, P. (1997) 'Constructivism and primary science', *Primary Science Review*, September/October. Reproduced with the kind permission of the author and the Association for Science Education (ASE).

Chapter 9: Kay, J. (2002) 'Supporting science in Key Stage 1' from *Teaching Assistants Handbook*. Reproduced by kind permission of Continuum Publications, New York and London.

Chapter 11: Jeffreys, B. and Woods P. (2003) 'Learning at Combes School' in: *The Creative School: A framework for success, quality and effectiveness*. Reproduced by kind permission of Routledge, London.

Chapter 13: Thomson, S. (2003) 'A well-equipped hamster cage', *Education 3–13*, **31** (2), Stoke-on-Trent: Trentham Books.

Chapter 14: Grugeon, E. (2001) 'Trainee teachers meet pocket monsters', in: Prue Goodwin (ed), *The Articulate Classroom*. Reproduced by kind permission of David Fulton Publishers, London.

Chapter 15: Burke, C. and Grosvenor, I. (2003) 'School buildings: "A safe haven and not a prison . . ." in *The School I'd Like*. Reproduced by kind permission of Routledge, London.

Chapter 17: Kenner, C., Arju, T., Gregory, E., Jessel, J., and Ruby, M. (2004) 'The role of Grandparents in Children's Learning', *Primary Practice*, **38**, Autumn. Reproduced with the kind permission of the National Primary Trust.

Chapter 18: Bastiani, J. (2000) 'Supplementary schools and their parents: an overlooked resource?', *Education Now – News and Reviews*, **29** (Autumn). Reproduced with the kind permission of Educational Heretics Press, Nottingham.

Chapter 19: Cremin, H., Thomas, G., and Vincett, K. (2004) 'Winning Teams', *Times Educational Supplement*, March. Reproduced by kind permission of the authors.

Chapter 23: Atkin, J. and Bastiani, J., (1986) 'Are They Teaching? An alternative perspective on parents as educators', *Education 3–13*, **14** (2), Stoke-on-Trent: Trentham Books.

Chapter 24: Brown, S. (2004) 'Effective Home–School Links' in *Primary Practice: The Journal of the National Primary Trust*, **37**, Summer. Reproduced with the kind permission of the National Primary Trust.

Chapter 25: Dann, R. (1996) 'Developing pupils' skills in self-assessment in the primary classroom', *Primary Practice: The Journal of the National Primary Trust*, **5**, June. Reproduced with the kind permission of the National Primary Trust.

Chapter 26: Eyres, I., Cable, C., Hancock, R., and Turner, J. (2004) ' "Whoops I forgot

David": Children's perceptions of the adults who work in their classrooms', *Early Years*, **24** (2) (September). Reproduced with the kind permission of the authors and Taylor & Francis.

Chapter 27: Atkinson, P. (2004) 'What do pupils and parents think?', *Primary Practice: the Journal of the National Primary Trust*, **36**, Spring. Reproduced with the kind permission of the National Primary Trust.

Chapter 28: Scrivener, C. (2003) 'Getting your voice heard and making a difference: using local environmental issues in a primary school as a context for action-oriented learning', *Support for Learning: The British Journal of Learning Support*, **18** (3) (August).

Chapter 29: Blackledge, A. (1999) 'Literacy, power and social justice: Bangladeshi women and their children's reading', *Primary Practice: the Journal of the National Primary Trust*, **21** (September).

Chapter 30: Williams, E. (2004) 'Social Outcasts', *Times Educational Supplement*, 8th October. Reproduced with the kind permission of the author.

Chapter 31: Pullman, P. (2005) 'Common sense has much to learn from moonshine', *Guardian*, 22nd January. Copyright Guardian Newspapers Limited 2005.

Chapter 33: Gershell, L. (2005) 'The special educational needs coordinator's role in managing teaching assistants: the Greenwich perspective', *Support for Learning: The British Journal of Learning Support*, **20**, 2. Reproduced with the kind permission of Blackwell Publishing.

Introduction

Carrie Cable and Ian Eyres

As with this book's companion volume, *Primary teaching assistants: Learners and learning*, two principles have played a role in the selection of all the chapters included: their relevance to the understandings and practices of teaching assistants in primary schools and their capacity to meet the needs of students following the Open University course E111, 'Supporting learning in primary schools'. This is a 60 point (600 hours) part-time course for teaching assistants, learning support staff and adult volunteers working in primary schools.

The role of those who work alongside teachers in the classroom has changed enormously over the past decade or so. Where there was once a clearly defined (and often vigorously defended) line between the duties of those whose job is to teach and those who 'just assist', now the working relationship is much more likely to be characterised by shared responsibility, partnership and a degree of overlap in the roles of teacher and teaching assistant. Several of the chapters that follow explore this relationship, sometimes explicitly, often implicitly.

Perhaps the most remarkable feature of the development of the teaching assistant role has been teaching assistants' increasingly active involvement in planning, teaching and assessing all aspects of the curriculum. In England the explicit inclusion of teaching assistants in both the framework and training for the National Literacy and Numeracy Strategies was in many cases important in initiating this kind of involvement, but teaching assistants support learning across a full range of curriculum subjects and contexts. The contexts in which children learn, and the curriculum (in all its senses) are the focus of this volume.

We should stress that we do not conceptualise 'curriculum' simply as a set of 'things to be taught', still less as a set of subjects. We have found it useful to think of the curriculum in terms of three distinctive aspects:

- the curriculum as *intended*
- the curriculum as *implemented*
- the curriculum as *attained.*

(Robitaille and Dirks 1982)

Working in the context of primary mathematics, Askew (1998) sees the intended curriculum as something to be found in published and official documents. In each of the four countries of the United Kingdom, the intended curriculum for primary schools is expressed in guidance documents and frameworks. It is worth noting that while these 'intentions' usually come from outside the learning context, it is a matter for teachers and teaching assistants to convert them into action, so creating the implemented curriculum. Everything teachers and teaching assistants offer children to support or influence their learning, from choosing learning objectives through creating a physical environment to ways of speaking to children, contributes to the implemented curriculum. Finally, what each individual child actually learns will be a different set of things again, and this is the 'attained curriculum'. Some of the chapters that follow will focus mainly on just one of these aspects: Cathy Nutbrown's treatment of assessment, for example, is concerned with the attained curriculum, while in Kathy Hall's interview, Stephen Anwyll gives his view of the intended curriculum for English (though he attributes many of its shortcomings to the implementation stage).

In choosing a title for this book, we felt very strongly that the word 'context' should occur alongside 'curriculum'. Of course, context is an important part of the view of curriculum outlined above, but we wanted to stress that learning always has a context, not least because of the crucial role played by teaching assistants in creating that context. An essential part of the context for learning – the reason why no two children will ever learn exactly the same thing from the same experience – is the knowledge and understandings which children bring with them from home, family, culture and elsewhere. Many of these contexts may be more familiar to teaching assistants than they are to teachers and headteachers. The situation of bilingual teaching assistants, as outlined by Carrie Cable, is an obvious illustration of this, but there are many others. Additionally, teaching assistants are often in the best position to really know the children they are working with.

In England, the recent history of the curriculum has been somewhat turbulent. As we write, it would appear that a period of intense central direction and demands for a rigidly subject-based curriculum is giving way to official encouragement (DfES 2003) for a way of working that is more contextualised and enjoyable and which allows for the fact that the same classroom experience can support a range of cross-curricular aims. We include many examples where this is the case, in particular in respect of the use of language and ICT. We also include several examples of teachers and teaching assistants taking an avowedly creative approach to teaching and learning across the curriculum.

When it comes to offering opinions about education, some voices are very loud. Loudest of all, in recent years, has been central government, but Her Majesty's Inspectorate, the press (often claiming to represent parents and the public) and employers have also been clearly heard. While some of these voices are (as is almost inevitable) included here, we have given prominence to a number of others we think are just as deserving of an audience: teaching assistants, teachers, parents, grandparents and, most importantly, children. And who better to talk about the process of writing than a highly respected writer?

Organising the chapters of this book into four sections has not been an easy task. The section headings we settled on reflect the major themes outlined above, but most chapters could easily fall under two, three or even four of the headings, and two chapters which might sit beside each other very comfortably may be found quite far apart in the list of contents. We feel this reflects the reality of teaching and learning and could only be avoided by choosing chapters which focused so tightly on particular themes that we felt they would not reflect the diversity of children's and teaching assistants' experiences. As we have argued above, for example, curriculum and context are largely indivisible, so the difference between these two sections is one of emphasis rather than substance. Students of E111, 'Supporting learning in primary schools', will find the course will provide a structure to their reading; readers wishing to research particular topics (e.g. mathematics or creativity) are advised to use the contents pages carefully and not expect to find everything they want in the same place.

We hope that you will find words in this book to encourage you to reflect on your practice, to inspire you in your support for children's learning and to support you on your professional journey.

A note on titles

We are aware of the many titles that are used to describe adults, other than qualified teachers, who provide learning support to children in schools. As the UK government has expressed its preference for the term 'teaching assistants' we have used this in the book's title. However, a variety of titles will be found within the selected chapters and this is important because it reflects the diversity of learning support roles that can be found throughout the UK.

References

Askew, M. (1998) *Teaching Primary Mathematics: A guide for newly qualified and student teachers.* London: Hodder & Stoughton.

DfES (2003) *Excellence and Enjoyment – A Strategy for Primary Schools.* London: DfES.

Robitaille, D. and Dirks, M. (1982) 'Models for the Mathematics Curriculum'. *For the Learning of Mathematics,* **2** (3), 3–21.

Section 1
Children and the curriculum

Carrie Cable and Ian Eyres

For this opening section we have selected chapters which both illustrate and raise questions about important aspects of the primary curriculum. In Chapter 1 Stephanie Northen argues that a curriculum based on formal teaching, and literacy and numeracy, fails to harness the natural impetus for learning reflected in children's learning through play, and needs to be much broader in its scope.

One reason why the curriculum can never stand still is the continuous introduction of new technology, especially Information and Communication Technology (ICT) into both everyday life and the classroom. The chapters by Neil Mercer and his colleagues (Chapter 2) and by John Ralston (Chapter 3) illustrate some of the opportunities created by ICT for learning across the curriculum, in the former case to help develop children's skills of discussion and thinking, and in the latter to support the mathematics curriculum.

The primary curriculum of all four UK countries is determined by nationally established policies and guidance, but, as Chapter 1 shows, many fundamental issues remain contested, and the official curricula themselves face regular revision. In Chapter 4, Kathy Hall interviews the last director of the National Literacy Strategy at a time when it was becoming clear that a mechanistic 'delivery model' has its limitations.

Both Chris Bills (Chapter 5) and Cathy Nutbrown (Chapter 6) consider the importance of what teachers and teaching assistants can learn from watching and listening to the children for whose learning they are responsible. Nutbrown, in particular is putting the case for placing children at the centre of the curriculum, offering learning opportunities which match their existing level of knowledge and understanding. This is essentially a *social constructivist* approach of the kind which Judith Watson outlines in Chapter 7. Many of the contributors to this book adopt a similar approach. This view of learning, where children are seen as constructing their own knowledge through interactions with peers and with adults not only capitalises on children's enthusiasm, argues Patricia Murphy (Chapter 8), but also leads to more secure scientific understandings. The two remaining chapters in this section, focusing on science, by Janet Kay (Chapter 9) and Joan Solomon with Stephen Lunn (Chapter 10), also emphasise the value of children's curiosity and excitement, with the former also outlining some of the subject knowledge essential for teachers and teaching assistants and the latter stressing the important role played by adults in helping children shape their scientific concepts.

Chapter 1

Play

Stephanie Northen

Stephanie Northen, a writer with the *Times Educational Supplement,* is concerned that children are becoming stressed by the over-emphasis on testing and the implications that this is having on their lives. English primary schools, she suggests, have pursued a pedagogy and a curriculum linked to formal learning to the detriment of both free and structured play. This, she argues, has squeezed music, art, PE, and fun out of the timetable, and this has not been in the interests of children's development or their engagement with learning. This chapter was first published as an article in 2003.

Take an unlucky five-year-old boy. At an age younger than the vast majority of children in Europe, he is plunged into full-time formal school. The building blocks and sandpits of his playgroup and nursery class have disappeared.

For the next 13 years he will be a conscript in the most tested pupil army in the world. The head of his school is not an early years specialist, but is conscious of league table scores. His teacher is under pressure to get the children reading and writing. The reception classroom environment is arid – desks, chairs, worksheets – and play becomes something that happens outside on an equally arid patch of concrete. The boy struggles to learn, finds it difficult to sit still, let alone hold a pencil. He doesn't talk much because what is there to say about worksheets? He becomes anxious and withdrawn. He doesn't like school; he would much rather be playing.

Too stressed to learn

This dismal scenario is driving a growing rebellion in English primary schools. Accounts abound of infants bored or distressed by being drilled for tests, and of music, art, PE – and fun – being squeezed out of the timetable. Exam stress is affecting more than one in two seven-year-olds, according to a survey carried out [in 2002] for the Liberal Democrats.

Some children lose their appetite, some start wetting the bed, while others become forgetful and depressed. The party's survey of 147 schools also showed that 68 per cent of teachers believe tests at such a young age are not good for pupils. A TES survey (25 April 2004) showed that one in five seven-year-olds spend so much time revising that they have less time to play with friends. By the age of 11, two-thirds show symptoms of stress as they revise for national tests.

Other research backs up the feeling that too formal too soon is counterproductive. Caroline Sharp of the National Foundation for Educational Research concluded that 'the best available evidence suggests that teaching more formal skills early in school gives children an initial academic advantage, but that this advantage is not sustained . . . an early introduction to a formal curriculum may increase anxiety and have a negative impact on children's self-esteem and motivation to learn'.

Playback time

Such alarming findings have put learning through play back on the primary agenda, to the relief of its great champions in the early years sector. In February 2004, Welsh education minister Jane Davidson proposed that Key Stage 1 be swept away and replaced by a play-based foundation phase for three to seven-year-olds. Many early years teachers in England yearn for such action, and a campaign is gathering steam, supported by the National Union of Teachers and the Liberal Democrats.

Tina Bruce, visiting professor at London Metropolitan University and author of books on young children and play, talks of a sea change supported by David Bell, the chief inspector. 'We are beginning to get some understanding that children in Key Stage 1 are often quite unhappy and we are not producing the goods at age 11 with this formal didactic transmission model approach. Children don't enjoy school in the way we know they can.'

In the early years, she says, the brain is geared up to language and play, to communication and movement. 'It is madness to sit children down at tables. It is actually stopping them from learning. Good creative writing and scientific thinking come out of first-hand experience. We are closing down learning, and the evidence is there because children at 11 are unable to write creative stories.'

Margaret Edgington, an early years consultant, petitioned MPs to protect the new play-based foundation stage for three to five-year-olds against the formality of Key Stage 1. She agrees things are moving forwards. Baseline tests of five-year-olds were abolished and progress is now assessed using the foundation 'profile'. This is built up over a year and based entirely on observation. 'More headteachers are aware of the foundation stage,' she says, 'and OfSTED is looking out for evidence of good play.'

Children need play as the route into learning until at least age seven, she says, so tests at Key Stage 1 must go and play-based learning be extended.

And if Professor Bruce had her way tests would go at Key Stage 2 as well, 'but we don't talk about that yet . . .'

Past imperfect

In 1905, a Board of Education inspector painted a grim picture of infant school life:

> Let us follow the baby of three years through part of one day of school life. He is placed on a hard wooden seat with a desk in front of him and a window behind, which is too high up. He often cannot reach the floor with his feet and in many cases has no back to lean against. He is told to fold his arms and sit quietly. He is surrounded by a large number of other babies all under similar alarming and incomprehensible conditions.
>
> . . . He usually spends the first day or two in tears . . . A blackboard has been produced and hieroglyphics are drawn upon it by the teacher. At a given signal every child in the class begins calling out the mysterious sounds: 'Letter A, letter A . . .' I have actually heard a baby class repeat one sound 120 times continuously.

Such inhumane treatment opened the door to the ideas of the great figures in the early years world: Friedrich Froebel, Maria Montessori and Jean Piaget. They stressed the importance of manipulative experiences for young children and the dangers of too early a launch into the world of symbols.

They created toys for children to use in their instructive play. 'Children must master the language of things before they master the language of words,' said Froebel, who believed youngsters must be free to follow their own interests. He was supported in the 1930s by Piaget, who argued that young children learn from their own spontaneous exploration, and that concepts such as volume and weight cannot be formally taught by adults.

A contrasting note was struck by the Russian psychologist Lev Vygotsky. Research backs his belief that infants only fully realise their abilities with the help of adults to guide them and 'model' appropriate behaviour. Vygotsky, who died in 1934, emphasised the teacher's role more than the other three educationists, who were happy to leave much of a child's learning to the child.

Free play

Piaget ruled in the child-centred 1960s and 1970s. It was accepted that the under-fives did most, if not all, their learning through freely chosen and self-directed play. The nursery teacher's role was to ensure they had appropriate toys and activities to choose from. But some were starting to question just how free 'free' play should be, sparking a debate that is still continuing. Teachers began to be encouraged to intervene in children's play and to talk to them more to develop their language.

By 2000 Margaret Hodge, then early years minister, had declared: 'I am fed up of hearing how unstructured play and free activity are all a young child needs.' The Conservatives and New Labour both set goals and targets for the under-fives. Mrs Hodge's draft proposals for nursery education drove 16 of the

Government's 18 early excellence centres to rebel. They argued, with some success, that the Government was trying to get the under-fives to do too much too soon – though, by then, most were offering their children something more complex than merely 'free' play.

Good play, bad play?

According to Margaret Edgington, many nursery staff say they believe in play, but they do not necessarily understand it. 'The open-ended nature of it, the lack of control, can leave them feeling uneasy. A piece of paper with some marks on it at least gives you some "proof" that "learning" has taken place.'

The foundation stage, introduced in 2000, emphasises learning and teaching, in that order. The children lead the way and the teaching is 'indirect'.

Professor Bruce says adults should not take over play so that it becomes overstructured. 'Then it isn't play any more. It has become an adult task.' Nevertheless, she says, 'we are not talking about no structure. The foundation stage is a highly structured approach, one that gives children the freedom to develop their own ideas.' Good teachers recognise the 'fine line' between supporting and extending play without taking control.

Sustained shared thinking

Drawing this fine line is not easy. 'It is not enough, as many early years staff believe, to create a stimulating environment and let the children play. Staff need to teach the children, which means modelling appropriate language and behaviour, sharing intelligent conversations, asking questions and using play to motivate and encourage them,' concluded researchers, in an influential report on effective pedagogy in the early years.

'It has caught the imagination of local authorities because it gives staff an idea of what early years teaching looks like,' says Professor Iram Siraj-Blatchford of the Institute of Education, who led the project with Professor Kathy Sylva of Oxford University. Play is an important medium for children, she says, and they will continue to develop if left to play in a rich environment. 'But the reality is that pre-school educators are being paid to help children move forward. While it might be all right to let more middle-class youngsters just get on with it, children who arrive with half their language skills need more support.'

Under-fives did best in terms of cognitive development in settings such as nursery schools where there was a good balance between child and adult-initiated activities, and where well-qualified staff were skilled in 'extending' or developing the children's activities. Free play was on the menu, but so were more focused group activities.

The best settings also promoted 'shared sustained thinking' between adults and children, and between the children themselves. Encouraging conversation through role-play games such as doctors and patients was one way, asking open-ended questions was another – though even in the best centres only one in 20 questions to children was open-ended.

Wales leads the way

When young children play, it is their work. This echo of Maria Montessori appears in the Welsh Assembly's consultation document on the foundation phase. Jane Davidson's drive for a more child-centred approach to three to seven-year-olds was inspired by visits to countries, including Cuba, where the early years agenda is focused on child development.

Ms Davidson says there is evidence that children need more time for well-planned play and less time sitting working at tables. Their language, creativity, self-reliance and decision-making skills are suffering. 'It is all about teaching children how to listen, how to talk, how to engage with each other, how to express emotion, how to develop confidence. It is not that we don't want any kind of structure, it's that we want the right kind.'

Summerhill

The subtleties of how best to plan and structure children's play would be anathema to the world's most famous progressive school. Summerhill, set up by A.S. Neill in 1921, is the oldest children's democracy in the world, where rules are set and reviewed weekly by pupils and staff. Lessons are optional and the pupils are free to play how they like and as much as they like. Their creative and imaginative activities are seen as an essential part of childhood, not something to be redirected or undermined by adults in pursuit of learning experiences.

That horrifies Zoe Readhead, daughter of A.S. Neill, and current principal of the Suffolk school. Her nightmare is the school inspector 'going up to children in a sandpit and saying, "Oh, that's really interesting, and how much more does that bit of sand weigh than that bit", and then telling us it's a really good learning experience, but we should be monitoring it and cataloguing it. We really don't go there. Play is for the kids, it is what they want to do and we just keep right out of it.'

Ms Readhead is well aware of the educational benefits of play. 'We have learned in 80 or so years of freedom that there are a lot more learning experiences in so-called play than the establishment imagines.' Take Warhammer, she says. This strategy war game, which involves armies, monsters, orcs and the undead, is popular with the older children. 'The kids love it and it involves strategic planning, and helps their literarcy when they read about the characters, and their fine motor skills when they paint the models. But that doesn't affect the way I feel about it. I don't think, "Oh goodie, that is going to improve so-and-so's literacy skills."'

Playing up

Teenagers need play, just as much as the under-fives. There is tremendous learning going on in a group of young people who are just 'hanging out', says Ms Readhead. 'There's interaction and personal relationships, and the exchange of information and knowledge, maybe about a film they saw last week. Even idle chat between teenagers can be a huge learning experience.'

So what happens to children who grow up free to play? Most Summerhillians go on to further study. They tend to be creative thinkers with quick minds, says Ms Readhead. They often make good entrepreneurs as well as architects, artists, professors, gardeners, carers and chefs. An ex-pupil wrote recently: 'We are the sort of people that Tony Blair would love. We're sociable, we're honest, we're law-abiding, we're not trouble-makers and we are just really good citizens.'

Zoe Readhead says the Summerhill message is again being heeded, particularly in terms of pupil power. 'There is a real swing and so much more interest,' she says. 'Summerhill raises questions that are good to be raised.'

Her view on the fear that tests at seven are stultifying children is simple: 'Well, bravo. Finally they've noticed.'

Chapter 2

Talk about texts at the computer: using ICT to develop children's oral and literate abilities

Neil Mercer, Manuel Fernandez, Lyn Dawes, Rupert Wegerif and Claire Sams

Both computers and talk have long been established as integral to the primary curriculum. Neil Mercer and his collaborators argue that there are different kinds of group talk, but one in particular, exploratory talk, has the potential both to allow groups to extend the knowledge they hold in common and to develop the psychological capabilities of individuals. They explain their method of fostering group talk, and the role played by computers as a focus for joint activity.

Introduction

In our recent and continuing research in British primary schools, computer-based collaborative activities have formed an important role in our attempts to develop children's skills in talking, writing and reasoning. The research is based on a sociocultural conception of language as a tool for collective sense-making, or 'thinking together' (Mercer 2000) and social interaction is treated as a potentially important formative influence on the development of individual, psychological capabilities (Vygotsky 1987). The research was also influenced by the pioneering work of classroom researchers Barnes and Todd (1977), who suggested that pupils engaged in joint tasks such as reading comprehension and problem solving should be encouraged to make their ideas explicit in ways that would not normally be required in 'everyday' discourse. In a more 'exploratory' mode of talk they would share relevant information, explain their opinions clearly and with justification, and examine each other's opinions and explanations critically but constructively. Barnes and Todd (1995) argued that the successful pursuit of educational activity through group work depended on this kind of communication, and on participants having a joint conception of what they are trying to achieve by it. One of our aims has been to investigate the educational benefits of encouraging and enabling children to engage in more explicit, reasoned dialogue. '

In its initial stages, our research was also strongly influenced by findings that primary school children often lacked a clear understanding of the purposes of group-based discussion activities and of how they might work effectively together in them. This might account for the fact that group work observed by researchers often seemed unproductive (Galton and Williamson 1992). One possible reason for this situation seemed to be that teachers – in all educational sectors, from primary to university level – rarely made explicit to students the purposes of classroom activities or provided guidance about what would constitute a 'good discussion', perhaps assuming that these things were self-evident (Mercer 1995; Sheeran and Barnes 1991). Having reviewed studies of group work in primary classrooms, Galton and Williamson (1992: 43) concluded: 'For successful collaboration to take place, pupils need to be taught how to collaborate so that they have a clear idea of what is expected of them.'

Ground rules for Exploratory Talk

An initial aspect of our investigation was to bring to the surface the tacit expectations or 'ground rules' about how language should be used in schools, and what children are meant to be learning to do with it. One way we did this was to ask teachers to say how they would like children to talk in joint activities – to specify the kind of features which they would use to identify a 'good discussion'. From their responses and from the results of other relevant research (such as that of Barnes and Todd 1977, 1995; Norman 1992) we attempted to define a kind of talk which would be good for solving intellectual problems and advancing understanding. Following Barnes and Todd, we called this *Exploratory Talk*. Our most recent definition of this way of communicating is as follows:

> Exploratory talk is that in which partners engage critically but constructively with each other's ideas. Relevant information is offered for joint consideration. Proposals may be challenged and counter-challenged, but if so reasons are given and alternatives are offered. Agreement is sought as a basis for joint progress. Knowledge is made publicly accountable and reasoning is visible in the talk (Mercer 2000: 98).

Our earlier observational research (as reported in Wegerif and Scrimshaw 1997) suggested that the following conditions were important for Exploratory Talk.

- Partners must *have* to talk to do the task, so their conversation is not merely an incidental accompaniment.
- Activity should be designed to encourage co-operation, rather than competition, between partners. There should normally be an expectation that partners should reach joint agreement at each decision point in a task.
- Partners should have a good, shared understanding of the point and purpose of the activity.

- Partners should have some critical understanding of how talk can be used for sharing ideas and solving problems effectively.

It is our view that the requirement that agreement should be reached means that children are more likely to consider all points of view within a group before proceeding with a task, and that members are more likely to develop a shared responsibility for their endeavours. When an activity involves the creation of a jointly authored piece of writing, the requirement that all agree on what it should include is likely to encourage children to make explicit the knowledge each of them has which is relevant to the task – which may include the results of what each has learned about creating a particular type of text. There is also empirical evidence that problem-solving activities that encourage children to reach agreement have more significant educational benefits.

Implementing the 'Thinking Together' programme

In a series of action research projects, we have worked closely with teachers to implement and evaluate the ideas described above. In summary the procedure has been as follows. Researchers first engage in professional development sessions with teachers, in which the notions of Exploratory Talk and 'ground rules' are made explicit and discussed. This way of talking is then introduced by teachers to their class, with teachers 'modelling' that kind of talk, and each class establishing its own 'customised' set of ground rules for use in its discussions (based on the teacher's awareness of the concept of Exploratory Talk). An example is provided as Figure 2.1 below. The children then pursue the rest of a specially designed programme of Thinking Together lessons, over a period of no less than ten weeks.

Our talk rules

1. Co-operate – try to get along with each other
2. Take turns to talk and to listen
3. Share your thoughts
4. Ask for reasons
5. Think together about everyone's ideas
6. Try to agree about what to do.

Figure 2.1 Ground rules for talk from one primary class

Computers as a focus for joint activity

Classroom-based observational research by ourselves and colleagues revealed that much of the interaction taking place at the computer in primary classrooms was not of any obvious educational value (Fisher 1993; Mercer 1992, 1994; Wegerif and Scrimshaw 1997). Very little Exploratory Talk was observed.

We have designed new items of software and software features specifically to encourage Exploratory Talk. We have designed classroom activities around existing software in a way intended to encourage Exploratory Talk.

The IDRF sequence and features of software design that encourage discussion

In earlier research, our colleague Eunice Fisher (1992) noted that the talk of pupils working together on tutorial software commonly had the same IRF (Initiation, Response, Feedback/Follow-up) discursive structure as most teacher–pupil dialogue (Mehan 1979; Sinclair and Coulthard 1975). We have since proposed a further possibility, the IDRF (Initiation, *Discussion*, Response, Feedback) sequence, where an element of productive talk *between pupils* is inserted into what would otherwise be a directive teaching exchange (Wegerif 1996). It is at this point that the computer provides its invaluable support for collective 'inter-thinking'. For this form of educational exchange to occur, active engagement with the software must be put on hold after the computer's 'initiation' while pupils jointly consider their next move. The interesting thing about this exchange structure is that it has the potential to combine interactive learning with directive teaching by steering peer-group activity towards appropriate curriculum goals.

We concluded from our observations that the following features of software design were beneficial:

- activities include problems which involve the rational consideration of available information, and which are sufficiently complex to benefit from being analysed through joint reflection and discussion
- problems and choices are embedded in a motivating narrative
- a clear purpose for the activity is made evident to participants and is kept in focus throughout
- on-screen prompts remind participants to talk together and encourage them to make predictions, proposals and reasons explicit
- information which can be used for reasoning about decisions is clearly presented on the screen
- instructions do not encourage rapid decision-making, competition within the group, or serial turn-taking
- unless the task is expressly concerned with writing development, responses should require simple keystroke responses rather than extensive typing (as this tends to damage the pace and continuity of discussion).

'Kate's Choice': an interactive moral tale

Using the above design principles, one member of our team (Rupert Wegerif) produced a program called *Kate's Choice*. Children are introduced to a girl called Kate, whose best friend Robert tells her a secret; he has stolen a box of chocolates from a shop near their school. He says that they are for his mother who is in hospital. Robert begs Kate not to 'tell'. She agrees, but subsequent events make it difficult for her to decide whether this promise should be kept.

Kate's Choice asks children to elaborate the perspectives and actions of characters in a fictional tale and to use their imagination to extend the narrative in new possible directions. It also foregrounds the importance of discussion and of considering other points of view in making moral decisions. The software does not simply present the story, but engages children in a structured task about it. At each stage, the children (working in groups of three) are asked to help Kate resolve her moral dilemma.

One of the main aims of the software is to stimulate talk about the conflict between personal morality (loyalty to a friend) and social morality (stealing is a crime). At each of several stages in the narrative, the children are asked to consider the relevant information at their disposal, and the points of view of each of the characters involved, before coming to a decision and proposing what should happen next. So although the content is focused on citizenship issues, success in the task involves the effective use of various kinds of language skills. Literate skills are required in reading the narrative, appreciating the perspectives of the characters involved, and projecting the narrative forward along hypothetical routes which would arise from each possible choice Kate could make; and oral skills are required in making proposals, presenting reasons, listening to the views of others and resolving different points of view. Taking a Vygotskian perspective, our hypothesis was that if children participated in the task using the appropriate 'ground rules' for talk, there would be good opportunities for them to practice these language skills and to learn new and effective ways of communicating and thinking from their partners.

Procedure and results

Through studying different groups of children working on *Kate's Choice*, we were able to assess its value for encouraging Exploratory Talk and generating a productive joint consideration of the narrative. Our analysis shows that the talk of the children in the target classes exhibited significantly more of the following features than did the talk of control groups:

- children asked each other task-focused questions
- they gave reasons to justify statements and challenges
- they considered more than one possible position before making a decision
- opinions were elicited from all members of the group
- members of a group reached agreement at each decision stage of the activity.

In contrast, the talk of control groups showed more of the following features:

- the child controlling the mouse made unilateral decisions
- the choice of the most dominant child was accepted without discussion
- arbitrary decisions were made without debating the alternatives
- children spent very little time at each decision point before moving on.

Target groups responded to the talk prompts provided by the software as an opportunity to engage with one another's ideas through Exploratory Talk. They also tended to spend much longer at each stage of the narrative as they considered the issues in more detail and made reasoned choices. There is little doubt that the target children achieved a deeper joint understanding of the moral issues embedded in the story and of alternative directions in which the narrative could be taken. We therefore concluded that the Thinking Together programme had encouraged children's more effective use of language as a tool for comprehending a narrative text and reasoning about it – and that *Kate's Choice* provided a good framework for exercising those language skills.

The following transcripts (Transcripts 1 and 2) illustrate typical differences between the discussions of the target and control class children. They both represent children dealing with the frame of *Kate's Choice* illustrated in Figure 2.1. This was an important decision point in the narrative activity and so was used to make systematic comparisons between the target and control conditions. Transcript 1 is the talk of a group from a control class.

Transcript 1: Do That

> Jared: (Reads from screen) Talk together and decide what Kate should do then click on one of the buttons.
> Tony: What should we do?
> Jared: Do that. (Jared points at the screen.)
> Tony: (Turning to call the teacher) Excuse me. (Turning back to group) We don't know what to do.
> Effie: (Clicks mouse)
> Jared: Yes we do.
> (Total time: 42 seconds)

The children in Transcript 1 did not use the narrative activity as an opportunity to 'think together'. Effie, who happened to have the mouse, decided the choice for the group. This assumption of control went unchallenged and the group moved rapidly through the task. The moral ambiguities of Kate's situation, and the ways that the character Kate might respond, were not explored. There was no explicit reasoning, and no requests for reasons to be given. Little time was spent discussing this frame or any other part of the programme.

Transcript 2 is an extract from the discussion of a target class group (who had been involved in Thinking Together lessons for several weeks at the time of the recording). [*Very obvious extended pauses are marked // and simultaneous speech is marked by square brackets at the beginning of the overlap.*]

Transcript 2: *What do you think?*

Gary:	Right we've got to talk about it. *(T looks at S.)*
Trish:	What do you think? *(T points at G.)*
Sue:	What do you think?
Gary:	I think even though he is her friend then um she shouldn't tell of him because em well she should tell of him em because was, was, if he's stealing it it's not worth having a friend that steals is it?
Trish:	No.
Sue:	Why do you think that?
Trish:	We said why//I think that one as well do you? *(T points to the screen and looks at S.)*
Gary:	I think she should tell her parents, do you? *(G looks at S.)*
Trish:	I think//I'm//I think even though he is her friend because he's stealing she should still tell her parents and her parents might give her the money and she might be able to go to the shop and give them the money.
Sue:	I think um//
Gary:	But then she's paying for the thing she stole so I think he should get the money anyway. He should have his . . .
Sue:	[I think that he should go and tell his mother.
Gary:	[. . . own money.
Trish:	Even though she has promised?
Sue:	Because he's// well you shouldn't break a promise really should you?
Gary:	What's it worth having a friend if he's going to steal?
Trish:	If he steals if you know he's stolen if she don't tell her parents then he will be getting away with it. *(T looking at S.)*
Gary:	It's not worth having a friend that steals is it?// *(3 second pause)*
Sue:	OK then. *(S puts hand on mouse.)*
Trish:	Ain't worth it is it?
Sue:	Tells her parents.
Sue:	*(Clicks mouse)*
Gary:	Yeh go on.

(Total time: 109 seconds)

In Transcript 2 – which, like Transcript 1, was quite typical of the group's discussion as a whole – the children presented their opinions in extended turns, justified their views, asked each other for their views and reasons, and challenged views with which they disagreed. The transcript illustrates how a group of children can engage in a debate about moral issues of fairness, justice, and loyalty. They took their time (there are several extended 'thinking' pauses), considering alternatives carefully before taking a shared decision. They were implementing their agreed ground rules for talk. This is not a perfect reasoned discussion; few additional reasons were given in support of the initial position taken by Gary, and it is hard to tell if Sue was persuaded by the reasoning or merely acquiesces to the strength of the majority view. The use of strategies such as asking 'What do you think?' or 'Why do you think that?' are a little formulaic. These children were in the process of learning a new way to engage with one another; their unpractised style showed through. Nevertheless, this discussion has some key features of Exploratory Talk.

It is interesting to speculate on how these two groups' discussions might inform a writing assignment based on this activity. Asked to create an ending to the narrative, or to engage in a discussion of crime in society, the members of the target group (Transcript 2) would each have some new and relevant 'common knowledge' generated by their discussion as a resource. Members of the other group, however, would not have gained such a resource from their interaction.

References

Barnes, D. and Todd, F. (1977) *Communication and Learning in Small Groups*. London: Routledge & Kegan Paul.

Barnes, D. and Todd, F. (1995) *Communication and Learning Revisited*. Portsmouth, NH: Heinemann.

Fisher, E. (1993) 'Distinctive Features of Pupil–Pupil Classroom Talk and their Relationship to Learning: How Discursive Exploration Might be Encouraged'. *Language and Education*, **7** (4) 239–57.

Galton, M. and Williamson, J. (1992) *Group Work in the Primary Classroom*. London: Routledge.

Mehan, H. (1979) *Learning Lessons: Social Organisation in the Classroom*. Cambridge, MA: Harvard University Press.

Mercer, N. (1992) 'Culture, Context, and the Construction of Knowledge in the Classroom', in: P. Light and G. Butterworth (eds), *Context and Cognition: Ways of Learning and Knowing*. Hemel Hempstead: Harvester-Wheatsheaf.

Mercer, N. (1994) 'The Quality of Talk in Children's Joint Activity at the Computer'. *Journal of Computer Assisted Learning*, **10**, 24–32.

Mercer, N. (1995) *The Guided Construction of Knowledge: Talk amongst Teachers and Learners*. Clevedon: Multilingual Matters.

Mercer, N. (2000) *Words and Minds: How we use Language to Think Together*. London: Routledge.

Norman, K. (ed) (1992) *Thinking Voices: The Work of the National Oracy Project*. London: Hodder & Stoughton.

Sinclair, J. and Coulthard, M. (1975) *Towards an Analysis of Discourse: The English used by Teachers and Pupils*. London: Oxford University Press.

Sheeran, Y. and Barnes, D. (1991) *School Writing: Discovering the Ground Rules*. Milton Keynes: Open University Press.

Vygotsky, L. (1987) 'Thinking and Speech', in: R.W. Riber and A.S. Carton (eds), *The Collected Works of L.S. Vygotsky: Volume 1: Problems of General Psychology*. New York: Plenum.

Wegerif, R. (1996) 'Collaborative Learning and Directive Software'. *Journal of Computer Assisted Learning*, **12**, 22–32.

Wegerif, R. and Scrimshaw, P. (eds) (1997) *Computers and Talk in the Primary Classroom*. Clevedon: Multilingual Matters.

Chapter 3

ICT, learning and primary mathematics

John Ralston

ICT has the capability to transform the way pupils understand and learn mathematics. When used with sensitivity and careful planning, it can act as a catalyst, contributing to a stimulating classroom climate which can bring mathematics alive. John Ralston, a lecturer at the Open University, takes a fresh and critical look at the use of ICT in mathematics teaching. He suggests that it is time to look carefully at the challenging, yet stimulating and exciting opportunities that these technologies present for teachers and teaching assistants.

Introduction

At a time when the numeracy strategy has dominated recent curriculum debate in Primary schools, teachers have been understandably reluctant to experiment with too many different approaches to mathematics teaching, outside of suggested guidelines and schemes of work. However, the emphasis on whole class teaching (in both numeracy and literacy strategies) and improved mathematics software has generated a growth in interest in the use of electronic whiteboards, data projectors and other technological aids to support classroom activities.

A techno-romantic perspective dominated the early introduction of ICT in schools, and sometimes led to scepticism about the contribution it made to mathematics teaching. This chapter takes the view that new technologies, when used with sensitivity and careful planning, can act as a catalyst, contributing to a stimulating classroom climate which can bring mathematics alive. However, there are hazards on the way; technologies are seductively diverting. As teachers and teaching assistants we need to consider carefully why and how we are using ICT. We need to have the confidence to reject its use when it is inappropriate and other approaches are better. Gaining this understanding of appropriateness takes time and requires us to experiment with the use of ICT, to take some risks in our teaching.

There have also been many obstacles to overcome, for effective ICT use; inadequate hardware resources, uncertain software and fragmented technical support dominated the use of ICT when the technology first appeared in classrooms. A degree of standardisation of hardware, the gradual implementation of broadband via National Grid for Learning initiatives, coupled with skills and curriculum-targeted professional development have moved the focus of ICT discussions in education to teaching and learning. This is a more satisfactory focus than previous deliberations about a school's ICT philosophy which frequently dwelt solely on the merits of various hardware configurations and where to put them.

It is also important to recognise that when we use the term 'ICT' we do not solely mean 'computers' but include the many devices which have emerged, following the convergence of computing, telecommunications and video-related technologies. These would encompass digital cameras, sensors, programmable toys, audio and video recorders as well as computers.

This chapter takes a fresh look at the use of ICT in mathematics teaching in primary schools, considering some of the key benefits that ICT can offer, reflecting on some of the approaches employed to exploit the potential of the technology. We begin by looking at some recent research.

ICT, learning and mathematics

The view taken is that teaching and learning is seen as essentially a social process such that the teacher can influence a child's development to cope with increasingly complex ideas. They need to be seen together:

> Teaching and learning may best be seen as two sides of the same piece of paper. We can choose to focus exclusively on one side only, but cut one and you cut the other (Merttens 2001: 12)

This chapter looks in detail at four areas in which ICT can be seen as an appropriate catalyst to enhance childrens' learning in mathematics:

- active participation
- frequent feedback and interaction
- opportunities for collaboration
- communications: interfacing with the outside world (adapted from Roschelle *et al.* 2000).

Active participation

To enhance learning, children need to be actively engaged in the learning process and the characteristics of ICT make it a particularly suitable medium for this type of learning. For example, data can be collected by children as part of a whole class experiment and the results speedily obtained and attractively presented by the children in graphical form for discussion and possible modification. Children are generally highly motivated in using ICT, encouraging their participation in learning, enabling both individual and collaborative active involvement in the process. This provides the opportunity for the teacher to exploit this enthusiasm to stimulate childrens' further learning.

When considering the different elements of a mathematics lesson; pace, know-how, investigating, conjecturing and proving, and 'struggle', Hatch (1999) promotes the idea of keeping pupils in a 'high-energy' state throughout their mathematical learning. 'Pupils in such a state will confront any problem, given to them or invented for themselves, with their previous learning in mathematics in an active and accessible state and with the assumption they have the ability to make progress' (Hatch 1999: 105).

Frequent feedback and interaction

Immediate feedback can be an invaluable incentive to encourage a child to maintain progress in learning. There are many examples that could be cited here – the use of calculators or software such as spreadsheets and tessellation programs. The most frequently quoted example, is that of the turtle.

Children can use a small programmable robot, such as a turtle, Pixie or Roamer, to move around a classroom floor or prepared surface, for a distance they have decided; then they can use the result to program another attempt. This provides the opportunity for a teacher or teaching assistant and child to work in partnership, investigating jointly situations which arise (Papert 1979).

Higgins (2001), however, highlights the complexity of feedback and the importance of ensuring it is of high quality and how it is then incorporated by the teacher into an appropriate range of learning activities. Some feedback can be unhelpful, for example, when it does not assist pupils in correcting their errors, merely giving the number of correct responses. Early computer software adopted this approach with some mathematics programs.

Opportunities for collaboration

Children need opportunities to discuss mathematics with others and so develop their abstract reasoning. Social contexts give pupils the opportunity to engage collaboratively in their learning. All UK national curricula now stress the importance of talk in mathematics learning, encouraging children to express ideas in a precise way, using technical language. ICT, when used carefully, can provide a stimulus to encourage discussion. Wegerif and Scrimshaw's 1997 study looked at the impact of different factors on the quality of children's talk around computers: type of software, interface design, role of teachers, composition of the group and the responses from children working on the computer. Adventure games, when well constructed with meaningful contexts, proved very productive in encouraging problem solving, developing children's reasoning capabilities. One concern in the design of some software, was the confusion being caused by mathematical terms being used in the program, in an unfamiliar form. For example, 'spot the difference' in one program was not understood by the pupils to mean 'subtract' (Wegerif and Scrimshaw 1997: 40). Again the role of the teacher or teaching assistant is crucial in guiding pupils and deciding when intervention is appropriate.

However, collaborative practice with ICT is not always used effectively by teachers. The IMPACT2 study, was a series of comprehensive investigations into the impact of information and communications technology (ICT) on educational attainment of ICT in education, carried out between 1999 and 2002. In the 15 case studies, the benefits of collaborative working using ICT were recognised, but not capitalised on. Teachers also described many tasks as 'collaborative' which merely involved pupils working alongside one another, rather than jointly addressing a problem (Harrison *et al.* 2002, Case studies).

Communications: interfacing with the real world

A common difficulty for many pupils learning mathematics is to transfer what has been learnt in school to real world situations. The ready availability of Internet-distributed information provides opportunities for school-based mathematical activity in a huge range of different contexts. The ease of computer communication allows authentic data to be used in school-based activities without the need for children to leave the classroom. For example, schools regularly make use of weather satellite data to enhance their work in mathematics, science and geography. In the Achilles project, Devon schools made use of authentic and regularly updated road traffic accident data, modified to remove personal identifiers, for children to analyse statistically on school computers as part of a mathematics activity and also identify issues of road safety. Many schools now chart the movement of expeditions or competitive races such as round the world yacht races, plotting progress, improving pupils' understanding of co-ordinates, mapping and different forms of representation of information.

So far we have considered a few of the ways that ICT might enhance mathematics teaching. However, many studies investigating the effectiveness of technologies in education often provide mixed results. For example, Rochelle *et al.* (2000) conducted a detailed analysis of recent major studies on the effectiveness of computers as learning tools. In one large-scale study, approaches to educational technology use showed an improvement in 8–10-year-olds' mathematical understanding, but were less effective with other ages. A further analysis of 500 research studies on computer-based instruction found generally positive effects on pupil attainment especially when the computer took on a 'tutorial' role; other computer applications, such as simulations, had very modest impact on attainment. The team found that software which encouraged in-depth mathematical reasoning, increased learning, while applications which tried to make repetitive skills practice more enjoyable actually decreased performance (Rochelle *et al.* 2000).

The research team attributed three reasons for these mixed results. Firstly, hardware and software varied considerably between the schools in the studies and was used quite differently in many of the classrooms. Secondly, there were other changes taking place at the same time within curricula, assessment and teacher professional development. Thirdly, it was difficult to separate the impact of the technology from other factors.

Levels of ICT use in mathematics

A different perspective is provided by McCormick and Scrimshaw (2001) and also Twining (2001) who have outlined three staged categories of analysing the use of ICT in the classroom, adapted here for a mathematical context:

Level 1 Where existing teaching becomes more *efficient* by using ICT in mathematics

Here the teacher or teaching assistant has the same mathematical objectives as when teaching without ICT, but makes use of ICT to achieve these more efficiently.

In an activity about measurement, the teacher is able to use a graphical program to present the results in a bar or pie chart and then discuss the implications with the class. This can be generated very quickly and efficiently and easily modified if necessary.

Level 2 Where the use of ICT extends the work of the teaching of mathematics

At this level, the possibilities of what can take place in the classroom are extended by the teacher by using ICT. This is more than simply the 'efficient' use of ICT.

Children in a rural school are taking part in a project about the cost of food. They have been collecting information about the cost of a shopping basket of bread, eggs and milk, vegetables and fruit when purchasing in a local shop. The school is twinned with another in a town area. An email is sent to children in the other school asking them to find out the cost locally of the same items. A reply is received the following day. The total costs of the shopping baskets are calculated and comparisons of prices discussed. Both schools can participate. The use of email has extended what can be achieved in the classroom.

Level 3 Where mathematics itself is transformed by the use of ICT

Here the nature of the subject itself has changed.

Being able to visualise how geometric shapes can be transformed is important in understanding ideas in geometry. Using dynamic geometry software, shapes can be changed by simply dragging a mouse. This allows pupils to see transformations which otherwise would be difficult to visualise. Similar software can be used to help explain ideas in angle work and so help children form their own mental images.

These studies illustrate the complexity of the issues surrounding the use of ICT in mathematics. As technologies become more sophisticated, so do the opportunities they provide to stimulate learning and the challenges for teachers to use them to best effect. We are just beginning to understand their likely impact in transforming subject teaching.

Challenging orthodox views

When we use ICT in mathematics, we need to try to avoid the 'solution' seeking a 'problem' model of the 1980s and 90s by using ICT for a specific purpose. How can we avoid a technology-focused perspective?

Let's look first at a parallel technology, which did undergo various transformations before appearing in schools in an electronic form: the calculator. On first reflecting about how calculators might be used in mathematics, the response is likely to be 'to add, subtract, multiply or divide numbers or find a percentage'. Now look at this description of the multiplicity of roles a calculator might play in a lesson:

- to accelerate the execution of routine computational tasks, releasing more time for conjectural thinking
- to provide valuable support for pupils who could otherwise be defeated or overwhelmed by the computational demands of a task
- to provide a neutral authority against which pupils can check their findings or test out mathematical conjectures
- to embody mathematical ideas, making them available for exploration and analysis through interaction with the machine (adapted from Ruthven 1995: 249).

It is important to look at the use of any new technologies with fresh eyes. When considering using ICT, we need to look beyond 'conventional' understanding and examine the many opportunities for using ICT creatively which might entrance children and enrich their learning. We now look at what might be described as a 'hidden feature of ICT'.

The opportunity to be a little bit wrong

Jane and David are two ten-year-olds working together on a computer in the corner of the classroom. The class has been investigating everybody's favourites: colours, books, sport, animals. They are using a simple database program and have been entering data, laboriously taking it in turn to key in the numbers.

> Teacher: *How many children prefer blue as a favourite?'*
> Jane: *26.*
> Teacher: *Are you sure, there are only 18 in the class?*
> David: *Look, you've put in 10 in that column, it should be 1.*
> Jane: *I'll change it quickly! You won't even notice. The nice thing about computers is it's easy to be a little bit wrong.*

The 'delete' button is one of the most powerful on the keyboard. Mistakes can be made to disappear as if by magic. As with computers, the opportunity to be 'a little bit wrong' in mathematics is an important idea for teachers to consider, when developing understanding of the subject for both young and old. We gain great satisfaction, when the 'correct' answer is achieved and certainly we do need to regularly verify and test pupils' facility with techniques. In a rigorously assessed curriculum, it is unsurprising that wrong answers can be difficult to contemplate, even seen as a sign that our teaching has failed. This is certainly not the case. However, it is also essential to probe and be aware of any misunderstandings or misconceptions which underpin pupils' work. A wrong answer provides a clue that can help uncover difficulties in a child's understanding of mathematics, a clue that can be followed up. A correct answer may not tell us whether the underlying concepts are fully understood.

Attempting to provide a rough estimate of an answer is often a key tactic to adopt, to show the result is of the correct magnitude, and avoid obtaining an answer which is totally unreasonable. So the fact that the use of ICT allows children to make changes easily, and be 'a little bit wrong', for example in text, a spreadsheet, a drawing, graph or a calculation and to obtain a result very speedily, is a genuine strength of computers, that teachers can exploit. It is one of the 'hidden' features of ICT.

Mathematics classrooms need to be interesting places which encourage meaningful learning, providing an atmosphere in which pupils can have the confidence to give answers, even wrong ones, but which pupils know will be listened to and not over-criticised.

Conclusion

Much of the early introduction of the use of mathematical computer software into schools, focused on what was possible, rather than what was desirable. Consequently there was an over-emphasis on sometimes quite trivial applications of mathematics which did have a use in teaching, mainly skills reinforcement, but really did not much to develop pupils' mathematical understanding, and in most cases was restricted by what the software would provide, rather than what the teacher of mathematics, or the pupils, needed.

The focus has now changed and readily available material such as dynamic geometry software can facilitate more transparent explanations of quite complex ideas and concepts.

We need also to keep in mind that just because children are performing tasks that look technologically complex it does not necessarily mean they are learning anything important:

> 'There was a tendency for the children to use the power of the technology to produce quick but meaningless graphs, which indicated they had no real grasp of the nature of the data with which they were working' – describing a classroom observation in the Primary laptop project (Ainley and Pratt 1995: 438).

ICT has the capability to transform the way pupils understand and learn mathematics. The technology can act as a 'bridge' between teaching and learning and between 'formal' and 'informal' mathematics teaching. It is time to look carefully again at the challenging, yet stimulating and exciting, opportunities that these technologies present.

References

Ainley, J. and Pratt, D. (1995) 'Integrating mathematics and technology into the Primary curriculum', in: Burton, L. and Jaworski, B. (eds), *Technology in Mathematics teaching – a bridge between teaching and learning.* Bromley, Kent: Chartwell-Bratt.

Harrison, C., Comber, C., Fisher, T., Haw, K., Lewin, C., Lunzer, E., McFarlane, A., Mavers, D., Scrimshaw, P., Somekh, B. and Watling, R. (2002) *IMPACT2: The Impact of Information Communications Technology on Pupil Learning and Attainment.* Becta: Coventry.

Hatch, G. (1999) 'Maximising energy in the learning of mathematics', in: Hoyles, C., Morgan, C. and Woodhouse, G. (eds), *Rethinking the Mathematics Curriculum.* London: Falmer, 104–17.

Higgins, S. (2001) 'Identifying feedback in mathematical activities using ICT' *Education 3–13*, March.

McCormick, R. and Scrimshaw, P. (2001) 'Information and Communications Technology, Knowledge and Pedagogy', in: *Education, Communication and Information*, **1** (1), 37–57.

Merttens, R. (2001) 'The baby with the bath water'. Mathematics Teaching, **176**, 12.

Papert, S. (1979) 'Computers in Learning', in: Dertouzos, M.L. and Moses, J. *The Computer Age: A Twenty-Year View.* Cambridge, MA: MIT Press.

Rochelle, J.M., Pea, R.D., Hoadley, C.M., Gordin, D.N., Means, B.M. (2000) 'Changing how and what children learn in school with computer based technologies'. *Children and computer technology.* **10** (2).

Ruthven, K. (1995) 'Towards considered calculator use', in: Burton, L. and Jaworski, B. (eds), *Technology in Mathematics teaching – a bridge between teaching and learning.* Bromley, Kent: Chartwell-Bratt.

Twining, P. (2001) 'Planning to use ICT in school?' *Education 3–13,* March, 9–17.

Wegerif, R. and Scrimshaw, P. (eds) (1997) *Computers and Talk in the Primary Classroom.* Clevedon: Multilingual Matters.

Chapter 4

Reflections on six years of the National Literacy Strategy

Kathy Hall

Here, Kathy Hall, a professor at the Open University, interviews Steven Anwyll, who was director of the National Literacy Strategy from 2001 until its replacement by the Primary National Strategy in 2004. Anwyll lists among the achievements of the Strategy an overall rise in standards and the development of a common language of literacy, used by all primary staff across the country. Readers who were working in English primary schools in the late 1990s may be surprised to learn of the flexibility then open to them in the implementation of the Strategy, but Anwyll takes pains to stress the importance of 'breadth and richness' in teaching literacy, and the scope for interpreting the framework creatively at school level.

KH: What do you see as the major achievements of the Strategy?

SA: One of the Strategy's big achievements has been to put literacy back right at the heart of what primary schools are about. I think possibly an underestimated impact of the Strategy has been the extent to which the framework has given teachers a common professional language. It struck me really forcibly when we did a series of conferences with headteachers from right across the country a couple of years ago. Irrespective of where you were, that common professional language provides a very powerful basis for professional development, for collaborative work, for networking, for sharing planning and resources.

If you think back to teachers' initial reaction to the framework – a Year 3 teacher would look at the Year 3 objectives and say 'that's a bit hard for our children, I don't think they can do this'. We just don't hear that now. It has actually raised expectations and it's raised attainment as a consequence. People would argue about how much it's raised attainment but I don't think anyone would dispute that the overall quality and consistency of literacy teaching has improved. The attainment of children has risen and that means the life chances of thousands of children have improved.

One of the frustrations I've always had as an adviser and an advisory teacher was that so many teachers didn't appreciate that teaching English or literacy involved considerable subject knowledge.

There was a kind of assumption that, if you could speak and read and write English, you could teach it. I think the Strategy has exposed that myth. It's said, 'look, there is substantial subject knowledge involved with effective teaching'. A huge investment in training and professional development has been made.

KH: What is your view of the notion of literacy underpinning the Strategy. How rich and balanced a view of literacy permeates the Strategy?

SA: Without doubt the conception of the Strategy involved a strong sense of the richness, the variety, the range, the engagement and the enjoyment of literacy.

Inevitably, how a national framework is then interpreted by 200,000 teachers will vary. I'm quite certain that there will be teachers who will feel that this is a framework that has been imposed on them and is restricting them.

Actually, I think the best teachers saw the framework as a very helpful way of setting out a skeletal progression. A scheme of work for English in a primary school was – and is – a very hard document to produce. It's not easy to chart progression through children's literacy development over a six or seven-year period. So, I think most teachers felt it was promoting range and variety and of course it's in the hands of teachers and schools to bring that richness and that sense of interaction with children and their lives.

Where it's being interpreted correctly, in my view, and with confidence, it's leading to greater breadth and richness, but I'm not suggesting for a minute that there aren't issues about its interpretation and that's the task that we are facing.

KH: But within the design of it do you think there is priority on the technical features at the expense of the construction of meaning?

SA: I think there is a balance there, and what we have always said is that the reason a Literacy Hour always starts with a shared text is because you start from making meaningful use of language. That's why you start from text and you work from there into the knowledge and use of language, the technical side. Currently, it is an issue of balance and it's an issue of interpretation, and I'd be concerned if teachers were getting too caught up with the technical side and losing sight of the broad aims of what language and language development are about.

KH: And in relation to that, are you concerned about the marginalisation of enjoyment, bearing in mind, for example, the PIRLS (Mullis et al. 2003) finding that England emerged relatively low in terms of positive attitudes to reading, despite overall high achievement?

SA: Without doubt there's a real issue because if we're increasing the attainment of children at the expense of their engagement and enjoyment, then we are failing to do the whole job and we have to take that seriously. I think this involves a whole set of issues there about children's interpretations of their reading, their definitions of reading and the whole change in pattern of reading on screen as opposed to reading in conventional books. It's about defining what is legitimate reading and I think some children maybe have too narrow a definition, so there are some interesting underlying questions there. We've now persuaded the government to put much more funding through the National Litercy Trust into a wider campaign of promoting reading for enjoyment. Again it's making sure that we keep the balance right and clearly one of the major responsibilities of primary schools, particularly for children where there isn't a reading culture in the home, is to do everything they can to provide that inspiration for children to read and make use of their skills. The whole purpose of developing reasonable attainment is to give children the opportunity to enjoy books: the two things should go together.

KH: Are you satisfied that all children benefit equally from the Strategy?

SA: No, I'm never satisfied, and I don't suppose I ever will be. The original design of the Strategy was not of absolutely equal resources being provided to all schools or LEAs. We deliberately skewed consultant support, resources and funding to those areas within LEAs which were serving the most disadvantaged communities. It is very satisfying that the biggest improvements have been made in those schools serving those disadvantaged communities. We still have the problem of a relatively large group of low-attaining children and frankly I don't think we've done enough to reduce that group. That's a big areas of focus for us at the moment.

KH: Do you think there may be an issue, at least for some children, of inadequate bridging between out-of-school literacy practices and those valued by the Strategy and the school?

SA: I'm sure that there's a great deal in that. From my own personal experience, I know it isn't just a question of what you can do in the classroom, there has got to be work with parents about support in the community. It's about children's understanding and perceptions of literacy, it's about the literacies they experience. I think it would be fair to say that we have rightly concentrated on the classroom because that has the biggest impact on children's outcomes. But for that lowest achieving group there's a much bigger context and it is about how the school approaches the communities and the families of those children to maximise the support and complement what goes on in the classroom; I think it's those children that will benefit most from the different facets of support in different contexts.

KH: You talked earlier about the importance of teachers' subject knowledge. What do you make of the PISA (PISA 2002) finding that high national attainment is associated with a high level of teacher education and a high degree of teacher autonomy?

SA: When you see really good teachers of English in primary schools, they are teachers whose confidence is born from a grasp of the subject, from an overview and ability to look ahead, to encourage children to move on in their learning. It comes from that confidence, so a well-qualified teaching workforce is essential. I think it's interesting that the notion of autonomy is important. If I think about the teachers who have made the best use of the Strategy, in many cases they are the most confident teachers. If you put materials in the hands of the really good teachers, they'll say, 'that's really good, I can use that', and they'll then improve and extend their repertoire.

So, teacher autonomy is very closely linked to confidence. It's about good subject knowledge which leads to confidence as a teacher, which leads to looking for support to improve.

KH: Do you see any tension in an emphasis on autonomy and the tendency in the Strategy to package and standardise?

SA: If there is, I think it's a false tension because the Strategy is designed to address that issue. When I was inspecting, primary English seven or eight years ago, in lots of schools you would see some very good teaching but you'd see some very poor teaching. What you'd want at least, is some kind of basic entitlement to good literacy provision for *all* the children, in *all* the classes in that school, and in different schools. That's an entitlement, it's not an option. The Strategy is about equity, it's not about trying to standardise or control. I'm not in any way wanting to cap or limit that sense of autonomy and confidence that comes from the best literacy teaching.

KH: But insofar as teachers are told what to do with a class in a particular term – there are expectations about objectives to be acquired say in term one for Year 1?

SA: What we've always said is, 'Look this is a framework – it's not more than that, it's not a straitjacket, it's not a something you can't interpret.' But it is saying, in order to raise expectations, let's at least say what are a broad set of expectations for children in each year group. Now we've always said to teachers, clearly you have to bring to that your knowledge of your children, your knowledge of the rest of the curriculum that you are teaching. I think there is a strong argument for defining a basic range and variety so children are encountering a wide range of texts over time. There is a progression in their learning through a set of objectives and there is coherence in their learning so that both teachers and children are clear about where they are going and what they are doing.

You see the best work when teachers are using the framework to then construct their own provision which relates to their children, their own school context and their own curriculum. Because nobody can centrally determine a set of experiences for children. A school has got to build that for itself.

KH: *What do you think of the argument that the Strategy's emphasis on highly detailed content and planning has the unintended consequence of curtailing the spontaneity and open-endedness of teacher–pupil interaction?*

SA: What you were meant to do with a set of objectives like that is orchestrate them, think long-term, think of sequences of work and build a unit that helps you think ahead. Obviously the objectives fit together, a lot of the reading and writing ones interrelate and a lot of the word and sentence objectives feed into the text-level objectives. So you need that sense of grouping, of clustering of objectives over time, around a sequence of experiences for children that move them forward in their literacy learning.

Nobody can really plan to meet the needs of a class of children except the teacher in their own context. I think that many of the commercial schemes have led to a very fragmented interpretation of the framework, which isn't helpful.

KH: *What do you think is the role of literature in children's literacy education?*

SA: Well it's key. All of us who are involved centrally in the Strategy are passionate about children's literature because that's what makes English teaching so enjoyable and fulfilling and engaging. Literacy is about a range of things; it's about ensuring that children have the functional ability to operate as an adult in society, but all of us understand that absolutely at the heart of what we're doing is giving children access to literature, which is that sense of other people's perspectives on the world, other people's feelings and imaginations. So the whole issue about children's personal development is central to what we're doing. It's not, it can't be, divisible from literacy, it's an absolutely integral part of literacy. I find it very sad when I come across primary teachers who aren't enthused by reading literature. Every child should have access to what is a key part of their own development; literature gives them access to the world as others experience it.

KH: *Do you think that it was a disadvantage within the Strategy to place so much emphasis on extracts from texts rather than whole texts?*

SA: Well, I'm not sure we did place undue emphasis on extracts; teachers generally have never spent a whole day reading a text with children. What they've done is a class novel, they've given children an experience of extended work, and there is absolutely no reason why that should have changed at all.

There are times in the Literacy Hour when you're looking at an extract because it illustrates a particular point or it's a short text or a poem, or a piece of non-fiction, but it's making sure that at different times, in guided reading for example, you're looking at full texts. There should still be times when the teacher reads to the class – gives them the experience of a whole text over a period of time – and we mustn't forget the experience of children's independent reading. Clearly they are encountering more texts.

We've tried hard to counter the interpretation that the Strategy is just about extracts; some of the planning exemplification illustrates the use of whole texts over time. Again it's that balance between fiction and non-fiction, it's a balance between different approaches, plays, scripts and different kinds of texts. Sometimes extracts are a perfectly valid way of looking at those texts, but at other times you've got to give children the experience of the whole development of a book.

KH: OfSTED recently noted the downward pressure of a formal pedagogical approach and its negative effects on Reception classes. To what extent do you think the Strategy is implicated in this?

SA: There is clearly an issue there. The full extent of it I'm not sure about because when the department has done telephone polls of reception teachers they'll often say, 'Well it's not a great dilemma for us; yes we've got the *Curriculum Guidance for the Foundation Stage* and we've got these objectives that are there for the Reception year in the strategies, but there isn't a great tension in bringing all those together.'

Many primary headteachers, particularly those whose background is largely in Key Stage 2, may have misinterpreted expectations and pushed for a more formal early introduction of the Literacy Hour. We've consistently said that in Reception you introduce that more coherent package within the Hour over time. We're just bringing out some new material around phonics called 'Playing With Sounds' and I'd defy anybody reading that to suggest that we are advocating formal, dogmatic approaches to teaching in Foundation and Reception, because what's described there are highly interactive, enjoyable activities based around play that will promote children's development in language and literacy.

I'm well aware of the fact that in some contexts and in some places there has been a view that a more formal approach is needed. But it's the way you provide that experience that matters and it seems to me that there's absolutely no reason why that shouldn't be done highly systematically. Teachers and practitioners in Foundation Stage usually plan extremely carefully, but it's about planning in such a way that what children do doesn't feel over-formal. I think it should be informed by the best that's there at Foundation Stage. So again, it's that idea of teachers' subject knowledge, having a really clear sense about what it is that the children need to develop in terms of their repertoire, their ability to discriminate sounds, their early development in that area, but doing it in a way that is enjoyable, engaging and fun, and reflects the best practice in the phase.

KH: *What do you see as the major changes to the Strategy since its introduction in 1998?*

SA: Inevitably in the early stages the strong emphasis was on establishing the Hour and changing the behaviour of many, many teachers. Although I don't believe there was any particular emphasis on reading, the immediate impact was felt most in reading because that's where the changes to practice were more apparent. So through the regular shared and guided reading, many children had a transformation of their previous experience. Daily encounters with texts for children in Years 4, 5 and 6 had not been happening before in many classrooms, and I think that had a big impact. Inevitably, as time has gone on, we've tried to ensure that writing was being given equal emphasis, because the teaching of writing was a challenge for many teachers. What you often saw was teachers introducing an issue, giving children vocabulary, talking through ideas, but then just getting them to 'write about it'. I think we've helped teachers develop a much clearer sense about how you teach the skills of writing effectively through active demonstration, and letting children see the decisions and choices that writers make. So I think over time stronger emphasis on writing, but that's probably to equalise the balance, not to change the balance.

In relation to what we're concentrating on now, it's less about teaching specific aspects of literacy – for example, focusing on guided reading or on shared writing – and more about orchestrating these components across the primary curriculum. So there's a lot more emphasis on speaking and listening and the place this has, not just in terms of how it relates to reading and writing but how it relates to children's learning overall. Schools are now giving more attention to the whole cross-curricular dimension of literacy and how it's applied in different subjects.

A big area that wasn't given early emphasis by the Strategy, but which I think is getting increasing attention now, is ICT and its contribution to literacy teaching. There's huge potential there for pedagogy, but also for the range and experience that children have of the changing literacies which they're encountering. I suppose the Strategy is maturing.

KH: *So are you saying this wider notion of literacy includes ICT, multimedia texts – multiliteracies?*

SA: Absolutely, yes. The work that we've been doing with consultants in the last year has put a lot of emphasis on the place of ICT and some of the most exciting work is about what that can now offer in terms of the creation of texts, multimedia texts of very different kinds, the integration of images, the exchange of texts and electronic collaboration; there's huge potential there for some incredibly exciting developments.

KH: *My last question. How do you see the future of the Strategy?*

SA: I think it's absolutely right that the Literacy Strategy and the Numeracy Strategy in a sense no longer exist as separate initiatives. The challenge is to retain the sense that literacy and numeracy are central to children's entitlement to a rich, broad curriculum experience. We've got to make sure that that has the maximum impact on children's life experience. I think the other issue for me in terms of how it develops is that it's more widely understood beyond the teaching force: everyone who supports primary schools needs to have an understanding of the centrality of literacy and the importance and the place of it. For example, it would include more emphasis on work with communities and parents, more emphasis on the lowest attaining children. So, it's about focusing on particular areas that still need further work, but doing it across the whole primary curriculum.

References

Mullis, I.V.S., Martin, M.O., Gonzalez, E.J. and Kennedy, A.M. (2003) *PIRLS 2001 International Report*. Boston, International Study Center, Lynch School of Education, Boston College.

PISA (2002) *PISA. Reading for Change: Performance and Engagement across Countries. Results from PISA 2000*. OEC Publishing, 19th November 2002.

Chapter 5

What can teachers learn from the language that children use?

Chris Bills

How can we tell whether children have really understood the concepts we ask them to work with? Chris Bills's research into the teaching and learning of primary mathematics led him to conclude that the words and metaphors children use can be a strong indicator of the depth and nature of their understanding. His findings have implications of relevance to the way teachers and teaching assistants talk to children about mathematics and underline the need to listen carefully when making assessments.

As a teacher of mathematics I am concerned to know what children have learned as a result of my teaching. I also need to know what they have learned from their previous teachers if I am to build upon their existing conceptualisations.

When I asked children to perform mental calculations and to tell me 'What was in your head when you were thinking of that?' I found that the words they used related to classroom activities I had previously observed. This leads me to suggest that the metaphoric language used in children's descriptions of how they have performed mental calculations can give teachers an indication of the experiences which have influenced the thinking of their pupils.

In addition to these echoes of previous classroom activities my study indicates that different modes of language use are associated with achievement. I discovered that the use of present tense, use of the pronoun 'you' and use of causal connectives are all most commonly associated with correct answers to mental calculations. These 'linguistic pointers' may help teachers gauge children's confidence in their mental calculation procedures.

Indications of previous learning

On my first visit to Bright Cross, a primary school near Birmingham, England, in October 1997, I watched a lesson with six- to seven-year-old children. The teacher, Mr K used Dienes Blocks to demonstrate addition of two two-digit numbers. First he balanced ten 'ones' on his hand, one on top of another, to show that they were the same height as a 'ten'. When the tower collapsed the 'ones' were laid along the 'ten' to show again that ten 'ones' made a 'ten'.

Two pupils were selected to help Mr K give Mandy two 'tens'.

Mr K: *Another way of putting it?*
Mandy: *Twenty.*

Mandy was then given four 'ones'.

Mr K: *How many altogether?*
Mandy: *Twenty-four.*

Mr K gave Nina one 'ten' and two 'ones'.

Mr K: *How many altogether?*
Nina: *Twelve.*
Mr K: *Now put them together in my hands.*

Mandy and Nina put their 'tens' in one of his hands and the 'ones' in the other hand. He then held out both hands for the pupils to see.

Mr K: *How many altogether?*
Pupils: *Thirty-six.*
Mr K: *Look how easy it is to add them instead of all individual cubes.*

One week later I interviewed several of the children and asked them to calculate 24 add 53, which I had printed on paper but asked them to work out in their heads. They had no materials or pencil and paper. The influence of the previous lesson seemed clear in the response of one girl, Elspeth:

I: *How would you do it?*
Elspeth: *Put those together. (Points at numbers.)*
I: *Why would you put those together?*
Elspeth: *Well you add the tens together then you add the units because it's like in one hand you have the tens and in the other you have the units.*

Elspeth made explicit the connection with the physical handling of objects by her use of 'like' but the metaphoric language of manipulation is also apparent in 'put those together'. This is a metaphor because we cannot 'put together' symbols yet use of these words may indicate that she was thinking about the manipulation of the symbols in terms of the manipulation of the physical objects.

Elspeth's response gives some indication of the way in which the language associated with manipulating physical apparatus may subsequently be used when talking about operations on number. In my subsequent observations of lessons and pupil interviews, I found that the language children used often related to previous classroom activities when talking about how they had performed mental calculations. Another example occurred in March 1998, when Mrs J gave this lesson about three-digit numbers to the Y2 class. Some language that was subsequently used by children is in ordinary type for emphasis:

> *Mrs J:*   *You have been throwing dice and all sorts of things. You also looked at rolls of raffle tickets like this:*

Mrs J drew on the white board: | | 186 | |

> *Mrs J:*   *What comes next?*
> *Pupil:*   *187.*
> *Mrs J:*   *What comes before?*
> *Pupil:*   *185.*
> *Mrs J:*   *Why wasn't the one or the eight changed?*
> *Pupil:*   *Because you are not adding tens or hundreds.*

Mrs J then replaced 186 on the white board with 199.

> *Pupil:*   *What comes before?*
> *Pupil:*   *198.*
> *Mrs J:*   *What comes after?*
> *Pupil:*   *200.*
> *Mrs J:*   *But that means* I'm altering the tens and *hundreds. That's because I can't have more than nine in any column.*

To illustrate *going to* the next number she held up three single-digit cards and then *changed* the units digit card for a different one. She indicated that only the *units digit changed* except when *the nine is changed for a nought* and then the ten digit is changed as well. She showed three-digit numbers by holding up three cards and suggested keeping two *the same* and only *changing the end digit* to add-on one. In this context 'change' means the physical exchange of one card for another.

In a subsequent interview I asked, 'When you are counting what comes next after 379?' The children's responses gave indications of their previous classroom activities:

> *Elaine:*   *I just* put away the three *um 300–79 – after that comes 80 and then – I do 380.*
> *Hazel:*   We have to change *the – seven to an eight and* we take nine to an oh.

Others used similar language but did not give the correct answer to the calculation:

> *John:*   *389 . . .* I changed the ten to the next.
> *Christine:*   *550 –* I added one more on to the units makes ten *and then I added it on so it was four made five.*

The language used by these children was sufficiently different to suggest that they had conceptualised from their own experiences, yet sufficiently similar to suggest that they had been influenced by their classroom experiences.

More metaphors

As the children learned more about written calculation procedures the language they used to describe mental calculations showed the influence of the algorithms. The expressions 'the units', 'put the five', 'carry the one', 'the tens' are all appropriate in the context of the written calculation. These expressions also, however, occurred in the language of children when they described how they had performed a mental calculation. This again suggests that the classroom experiences had influenced the way they communicate. These expressions are also metaphoric in the sense that the language of one context (written algorithm) is used in describing another context (mental calculation).

Expressions related to written calculation were common when children were asked to calculate mentally questions such as '48 add 23'. For instance these were typical responses when, having given the answer, 44 children were asked. 'What was in your head?':

Dennis: I was adding the eight and the three, *which makes 11, and then I was adding* the two and four *and that equals six. But then* it needs to be carried by one.

Irene: *Well I added eight and three, which makes 11, then I added the four and two which makes six but the 11 is over 10 so I added another one,* another ten to the six *to make 70.*

The use of the language of the algorithm indicates that the pupils conceptualisations for calculation seem to have been influenced by these experiences.

It is important to realise that not all the children used this language. Others seemed to have been less influenced in their thinking by these written procedures. Some simply counted and one seemed to have been influenced by numberline activities:

Myles: *It was like a ruler.* I counted along *it, I think it was in fives. And when* I got to 70, *I counted another one.*

Notice the the metaphors of movement and position apparent in 'when I got to'. Language related to numberlines was relatively uncommon in this classroom and this may reflect the low proportion of time given to these activities.

Other pupils used mental calculation strategies:

Bobby: I added *20 which makes 60* and *then you* add *two to make 70 and added one more which makes 71.*

Bobby's response is also interesting because of his use of tense and pronouns. Notice that 'I' and past tense were used initially but then he changed to 'you' and the present tense when he seemed to be giving the rule he was following. This aspect of the children's language will now be explored.

Pronouns and tense in descriptions of mental calculations

The use of 'you' and the present tense is common in rule-giving in everyday life and in the classroom. Rowland (1999) noted that children may also start to use 'you' when they discover a generalisation. In his study children used 'you' to distance themselves from a statement and thus indicate that it was not peculiar to them but was in general true. He suggested that pronouns are 'linguistic pointers' which indicate a mode of thought.

In the classroom teachers and pupils frequently use 'you' instead of the more formal 'one'. The present tense is also appropriate in the classroom when a rule is being described when a calculation is being performed. Here is an excerpt from a typical Year 3 lesson in which Miss P reminded pupils of the method she had shown them to halve an odd number. A pupil described what to do as Miss P drew on the board:

Miss P:	*How to half an odd number equally? Do you remember what to do?*	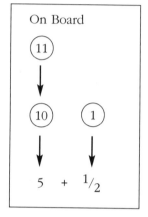
Pupil:	11 is made out of 10 and one and you put . . .	
Miss P:	*Carry on* 'you put . . .'	
Pupil:	You put *half of 10 is five and half of one is half so it's five and a half.*	

In a subsequent interview I asked, 'What is nine split in two?' and then 'What was in your head?' My past-tense question was frequently answered in the present tense when a rule seemed to have been used. Similarly instead of the expected 'I' to describe what the individual had done, the use of 'you' indicated the influence of the classroom activities and language:

> Nora: Well – you *get nine is made out of eight add one, and half of eight, is, four, and half of one is half,* – so you *add eight and a half together and* you *get – four and a half.*

My analysis indicates that use of 'you' was more frequently associated with correct answers. When 'you' was used exclusively, 79 per cent of the answers were correct. When 'I' was used, 65 per cent were correct. This seems to indicate that when the pupils have mastered the rule it tends to be expressed in the general 'you' mode. Similarly the use of tense indicated differences. When the past tense was used exclusively 62 per cent of the responses were correct. In comparison 71 per cent of the responses using present tense accompanied correct answers to the calculations.

When the children had difficulty performing the mental calculation their responses to 'What was in your head?' were often descriptions of what they had done in that particular instance. When they had given the answer easily they more frequently gave the rule using the classroom mode of description (i.e. present tense and use of 'you').

Language associated with explanations

Since the use of 'you' for descriptions of procedures is common in everyday life it is not surprising that it is also common in the mathematics classroom. Its use, as we have seen above, is also actively encouraged in the classroom discourse. There were other examples in my observations that illustrate the similarities in language used by teachers and pupils. There was evidence that pupils were being encouraged to adopt the speech styles common in mathematics. For instance, explanations involving 'because' were used both by teachers and pupils. Again this is not uncommon in everyday life but pupils frequently followed the teacher's lead in the use of the word. For example in a lesson on 'adding and subtracting near-multiples of ten' Mrs F first talked to the Y4 children about 36 add 19. She used a hundred square:

> Mrs F: *What is 19 nearly?*
> Lynne: *20.*
> Mrs F: *If you wanted to add 20 to 36 how would you do it?*
> Lynne: *Go down.*
> Mrs F: *So 36 go down two is 56 but we have to take one* because *we are only adding 19 not 20.*

More examples of addition were worked through with the class, then subtraction was described in a similar way. Mrs F wrote 55−19 on the board.

> Mrs F: *See if you can do it in your head but using that strategy.*
> Peter: *36.*
> Mrs F: *Tell us how you did it.*
> Peter: *'Cause 19 is near 20 so I just took two tens from 55 and added one.*

In this example 'because' was used by the teacher and the pupils immediately followed suit. The use of 'because' is part of the speech style of mathematicians.

Since deduction is an essential element of mathematics the use of 'if', 'then', 'so' and 'because' are inevitably common in the mathematics classroom. Children's use of these words can be an indication of their adoption of a mathematical style of reasoning.

In my interviews, many children spontaneously used causal connectives. Having given an answer to a mental calculation there was no necessity to give explanations in reply to 'What was in your head?' yet many children did so:

> 17+8   *You add three on* because *five add three is eight*
> 97+10   *I can't add a ten* so *I put the one in front of it.*
> 17+9   *If you take off one, because it was the nine, it would be 26.*
> Round 239   *If it's 30* then *it's under 50.*

Use of causal connectives was associated more frequently with correct answers to the mental calculations. This seems to suggest that children who are secure enough in their calculation strategies to give correct answers are more likely to describe their methods in the language associated with explanation. They do not simply *describe* what they did. They *explain* why they do it that way.

What can we learn from children's language?

I have given three examples where the language children use to describe their mental calculations can inform teachers of the ways in which the children may be thinking.

- When children use words associated with particular classroom activities such as the manipulation of blocks or cards there is an indication that experiences with these materials have influenced their thinking.
- When children adopt a classroom speech style involving use of 'you' and the present tense there is an indication that they have internalised the rules and follow them when making their own calculations. Children in my survey seldom adopted this mode of expression when they used their own idiosyncratic methods.
- Children also spontaneously used causal connectives in an explanatory mode of expression even though they had been asked simply 'What was in your head?' There was an indication that this style of language was associated with correct answers. This seems to suggest that this mode of language use points to the use of a familiar routine that is well understood.

Listening to children's language can assist teachers in identifying the differences in their conceptualisations. An understanding of the significance of the words that are used can thus be an aid to formative assessment.

My study suggests that the 'image like' nature of children's language (Bills 1999) is indicative of the influences on their thinking. This may only confirm what we have always known: teachers need to listen to what children say if they wish to find out what is going on in the children's heads. I hope, however, that I have also given some pointers to help interpret the words that they use.

References:

Bills, C.J. (1999) 'What was in your head when you were thinking of that?' *Mathematics Teaching*, **168**, 39–41.

Rowland, T. (1999) 'Pronouns in Mathematics Talk: Power, Vagueness and Generalisation.' *For the Learning of Mathematics*, **19** (2), 19–26.

Chapter 6

Watching and learning: the tools of assessment

Cathy Nutbrown

Assessment is a key feature of the work of teachers and many teaching assistants. However, all too often, external demands and considerations can mean that the focus is on outcomes and measurable achievement – assessment *of* learning rather than assessment *for* learning. Cathy Nutbrown, a distinguished early years academic, argues that we need to reconsider why we assess young children's learning and to develop assessment practices that begin with and respect the learner, and that will provide us with information to engage with and support children's learning and understanding. She suggests that observation is an essential tool in achieving this. Although the focus here is on young children, the conclusions have implications for those working with older children as well.

This chapter focuses on how early childhood educators can understand the capabilities of the children they teach. It begins by asking *why* assessment is important, discussing why educators need a broad picture of children's capabilities, and considers *observation* as one of the best 'tools of the trade'.

Why assess young children's learning?

To ask 'Why assess children's learning?' is to question one of the most fundamental components of teaching young children. Children's learning is so complex, rich, fascinating, varied and variable, surprising, enthusiastic and stimulating, that to see it taking place, every day, before one's very eyes is one of the greatest privileges of any early childhood educator. The very process of observing and assessing children's learning is, in a sense, its own justification. Watching children learn can open our eyes to the astonishing capacity of young children to learn, and shows us the crucial importance of these first few years in children's lives. But there is much more to say about assessing children's learning. There is much more to be gained from watching children learn than to make us marvel at children's powers to think, do, communicate and create, for there is an important piece of work for educators to do to help them to understand – really understand – what they see.

The legacy of some of the pioneers of early education (such as Froebel, Piaget, Vygotsky and Isaacs) and of those whose work in the latter half of the twentieth century has illuminated children's learning (such as Donaldson 1983; Athey 1990; Abbott and Rodger 1994) helps educators to consider their own observations of children in the light of a rich literature which opens up the meaning of children's words, representations and actions. Educators' personal experiences of individual children's learning can help them to see more clearly the general principles that other researchers and educators have established as characteristic of that learning.

Some of the pioneers of early childhood education learnt about children's learning by watching and learning themselves, by observing children and thinking about what they saw. Those published observations can be useful to educators now as tools for reflection on children's processes of learning and as a means of moving from the specifics of personal experiences to general understandings about children's thinking. Susan Isaacs, for example, ran an experimental school, The Malting House, in Cambridge from 1924 to 1927. Her compelling accounts of the day-to-day doings of the children in the school show clearly how her analysis of children's intellectual development is the product of a mass of detailed anecdotal insights. For example, she describes the development of the basic concepts of biology, change, growth, life and death, illustrating this process with a wealth of evidence:

18.6.25
The children let the rabbit out to run about the garden for the first time, to their great delight. They followed him about, stroked him and talked about his fur, his shape and his ways.

13.7.25
Some of the children called out that the rabbit was dying. They found it in the summerhouse, hardly able to move. They were very sorry and talked much about it. They shut it up in the hutch and gave it warm milk.

14.7.25
The rabbit had died in the night. Dan found it and said: 'It's dead – its tummy does not move up and down now.' Paul said, 'My daddy says that if we put it into water it will get alive again.' Mrs I said 'shall we do so and see?' They put it into a bath of water. Some of them said, 'It is alive.' Duncan said, 'If it floats, it's dead, and if it sinks, it's alive.' It floated on the surface. One of them said, 'It's alive, because it's moving.' This was a circular motion, due to the currents in the water. Mrs I therefore put in a small stick which also moved round and round, and they agreed that the stick was not alive. They then suggested that they should bury the rabbit, and all helped to dig a hole and bury it.

15.7.25
Frank and Duncan talked of digging the rabbit up – but Frank said, 'It's not there – it's gone up to the sky.' They began to dig, but tired of it and ran off to something else. Later they came back and dug again. Duncan, however, said, 'Don't bother – it's

gone – it's up in the sky' and gave up digging. Mrs I therefore said, 'Shall we see if it's there?' and also dug. They found the rabbit, and were very interested to see it still there.

The diary entries by Isaacs and her colleagues were more than entertaining anecdotes: they formed the basis for her analysis of children's scientific thinking. Isaacs was able to learn about learning by intently studying her own detailed observations. Thus, assessment of children's learning through the tools of observation is not at all new, though for some who have not had the opportunities to continue to practise their skills of observing and reflecting upon their observations, those tools may well have become somewhat rusty. However, many have followed Isaacs' observational practice; indeed, much of my own earlier work on children's learning has been informed by my diary jottings (made while teaching) of children's words, actions and graphic representations (Nutbrown 1999). Similarly, the pioneering practice of Reggio Emilia in northern Italy is developed largely through careful observation, documentation and reflection upon the children's work (Filippini and Vecchi 1996; Abbott and Nutbrown 2001).

The 1990s saw a proliferation of criteria for high-quality provision for young children's learning. Such statements represented attempts to identify and specify necessary conditions for this learning and development but, as Woodhead (1996) illustrates, quality is often culture and community specific and it is difficult to agree universal statements of quality. What might suit the discussion of quality in the UK may well be quite unsuitable in, say, the Caribbean. That said, it is true that – whatever their setting and whatever their international location – where educators observe children and use their observations to generate understandings of their learning and their needs, they are contributing to the development of a quality environment in which those children might thrive. The evaluative purpose of assessment is central for early childhood educators, for they cannot know if the environments they create and the support they provide for children as they work are effective unless they watch and learn from what they see.

Observation can provide starting points for reviewing the effectiveness of provision, and such observational assessments of children's learning can be used to identify strengths, weaknesses, gaps and inconsistencies in the curriculum provided for all children.

Assessment can be used to plan and review the provision and teaching as well as to identify those significant moments in each child's learning which educators can build upon to shape a curriculum that matches each child's pressing cognitive and affective concerns.

Observation and assessment can illuminate the future, as well as provide information with which to improve the quality of the present. This forward-looking dimension of assessment is the means by which early childhood educators can explore the possible outcomes of the provision they offer; the curriculum, pedagogy, interactions and relationships. Increasingly, formal assessments are being used to diagnose children's abilities. There is a danger that formal assessment of four-year-olds on entry to school limits the opportunities they are offered rather than opening up a broad canvas of learning. It is important, however, to use the active process of assessment to identify for each individual the next teaching steps so that learning opportunities in the immediate future are well matched to the children they are designed for.

This focus on the *next steps* in teaching (and learning) takes us into the area of development Vygotsky called 'the zone of proximal development'. He used this concept to argue passionately that assessment does not end with a description of a pupil's present state of knowing, but only begins there. He wrote: 'I do not terminate my study at this point, but only begin it' (Vygotsky 1978: 85). Effective assessment is dynamic, not static, and can identify for the educator what the learner's next steps might be; assessment reveals learning potential as well as learning achievements. Vygotsky's arguments show how 'learning which is oriented toward developmental levels that have already been reached is ineffective from the viewpoint of a child's overall development. It does not aim for a new stage of the developmental process but rather lags behind this process' (Vygotsky 1978: 89).

Observation and assessment are the essential tools of watching and learning by which we can both establish the progress that has already been made and explore the future – the learning that is still embryonic. The role of the adult in paying careful and informed attention to children's learning and reflecting upon it is crucial to the enhancement of children's future learning.

Early assessment for the future

Children's early learning and development are exciting. It is stimulating and rewarding for teachers (as well as children and their parents) to see a child taking new steps in learning. But the prevailing conditions for effective teaching must include *a fair breeze with a following wind.* Everything must be heading in the same direction – charting the same course, running the same race. It will not do for those who teach and those who are responsible for teachers and education in terms of policy to be in opposition – a team effort is what children need. The status of *assessment for teaching* is essential to optimum early education experiences for young children. But there are other conditions that make up a *fair breeze* for early education: *time* for children (enough teachers to work with them), *time* for assessment, *confidence* in teachers' teaching and assessments, and *recognition* of the judgements teachers make about what they teach, how they teach and when. These together can make for teaching that enhances learning.

So what might the future hold for the improvement of assessment for learning in the early years of education? First, the elevation of the status of ongoing teacher assessment as the main tool for understanding children's learning needs and progress; second, professional development opportunities that challenge teachers and other early childhood educators to observe children's learning and understand what they see.

With due respect . . .

In this chapter I have discussed why educators should observe and assess young children. Future policies and pratice must support the full involvement of parents and educators towards respectful understandings of children's learning. The 'one-stop' summaries of children's abilities according to predetermined lists (that miss the true riches of children's minds) do nothing to truly focus the minds of educators on children's learning.

Time for teaching and assessment, *confidence* in teachers' teaching and assessments, and *recognition* of the judgements teachers make can create the important climate of *respectful* teaching. The concept of respect can underpin and inform the way adults work with children and the ways in which policies are developed and implemented, but the notion of respect in education can be misunderstood (Nutbrown 1996, 1997). What do I mean when I speak of *respect* in education? 'When advocates of respect for children are accused of being "idealistic", of "romanticising early childhood" – their meaning is misunderstood. Respect is not about "being nice" – it is about being clear, honest, courteous, diligent and consistent' (Nutbrown 1998).

The concept of respectful assessment and respectful teaching may still raise an eyebrow or two, and could be dismissed by some as an over-romanticising of work with and for young children. So the careful articulation of our terms is important, and it is worth examining here what the concept of respectfully working with children might include. Table 6.1 shows some aspects which I

Table 6.1: What is a respectful educator? What is respectful teaching? What is respectful assessment?

Respectful approaches	*Disrespectful approaches*
Taking account of the learner – 'children as participants'	Ignoring the learner – 'children as recipients'
Building on existing learning	Disregarding/unaware of existing learning
Based on tuning into learners' agendas	Based on predetermined curriculum
Responsive to learners' needs and interests	Unresponsive to learners' needs and interests
Informed by children's developmental needs	Informed by targets/key stages/ages
Curriculum based on children's identified needs	Curriculum based on external definitions of needs
Includes/embraces issues of children's rights	Ignores/disregards issues of children's rights

(Continued)

Table 6.1: Continued

Respectful approaches	Disrespectful approaches
Clarity for learner	Lack of clarity for learner
Authentic assessment to inform teaching	Inauthentic assessment used to track progress of cohort
Challenge	No challenge
Opportunity for extension and diversity	Closed to extension
Holistic	Compartmentalised
Involves parents	Excludes parents
Evaluation	'It works' – no evaluation
Revision in the light of experience	Carrying on regardless
Recognises all achievements	Values achievement of specific prespecified goals
Purposeful	Lack of purpose
Knowledgeable teachers	Teachers with limited knowledge
Professional development for teachers and other educators	Lack of professional development for teachers and other educators
Teachers and other educators with appropriate initial training and qualifications	Teachers and other educators with limited/inappropriate training qualifications
Each learner matters	The cohort/group/majority matter
Equality for all children	The 'same' for all
Includes all children	Excludes some children
Sufficient and appropriate equipment/resources	Insufficient and inappropriate equipment/resources
Appropriate ratio of adults to children	Too many children – too few adults
Sufficient/appropriate space and access to learning areas/experiences	Insufficient/inappropriate space and limited access to learning areas/experiences

suggest might constitute respectful teaching, and it is worth noting that the opposite of respectful approaches is *dis*respectful. (I doubt that anyone would endorse such a term!)

Teaching young children needs those qualities of clarity, honesty, courtesy, diligence and consistency. It means identifying what children *can* do, what they *might* do and what their teachers need next to teach. This is indeed a task that – despite repeated attempts to make it simple – can never be other than complex. Watching children as they learn and understanding the significance of those learning moments are complex tasks that make high demands on all who attempt them.

References

Abbott, L. and Nutbrown, C. (2001) *Experiencing Reggio Emilia: Implications for Pre-school Provision.* Buckingham: Open University Press.

Abbott, L. and Rodger, R. (1994) *Quality Education in the Early Years.* Buckingham: Open University Press.

Athey, C. (1990) *Extending Thought in Young Children: A Parent–Teacher Partnership.* London: Paul Chapman Publishing.

Donaldson, M. (1983) *Children's Minds.* Glasgow: Fontana/Collins.

Filippini, T. and Vecchi, V. (eds) (1996) *The Hundred Languages of Children: Exhibition Catalogue.* Reggio Emilia: Reggio Children.

Nutbrown, C. (ed) (1996) *Respectful Educators – Capable Learners: Children's Rights in Early Education.* London: Paul Chapman Publishing.

Nutbrown, C. (1997) *Recognising Early Literacy Development – Assessing Children's Achievements.* London: Paul Chapman Publishing.

Nutbrown, C. (1998) *The Lore and Language of Early Education.* Sheffield: University of Sheffield Division of Education Publications.

Nutbrown, C. (1999) *Threads of Thinking: Young Children Learning and the Role of Early Education,* 2nd edn. London: Paul Chapman Publishing.

Vygotsky, L. (1978) *Mind in Society: The Development of Higher Level Psychological Processes.* Cambridge, MA: Harvard University Press.

Woodhead, M. (1996) *In Search of the Rainbow: Pathways to Quality in Large Scale Programmes for Young Disadvantaged Children.* The Hague: Bernard van Leer Foundation.

Chapter 7

Social constructivism in the classroom

Judith Watson

Children can often feel alienated by the experience of school when they feel no account is taken of their interests, experiences or opinions. Social constructivist approaches view teaching and learning as a shared social experience in which meanings are jointly and actively constructed and where more knowledgeable 'others' such as teachers, teaching assistants or other children or adults help to build and develop children's understandings. In this chapter Judith Watson, from the University of Edinburgh, explores how this approach could support children who experience difficulties in learning, although her arguments also have implications for teaching and learning for all children.

This chapter follows a recent discussion of research indicating the potential of social constructivist approaches with pupils who experience difficulty with their school learning (Watson 2000). These embody ideas of learners actively building their understanding, helped (or 'scaffolded') by other more knowledgeable persons such as their teachers, in their Zone of Proximal Development (ZPD), and gradually becoming more aware of and able to regulate their own learning through metacognition. Learning is regarded as a shared social activity, embedded in classroom interactions.

Constructivist teachers

Emphasis on the power of the learner must seem to many a radical perspective, which can briefly be summarised in Wells's (1999:329) masterly summary of the application of Vygotskyan ideas in Canadian classrooms in inner city schools:

> . . . the increased understanding among educators that teaching involves much more than appropriately selecting and delivering a standardised curriculum and assessing the extent to which it has been correctly received. Teaching certainly involves preparation, instruction and assessment; but to be truly effective it also involves the

ongoing co-construction of each student's ZPD and on-the-spot judgements about how best to facilitate his or her learning in the specific activity setting in which he or she is engaged.

In providing examples of pupils' active engagement with learning, and their teachers' vital role in helping them to build on what they already know, I have chosen to use twelve headings used by Brooks and Brooks (1993) to describe constructivist teachers. I consider each descriptive heading's application to pupils who have learning difficulties by means of recent illustrations from British classrooms.

According to Brooks and Brooks (1993) constructivist educators:

1. Encourage and accept student autonomy and initiative

Research evidence indicates that pupils with learning difficulties are especially likely to show dependence rather than autonomy and are unlikely to show initiative, that this increases over time, and may be unintentionally fostered by the tendency of many teachers to dominate classroom interactions, to be controlling, and in their teaching style to convey low expectations of their pupils (Goddard 1997; Norwich 1997).

It is essential therefore that at least some of their classroom experience should be under pupils' control. Teachers naturally are always concerned to cover the curriculum but it should be possible to foster meaningful choice and autonomy within this. If pupils are encouraged to follow up their own ideas they are more likely to see relationships between ideas and concepts, and to become problem finders as well as problem solvers.

In the following example pupils with learning difficulties were decision makers and gained a sense of ownership of their learning; their teachers made it plain that the video content was the pupils' responsibility.

In a special unit in a mainstream school 13-year-old pupils with moderate learning difficulties made a video showing the work in their term-long project, to be given to their parents. They decided on content and presentation. Their planning was impressive for the range of ideas, their animated talk, and their awareness of different possibilities. It was also marked by their pride and clear sense of achievement.

James: *Somebody could come out and then introduce it.*
Dave: *We could make up two posters, saying 'here comes the video' and 'thank you for watching the video'.*
Lucy: *We could make up a book.*

2. Use raw data and primary sources, along with manipulative, interactive and physical materials

Even expertly presented, interesting information may have little meaning for pupils who lack the basic general knowledge to which it could have been linked.

Teachers have somehow to create the conditions for building up appropriate conceptual foundations for subsequent learning.

Direct physical interaction with materials is often effective in enhancing pupils' thinking, especially as many do not spontaneously use verbalisation. Handling physical materials extends their sensory experience, is relaxing and satisfying, and may facilitate mental reasoning as in the following example.

Twelve-year-old Andrew in his special school was involved in the task of making a safe, strong go-cart, with two classmates, from a set of model parts. His teacher had planned initially to provide a model for his group of eleven-year-olds to copy using the kit of parts. However she decided, with a degree of apprehension, simply to give them the much more difficult and creative task of making it in accordance with her verbal description, with the notion that it would be strong enough and safe enough to carry a five-year-old from one of the younger classes. This paid dividends. With the occasional interested and responsive participation of his teacher, Andrew experimented, tested, reorganised the parts, tested again, made predictions, looked for more parts, tested and explained again. He discovered for himself the principles on which axles of wheels worked and was able to explain this to the rest of the class.

3. Use cognitive terminology when framing tasks

Pupils' own language and thinking are powerfully affected by that of their teachers, as when teachers think aloud, plan, and check. Teachers who say explicitly that they need time to think, or that they will need to check on their facts, or are puzzled, are providing models of thinking in which pat answers are not always available, and speed of response is not at a premium. When they encourage their pupils to take time to think, they are conveying powerful expectations. Likewise, pupils' cognitive language provides their teachers with the opportunity to tune into their understanding at its most advanced, through sharing and helping them to make progress in their current ZPD. In developing use and understanding of the language of thinking and knowing, evidence and proof, high expectations are conveyed, and metacognitive understanding enhanced.

The following conversation took place in a maths class for 13–15-year-olds, in a special school for pupils with moderate learning difficulties. The pupils' talk resembled that of their teacher, containing many predictions, logical deductions, and references to causal relationships. In this example the teacher was able to accept and expand on Sam's contribution to help them develop new understanding.

Teacher:	*Now here's a true or false statement. Is it true or false that a longer perimeter always has a larger area?*
Jake:	*Just because it's longer doesn't mean it's bigger.*
Sam:	*Perimeter and area don't have anything to do with each other.*
Teacher:	*They don't relate in a simple way.*
Jess:	*Why didn't I think of that in the first place?*
Sam:	*Because area is times and perimeter is adding.*

4. *Allow student responses to drive lessons, shift instructional strategies and alter content*

A good deal of evidence indicates that planned learning experiences often appear to be meaningless and uninvolving to pupils with learning difficulties, when they are not related to their current focus of interest or state of knowledge. With some pupils who are communicating at pre-verbal levels or who are on the autistic spectrum, the principle of following their lead is clearly demonstrated in intensive interactive teaching. A major challenge in constructivist approaches to teaching is to enable pupils to engage better with learning. Whereas teachers may have limited decision making about the content of their lessons, some demonstrate this principle very effectively in their contingent responding to their pupils' expressions of understanding, whether verbal or non-verbal, or through drawing, signs, or other means.

Many teachers, as a matter of course, use pupils' ideas to help determine the course and content of their teaching, as in the example given by Quicke (1995) in a mainstream secondary class on poetry:

> Bob the English teacher asked pupils to bring in any poetry they wished from home. They brought lyrics from pop songs, verses from greetings cards, limericks and nursery rhymes. Each was shared, talked about and evaluated. Other examples of this teacher drawing on pupils' out-of-school knowledge included the activity of predicting the story on the basis of a front cover illustration of a novel. The strength of this task from a Vygotskyan perspective lies in the connection explored between the thinking of the author, the illustrator and the groups of pupils who were about to embark on reading the novel. Pupils were being asked to enter the 'zone' of the writer and to use this meeting point as a foundation for the creation of a story of their own.

5. *Inquire about students' understandings of concepts before sharing their own understanding of those concepts*

Concepts are built up by each of us over time. True understanding and advances in understanding occur when new information we encounter is not too different or discrepant with what we aready know, as it has to fit in some way with our existing cognitive structures.

When teachers are in the habit of introducing their own ideas and information before pupils have a chance to think out theirs, pupils are unlikely to engage in reflection and will probably take the easier route of accepting unthinkingly what their teacher says. Teachers then lose the opportunity to get into their pupils' minds, which may in fact be through their misconceptions.

Anita, a science teacher, was amazed at the ideas from her pupils in a brainstorming session in a mainstream school:

> I started off the lesson just by putting the word 'gravity' on the board and we ended up filling the whole of the board with all their ideas about gravity. They were all putting their hands up saying what they thought. Everybody was contributing to it, they were all quite enthusiastic about it. And we didn't stop asking questions. Every statement that was said was put down and other people would put their hands up

and comment on that statement and by the end we'd got a good understanding of what gravity was. Some people were saying 'there's gravity on earth but there's no gravity anywhere else.' And then came the argument, 'well there must be gravity because otherwise a flag couldn't stay on the moon, you wouldn't be able to land on the moon' and all these other things. So they started to discuss each other's points to come up with the right answer. And that was without me feeding any information at all. That is what impressed me most.

(Quicke 1995)

6. *Encourage students to engage in dialogue both with the teacher and with each other*

The social aspect of social constructivism is vitally important. For it is mainly through the mediation of one or more other people that pupils make intellectual progress. This is especially true of pupils who have learning difficulties, whose metacognitive awareness, use of effective learning strategies, and self-regulation of their learning is likely to be relatively undeveloped. In other words they are less likely than their peers to be able to engage in formal learning on their own.

Observations show this aspect of pupils' learning to be under-used and undervalued. Yet it has great potential, for the following reasons among others:

• Pupils can enrich each other's learning. They may spark off ideas in each other: 'That's a good one. I wish I'd thought of that.'
• Explaining to others and justifying their own views are intellectually stimulating experiences:
    'I like being in a group because I get good ideas.'
• Understanding different viewpoints can increase metacognitive awareness:
    'It's awkward trying to be in a group because we're all different people, we're not the same people because some person says something and someone says something else.'
• Learning tolerance and respect for others' views is an experience in democracy, and enhances social understanding:
    'No matter how much you don't like them you've got to try and make an effort.'
• Pupils often feel less vulnerable and exposed than in individual working:
    'We were working as a team. We were all working together.'
• This is the ideal and natural context within which to practise and learn social skills which are often relatively undeveloped and without help may prove obstacles in later life and work:
    'You shouldn't make a fool of people and you shouldn't call people names. We've all to stop embarrassing each other.'
• Not least, it is usually more engaging and more fun.

In introducing group work to the pupils whose talk is illustrated in this section, their teacher was initially dubious about the likely benefits. However after one term of working together, not only had they enjoyed and learned socially and academically from the experience, they were also at times congratulating each other on their contributions (Watson 1999).

7. *Encourage student inquiry by asking thoughtful, open-ended questions, and encouraging students to ask questions of each other*

8. *Seek elaboration of students' initial responses*

9. *Engage students in experiences that might engender contradictions to their initial hypotheses and then encourage discussion*

These three descriptions of classroom talk make up what I have identified as talk that encourages pupil reflection (Watson 1996). The nature of the classroom interactions experienced by all pupils are vitally important in their learning and understanding. They convey teachers' expectations, at verbal and non-verbal levels. Constructivist approaches place great stress on the power of dialogue to challenge and extend pupils' levels of understanding.

A Scottish study of classroom conversation, which involved recording on four separate occasions, concerned the role of questions and control of classroom conversations. A group of five children had been placed in a special primary unit because they had not coped well in mainstream. All had moderate learning and general language difficulties. Their teacher decided to play a less dominant role by reducing her questions and waiting longer for the pupils' contributions. The overall effect was that the pupils now were not just sitting in a group to answer questions: they were taking part in a conversation . . . They were talking more, thinking more about what they were saying, listening to, learning from and communicating with each other. Talk was becoming an important feature of the classroom. Over the four sessions, the mean length of pupil utterances and their contributions to the discussion doubled and they made many fewer irrelevant comments. The teacher concluded that deliberately making fewer controlling moves and handing over some of the control of the flow of ideas to the children involved more than just a change in strategy. It was effective because it also involved changes in her attitude and perception. She became more aware of the children's ability in group conversation, because they were now able to be more in control of what was happening (Togneri 1984).

Classroom observations have shown that where a high proportion of teacher talk aimed to encourage pupil reflection, more reflection did happen, and that pupils enjoyed the challenges involved. In contrast to interactions where pupils' thinking was challenged and extended, and their understanding increased, which were satisfying and enjoyable experiences, some were left incomplete and were a source of frustration. It was as though pupils were wanting engagement and reflection and not achieving it. Such experiences almost never occurred in sessions in which the teacher's talk was mainly responsive to pupils. The main causes of episodes remaining unresolved included:

- Very occasionally a teacher failing to respond to a specific request for help:

  Paul: *I don't know what to do.*
  Teacher: *I know it's a bit difficult for you but keep trying.*

- A teacher's determination that the pupil should produce a specific answer, and a consequent failure to tune into their thinking:

  Trudy returns to class from seeing the dentist and says she has had cement. Another pupil asks in an amazed tone what that is, but the teacher asks whether Trudy got a sticker from the dentist.

- Misinterpretation of a pupil's initiative, and the teacher's lack of awareness that this caused a problem:

  Alan corrects another who has confused 'news' with a diary account, saying 'that's not news it's a diary'.
  Teacher: *Now that's a good question.*
  Alan: *No I was meaning that's a diary, it's meant to say news.*

  The teacher persisted in her belief that he was asking what a diary was.

- Failure to respond appropriately when pupils identified errors or ambiguities in their work:

  Teacher: *Now have a look carefully. How many seasons does it give there?*
  Stewart: *Five.*
  Teacher: *But there are only . . .*
  Stewart: *Four.*
  John: *Why has it got winter there?*
  Teacher: *There is one month [sic] that is repeated again.*
  John: *I'll scribble it out.*
  Teacher: *It's winter, quite right. No need to rub it out, When it's January it's all cold . . .*

- Failure to take seriously pupils' rarely expressed opinions about their work.

  Teresa: *It's boring.*
  Teacher: *Is it boring? Well why is it boring? Have you read it yet? What does it say? It's boring when you don't do anything but when you start reading then it becomes interesting.*

What seems to be dominant in the teacher's mind in these examples is not pupils' understanding and how to enhance and stimulate it, but the carrying out of restricted low level tasks that will involve the minimum of challenge and presumably less risk of emotional upset.

Any teaching session under scrutiny will appear to contain missed opportunities to develop reflection, and for a range of good reasons. Nonetheless these are far less frequent in the classrooms of constructivist teachers.

10. Allow wait time after posing questions

When teachers wait longer for replies from pupils and reduce the number of questions they ask, for example by replacing them with their own personal contributions or simply indicating their interest and wish to hear more (non-verbally or by phatics like 'Uhhm'), this is reliably found to lead to more and more complex pupil talk, including questioning and the production of more ideas (Wood 1991). In general, the greater the understanding we believe a person to have, the more time we wait for their answer, but we are all too ready to jump in to 'help' the halting communications of those whom we believe to be less competent. Contributory factors may be embarrassment, impatience and probably the belief that we know what they want to say anyway. But cutting short or preventing a response from someone who has difficulty in communicating their thinking is not helpful. And it is far from the contingent responsiveness of social constructivism, in which thoughtfulness is prized and expected to take time and effort.

Classrooms are brisk and busy places, which do not naturally lead pupils to believe that they are expected to take time to think. Teachers are often aghast to discover that they ask and often answer their own question in virtually the same breath. Pupils' awareness of their own thinking can also be helped by encouraging them to reflect about their own strategies and learning styles, and this takes time, especially for less confident pupils.

11. *Provide time for students to construct relationships and create metaphors*

Research by Cooper and McIntyre (1993) highlighted the importance of pupils incorporating newly encountered learning into their previous knowledge and understanding in a very active process, and in a range of different, perhaps idiosyncratic, ways. Reconstruction, turning ideas around, and considering their possible conflict with others that are firmly held, are mature intellectual processes, desirable outcomes of teaching, and fostered by constructivist pedagogy which leads toward more critical independent thinking. The use of pictorial symbols and representations, the creation of appropriate analogies and metaphors stretch pupils' imagination and can enhance their understanding.

However, many pupils with learning difficulties do not spontaneously relate their current learning with other experiences either in or out of school, and teachers often do not take up the opportunities to help pupils to extend the context of meaning in this way. Besides explicit reminders by teachers, modelling can be powerful both in encouraging pupils to develop the habit of looking for links and relationships for themselves, and also because it is a powerful way of increasing their understanding.

In my classroom recordings involving pupils with learning difficulties it is quite unusual to hear pupils make spontaneous connections with earlier classroom experiences, such as:

Pete: *Mr Jones told us that all the planets are getting nearer to the sun.*
Tony: *He said it's pushing all the planets together.*

Teachers using a constructivist framework explicitly encourage their pupils to look for links and relationships, introduce them to analogy and metaphor and will respond very positively to their pupils following suit.

12. Nurture students' natural curiosity through frequent use of the learning cycle model

This model consists of a three-stage cycle of learning in which metacognition is emphasised. Initially pupils generate questions and hypotheses from, for example, working with science materials; next the teacher extends and focuses the students' thinking; and thirdly there is generalisation as students apply their understanding to new problems. In this way their understanding and control of their own learning will be enhanced.

An example of the learning cycle model in practice comes from a learning support unit attached to a large Scottish comprehensive school. Here, as a matter of whole school policy, special attention is paid to the sequence of planning, doing and reviewing, with pupils participating at each stage. The procedure includes different stages, initially aiming to increase pupils' sense of ownership, by including them in planning their learning, and inviting and considering their ideas and suggestions. Visible plans are also created and displayed to help as reference points for both pupils and staff, showing where they have reached, and the planned end product, and helping recapping and self-assessment. Then reviewing – pupils' reflection on their work during or after its completion – is the ideal locus for emphasising metacognition, pupils' awareness of their individual learning styles, and their strengths and weaknesses. This in turn contributes towards the development of autonomy and initiative with which this article on the characteristics of constructivist teaching began.

Conclusion

This article describes teaching that is especially helpful to pupils who experience difficulty in school. It demonstrates how often quite minor changes in teachers' practice can be effective in conveying to pupils that what they think and say matters, that learning depends on them and can give them great satisfaction, individually and as part of a class community. A general framework of social constructivism can promote effective teaching in pupils of all ages and levels of ability and across the curriculum.

References

Brooks, J. and Brooks, M. (1993) *In search of understanding; the case for constructivist classrooms.* Alexandria, VA: Association for Supervision and Curriculum Development.

Cooper, P. and McIntyre, D. (1993) 'Commonality in teachers' and pupils' perceptions of effective classroom learning.' *British Journal of Educational Psychology*, **63**, 381–99.

Goddard, A. (1997) 'The role of individual education plans/programmes in special education: a critique' *Support for Learning*, **12** (4), 170–4.

Norwich, B. (1997) 'Exploring the perspectives of adolescents with moderate learning difficulties on their special schooling and themselves: stigma and self-perceptions.' *European Journal of Special Needs Education*, **12** (1), 38–53.

Quicke, J. (1995) 'Differentiation; a contested concept.' *Cambridge Journal of Education*, **25** (2), 213–24.

Togneri, K. (1984) 'Conversation in the special class: a teacher's change of strategy in group conversations', Dip SEN dissertation (unpublished). Edinburgh: Moray House College.

Watson, J. (1996) *Reflection through interaction: the classroom experience of pupils with learning difficulties.* London: Falmer Press.

Watson, J. (1999) 'Working in groups: social and cognitive effects in a special class'. *British Journal of Special Education*, **26** (2) 87–95.

Watson, J. (2000) 'Constructive instruction and learning difficulties.' *Support for Learning*, **15** (3), 135–41.

Wells, G. (1999) *Dialogic Inquiry: Toward a Sociocultural Practice and Theory of Education.* Cambridge: Cambridge University Press.

Wood, D. (1991) 'Aspects of teaching and learning', in: P. Light, S. Sheldon and M. Woodhead (eds), *Learning to think.* London: Routledge.

For permission to use illustrative examples I am most grateful to the Edinburgh schools which participated in Watson (1996), and to staff and pupils at Balwearie High School, Cambridge School and Woodmill High School.

Chapter 8

Constructivism and primary science

Patricia Murphy

A curriculum that emphasises the teaching of content or subject knowledge can leave little space for children to develop their own ideas and feel in control of their learning. Patricia Murphy, a lecturer at the Open University, argues that how we teach children is as important as what we teach them and that this should include opportunities to think, question and make decisions. In this chapter she explores 'constructivist' approaches to teaching in science and suggests that these will encourage children's curiosity and enthusiasm and ultimately the quality of their scientific understanding.

Joan Solomon (1997: 4) argues that 'no one who is without curiosity has a hope of understanding what science is about'. For this reason she believes that *how* we teach children is at least as important as *what* we teach them, if not more so. She identifies two ground rules for fostering children's curiosity:

- the '*locus of control*' must reside with the learner
- the '*instructional density*', that is the amount of teaching, must not inhibit or get in the way of the child's thinking and decision-making so as to remove the activity completely from them.

The theory

Mike Watts, Brenda Barber and Steve Alsop (1997: 6) highlight research into '*question-rich environments*'. Such an environment, they argue, nurtures learners' natural curiosity. The children in the classrooms observed were encouraged to formulate questions after having been given the means and opportunities to '*speak their minds*' (Watts, Barber and Alsop: 7). This approach, like Joan Solomon's, places the locus of control with the children. However, there is also an important and demanding role for the teacher, that is to know what activities to select and when to give help and in what form. Children need to learn how to collaborate and be given tools to assist them in making their thinking explicit to themselves, other children and their teachers. They also need to be able to identify a 'good' question in science and, importantly as Mike Watts and colleagues point out, where and how they might find a 'good' answer.

Concerns about how to teach effectively in science have emerged as understanding about children and how they learn has progressed. Pamela Wadsworth (1997) refers to a *constructivist approach* to teaching and learning. Constructivism is a general term which is open to numerous interpretations. However, central to a constructivist view of learning is the notion of *agency*. Jerome Bruner described agency as one of the crucial ideas that educators have learned in the last decade (Bruner 1994).

Agency in learning means that knowledge is not passively received by learners, rather it is actively built up by them. It is the learner who makes sense of his or her experiences. In making sense of new experiences children draw on their pre-existing knowledge and beliefs. There is therefore an essential link between the ideas children bring to science and the sense they make of the experiences provided for them. In a constructivist approach to learning, as Pamela Wadsworth points out, children's ideas matter.

A teacher who adopts this view of learning has to pay attention to children's ideas but also, and importantly, has to help them to learn about their learning precisely because they are the ones in control of it. Learning about learning is another central idea in a constructivist approach. Bruner referred to it as *reflection*, 'not simply learning in the raw but making what you learn make sense, taking it inside you' (Bruner 1994). In a report into the effectiveness of existing teaching approaches used to introduce scientific ideas in Key Stage 2 classrooms (Sizmur and Ashby 1997:24), it was observed that 'for meaningful learning to take place there must, at some level, be a need for that learning'. An important way that the teachers observed in the study established 'a need to learn' was to use tasks that promote reflection and to provide tools to enable this. For example, children would be asked in a variety of ways to record their ideas and thinking and at various points in learning activities be given opportunities to reflect on and record any changes in them. The use of concept maps is a good example of an activity that elicits children's thinking and supports reflection.

The practice

Constructivism in its various forms is a major influence on research and curriculum development in science but what of teachers' practice? I decided to ask local teachers about their approach to learning in science. It was interesting but not surprising that some teachers were not convinced about a constructivist approach, in particular whether it was appropriate at all ages. Others had never heard of constructivism but were nevertheless committed to investigative learning where the children had 'freedom in the practical sense to decide what they wanted to find out and how to set about doing it'. Some described a constructivist approach as the children 'doing the doing'.

Those who had heard of the term were usually strong advocates of the approach and described it as 'children building on their previous experiences through practical investigation, learning through investigative, open learning situations within the classroom'.

An important element of the approach from the point of view of the teachers interviewed was that the classroom activities had to match the science learning objectives. 'If what we are wanting to do is to teach them about science they're not going to learn that just by watching and listening to somebody else. They only get that by being scientific themselves.' In the interviews I asked teachers if they tried to establish children's ideas about a topic: 'I would start a new session perhaps with a discussion about what they [the children] already know: Who can remember about . . . ? What do you know about . . . ? What do you think might happen . . . ? So building on what they already know, not discussing it starting from where they are.'

For other teachers it was more problematic. For instance, one teacher said that she typically would find out what the children knew about a topic before any activity. However, when asked if that influenced what she did she said that it did not. The Sizmur and Ashby study (1997) found that few teachers elicited children's views in any systematic way. Furthermore, the lessons observed were structured in advance and were rarely reactive to children's pre-existing ideas. As one teacher I interviewed explained: 'There is so much that you have to pack into such a short time and the constraints are so rigid that they [the children] don't have an awful lot to say in what they're doing.' Another observed: 'It is so directed with the National Curriculum and we know they've got to understand this, this and this . . . it's as much a time constraint as anything else.'

The problem

If children have to make their own sense, then attempting to impart knowledge will either fail altogether or result in only superficial short-term learning. It would seem that for a constructivist approach to flourish in classrooms the curriculum structure and load in science need to change, and its assessment. Different kinds of understanding need to be valued and elicited by a wider range of assessment tasks and methods than is presently the case.

Guy Claxton (1990: 29–31) has some useful images to apply to different views of the relationship between teacher and learner. For example, a belief that we can 'give' knowledge to children assumes a model of the teacher as 'a petrol pump attendant' and of the child as the passive recipient of knowledge. Teachers who want to 'fix' children's 'unscientific' ideas Claxton would label as 'watchmakers' tinkering with the children's brains. This approach, like the former, denies the learner's active role in learning and the essential requirement for the learner to perceive a need for learning. Although, as Claxton describes it, the children are involved in the construction of the watch they do not get to question the components or the objectives. A more constructivist-oriented image is that of teacher as 'gardener' where the 'growing' is done by the learner as she converts the nourishment she receives from the learning situation into her 'own fabric'. The gardener assists but cannot determine this process. Another useful image he offers is that of the 'sherpa' acting as a knowledgeable guide to an explorer of unfamiliar terrain.

One of the teachers interviewed described science as 'like teaching a foreign language', a language she had never learnt. Sutton (1996) uses a similar metaphor to make the point that science is a strange language and understanding how it is used by people to make sense is what teaching should focus on. This resonates with Claxton's image of the teacher as 'sherpa', helping children to negotiate a strange terrain.

Strategies

The Nuffield Primary Science materials offer a range of ways of eliciting children's ideas. I found that some teachers used these methods, such as annotated drawings, to elicit children's ideas about a concept and these informed the way they grouped children, usually on the basis of shared interests and questions. Sizmur and Ashby recommend an approach that is similar. They observed how in some classrooms children were given opportunities to discuss their ideas and to collaborate in the development of a set of shared questions or statements with which they could agree or disagree. The children then chose the best approach to address their chosen question. Their approach might be an investigation but it had to 'fit' the question. This strategy gives the locus of control to the children, both in deciding what is a good question and in identifying the approach to find a 'good' answer. It also requires the children to share their thinking with each other and with the teacher, and so promotes reflection on their own learning. Requiring children to organise their ideas into good questions is therefore an effective teaching and management strategy. It helps make manageable what some teachers fear, that is the potential range of children's interests and ideas.

This approach might help those teachers who expressed regret that prior to the National Curriculum there was more opportunity to explore children's ideas. This they saw as important because 'they [the children] see what they think is valued and what they are interested in as valued'.

Children's views

I also talked to children from Years 5 and 6 to see whether 'constructivist' approaches were affecting their view of the importance of their ideas. I asked them what they thought about the 'control' they had over their learning in science. The children liked science and identified two reasons for this: the opportunity for finding out, and the ability to have their own ideas explored. The children all agreed that their ideas were important in science, more so than in other subjects. They saw the teacher as the person who decides what is to be done, that is the topic selector, but it was they who decided the best way to find things out: 'We make up our own mind how to do it.' In explaining why they thought it was good to explore their own ideas, one child observed: 'Sometimes even though the teacher's ideas might be better we've got something to go on for ourselves.' Another child added wisely: 'It's also a way teachers can see what we think and know and that's important.'

It may well be that opportunities for working with children in the way described are difficult to find. Nevertheless, children welcome being the decision-makers and want their thinking and ideas to be valued. The pay-off for teachers is both in the enthusiasm for learning science that such an approach fosters and in the quality of children's scientific understanding that results.

Acknowledgement

My thanks to all the teachers whose views were drawn on, particularly the children and staff at Gifford Park County Combined School, Milton Keynes, who provided some of the information reported.

References

Bruner, J. (1994) 'Four ways to make meaning'. Invited address to the 1994 Annual Meeting of American Educational Research Association. New Orleans.

Claxton, G. (1990) *Teaching to Learn: A direction for education.* London: Cassell.

Sizmur, S. and Ashby, J. (1997) *Introducing Scientific Concepts to Children.* Slough: NFER.

Soloman, J. (1997) 'Is how we teach science more important than what we teach?' *Primary Science Review*, **49**, 3–5.

Sutton, C. (1996) 'The scientific model as a form of speech', in: G. Welford, J. Osborn and P. Scott (eds), *Research in Science Education in Europe.* London: Falmer Press.

Watts, M., Barber, B. and Alsop, S. (1997) 'Children's questions in the classroom'. *Primary Science Review*, **49**, 6–8.

Wadsworth, P. (1997) 'When do I tell them the right answer?' *Primary Science Review*, **49**, 23–4.

Chapter 9

Supporting science in Key Stage 1

Janet Kay

Teaching assistants have much to contribute to children's learning across the primary curriculum. In this chapter Janet Kay, author of books for teaching assistants, explores the contribution they can make to children's learning of science through encouraging children's curiosity, clarifying and extending children's knowledge and understanding and addressing misconceptions. 'Misconceptions' usually arise because children have not been provided with accurate information or the opportunity to explore their ideas and the author highlights the importance of conversation and careful questioning in supporting children's learning of science. This chapter focuses on the curriculum guidance for Key Stage 1 in England. Readers working in other countries might like to compare and contrast this with the recommendations in their own curriculum documents.

The idea of children as 'natural explorers', who will seek explanations for the things they see and experience in their environments, is one that is commonly held. Bloomfield *et al.* (2000: 149) state that: 'We are explorers from the cradle to the grave. We seem to be born with curiosity, "a need to know".' However, Siraj-Blatchford and MacLeod Brudenell (1999) argue that although children may be natural scientists they need guidance to ensure that what they find out about the world around them is accurate. Otherwise, they may reach conclusions about events in their environment, which are basically incorrect.

Harlen (2000: 57) suggests the following may occur and lead to misconceptions:

- Children take account of only some factors that are relevant.
- Things are considered from only one point of view, their own.
- Inappropriate links are made.
- Predictions may be no more than stating what is already known, so that they are bound to be confirmed.
- Evidence may be selectively used to support an existing idea, ignoring what may be in contradiction.

Examples of these misconceptions include children who believe that objects float or sink because of their colour; that bigger objects will sink because of their size; that ice melts because it is placed in a drink, not because of changes in temperature.

It is important to encourage an enquiring mind and to help children formulate and ask questions about their environment. Children need to know that scientific enquiry does not take place in a vacuum. It is part of an ongoing and developing body of knowledge, understanding, developments and applications that is part of the past, present and future.

The role of adults

Siraj-Blatchford and MacLeod Brudenell (1999) argue that adults need to become active role models to young children, exploring and investigating the world with them and acknowledging the widespread existence of science. They need to role-model observational skills, investigation skills and effective methods of enquiry. Adults also have a very important role in clarifying and extending the children's knowledge and understanding, reversing misconceptions and making sense of outcomes. Without adult guidance, children may reach understandable, but incorrect, conclusions about their discoveries. For example, children in a nursery class were choosing and placing different objects in water to see which floated and which did not. By coincidence, the large objects floated and the smaller objects sank, leading the children to start to believe that this would always be the case. The parent helper suggested a few more trials and quietly introduced some objects, which she knew would reverse the trend, to 'head-off' the mistaken conclusion the children were about to reach.

Conversation with children can be used to develop and refine ideas, and to help them produce a sequence of small steps towards achieving their desired goals. For example, when Dan was planning his trip to the pond, he shared his ideas about how to conduct his experiments with the adult, and between them they established a simple sequence of activities with which to complete the investigation. Through this discussion, Dan's plans became clearer and more achievable. The adult also asked questions and made suggestions to extend Dan's understanding and areas of investigation. Conversation was a crucial part of the process of completing the investigation and reaching conclusions.

Bloomfield *et al.* (2000) suggest that adult questions can stimulate children's enquiry in the following areas:

- Observation – What do you notice? What do you see?
- Classification – What does it remind you of? Which are the same as each other?
- Predictions – What will happen next? What will happen if?
- Testing – How can we find out? Shall we do it again? Shall we change anything?

(Adapted from Bloomfield *et al.* 2000: 150)

Riley and Savage (1994: 139) argue that adult involvement is important to guide children where multiple solutions present themselves, particularly if the child lacks confidence. 'Open-ended enquiry' can seem daunting if a myriad of different answers present themselves. Children may need support to structure their approach and make sense of what they find. They may also need support to feel able to make mistakes, try out new experiments and draw reasonable conclusions from these. Adult involvement is also important in developing the language of science, teaching children new words to describe the things they are observing or making happen through their own activities. Recording of experiments or investigations can be supported through diagrams and pictures, mark-making and emergent writing, although O'Hara (2000) points out that formal recording may not be desirable or necessary with younger children, and concentrating on conversation may be more useful on some occasions.

Key Stage 1 Science

Guidance as to how and what should be taught to develop science at Key Stage 1 is found in the National Curriculum for England (DfEE/QCA 1999). There are four areas of knowledge, skills and understanding for science at Key Stage 1:

* scientific enquiry
* life processes and living things
* materials and their properties
* physical processes.

The skills and knowledge for scientific enquiry are taught through the other three areas of study rather than as a separate subject. For example, children will learn methods of and approaches to scientific enquiry into materials and their properties.

Key skills that are developed through the science curriculum are:

* communication
* application of number
* IT
* working with others
* improving own learning and performance
* problem solving.

The opportunity for development of these key skills is embedded in the activities children do in science at Key Stage 1. However, it is important to recognise and promote this development through supporting children to use their skills in science and to work independently and as part of a team.

The role of science in the primary curriculum is often seen as having several layers. These include helping children to develop enquiry skills; understanding about the wider meaning of science (becoming literate in science); and making small investigations and understanding basic ideas on which more complex scientific understanding can be based.

Holland and Rowan (1996: 1) suggest that at Key Stage 1, '[by] channelling the children's natural curiosity into scientific investigation we can help them to acquire strategies to develop more formal and complex concepts'. Siraj-Blatchford and MacLeod Brudenell suggest that children should be both introduced to key ideas in science and also develop their own investigative skills. They describe this as 'playing the scientist game'.

> The central task of a science education is therefore to give children an appreciation of the historical accomplishments of the scientific community and an introduction to the scientific practices that provide the means by which they are achieved.
>
> (Holland and Rowan 1996: 6)

They also argue that the key skill within the 'scientist game' is that of reasoning, and that this is developed through scientific enquiry based on experiments and accurate measuring.

Harlen (2000: 13) states that:

> The role of primary science is, therefore, to build a foundation of small ideas that help children understand things in their immediate environment but, most importantly, at the same time to begin to make links between different experience and ideas to build bigger ideas.

Scientific enquiry

Children are laying down the basic skills for scientific enquiry at Key Stage 1 as well as learning about specific aspects of the world around them. To some extent, the development of enquiry skills is the key issue in Key Stage 1 Science, laying the foundations for more structured investigations at Key Stage 3 and 4, and setting the children on the 'road to discovery' (Wynn and Wiggins 1997). Scientific enquiry can be achieved through different methods of testing ideas and beliefs about aspects of the environment in which we live. Newton (2000) suggests that the following features are common to most types of scientific enquiry. The process is not linear, but can be repeated again and again as knowledge is increased and refined.

- Something is noticed or observed.
- A tentative hypothesis (explanation) is created to explain what is observed.
- The hypothesis is used to make a prediction about the event.
- An experiment is carried out to test the prediction.
- A conclusion is reached as to whether or not the hypothesis is valid.
- If not, then a retest is carried out to check a revised hypothesis.

(Newton 2000: 33)

For example, the children may observe that plants that do not get water may die. They may form the hypothesis that plants need water to live. They may *predict* that if they do not water the plants in the classroom they will wilt and die. They can experiment by growing or buying some plants and then depriving them of water and observing the outcome over a period of time. They may conclude that some plants do die quite quickly without water, but that others seem to survive longer. They may revise their hypothesis to say that some plants need more water to live than others and retest by experimenting with the watering needs of different types of plants.

The children could then go on to look at the other needs of plants, warm or cool conditions, light or shade, and make further experiments to confirm that plants have common needs which vary considerably between varieties of plant. In this experiment, it is important to make sure that some variables are kept constant to ensure they do not affect the outcomes of the experiment. These could include warmth, light and air flow. Changes in any of these conditions may also impact on the survival of the plants and therefore must be kept the same for all the plants in order to ensure that we can safely conclude that it is water deprivation that is making the plants die, not something else.

Newton (2000: 43) suggests that exploration is a key skill in scientific enquiry. Exploration is about noticing and observing and describing things and events. Exploration is a skill, which is usually initially developed through activities in the Foundation Stage and the home. This leads to the development of two other types of activity in science, *investigation* and *experimentation*.

Investigation

- weighing evidence
- comparing evidence with existing ideas
- spotting patterns and relationships
- explaining what the evidence suggests
- drawing some sort of conclusion.

Experimentation

- observing something
- coming up with an idea to explain what is observed
- predicting what will happen if
- designing a fair test to check out the prediction
- collecting the evidence
- comparing evidence with the original idea
- where to from here?

These different approaches will be applied to the other areas of study in Key Stage 1 Science in order to promote pupils' skills in scientific enquiry. However, it is important to remember that it is not possible or desirable for children to investigate every scientific aspect of their world through practical activities.

Life processes and living things

Children will study humans, animals and plants in the local environment in order to cover this part of the National Curriculum. Within this area of study children may explore their own bodies, how they grow, what they can do and the differences between themselves and others. They will learn to identify the factors that differentiate living things from things that have never been alive. They will learn about the different parts of the body, healthy living and what humans, animals and plants need for life.

Newton (2000: 51) lists the seven indicators of life, the presence of all of which differentiates living from non-living things:

• maturation (growth and change)
• locomotion (movement)
• nutrition (feeding)
• respiration (breathing)
• excretion (waste elimination)
• irritability (sensitivity to environment)
• reproduction (producing offspring).

These criteria apply to all living things – humans, animals and plants. Children do not have an instant understanding of the difference between living and non-living things. This develops gradually over time and through experience. Some non-living things fulfil some of these criteria and this can cause confusion. For example, cars and buses, wind and rain all move. It takes time for children to understand the different processes of life, and studies show that it is easier for children to understand growth and movement at an earlier age, and the more complex aspects of life later.

As part of the curriculum for science at Key Stage 1, children may be asked to bring in photos of themselves at a younger age, or as a baby. At the age of 5, Laura was asked to bring a baby photo into class to be put up as part of a display which was being prepared to help the children start to understand the process of maturation. Laura did not mention this project at home until the day it was due, and then she tearfully refused to go to school. As an adopted child, she and her family had no photos of her as a baby, because none had been taken. A photo of Laura at two was substituted and calm restored.

However, this incident reminds us that children do not all have rosy pasts and happy beginnings. Even children as young as 4 and 5 may have complex and difficult histories, reflecting failures in parenting or family breakdown, abuse, loss and separation. Children can feel acutely sensitive about being 'different' and therefore it is important to be aware of the possibility that any activity that delves into family life may be painful for some children. Teachers and teaching assistants need to be aware of the possible sensitive issues and have contingency plans if the activity may cause problems for some children. However, learning about humans is an important part of helping children to develop positive attitudes and values to each other, across cultural, religious and linguistic differences.

Materials and their properties

Materials are the substances from which our physical environment is structured. They include metals, glass, fibrous materials (polymers), composites (combinations of materials) and alloys (combinations of metals). Children need to know about the range of materials that are in the environment and different ways of classifying these. For example, we can classify a house brick as manufactured (not naturally occurring), a composite (made of several other materials), a solid (not liquid). We can also look at the substances that are used to make a brick and the processes involved, including the application of heat. Is this reversible? Are the substances in different states before they are combined to become a brick, i.e. liquid or gas? Why are these particular materials chosen for building houses?

There are any number of materials that can be investigated in this way, by exploring their properties and classifying them according to those properties. Children need to recognise the link between the properties of materials and their uses. For example, bricks are used for building houses because the application of heat makes the combination of materials used hard and strong and this is irreversible. Bricks do not absorb much liquid, they do not dissolve and they will not revert to a liquid state.

Young children may have lots of information about materials from their day-to-day experiences of life at home and in the wider world. This information needs to be extended on and clarified. Cooking is an excellent example of exploring materials and their properties. Combining ingredients such as flour, fat and water can make another material – dough. By applying heat to this dough we can make another material – pastry. Children are often very unclear as to whether materials are manufactured or natural. They may simply not know where flour comes from or how it is processed. Discussing the origins of different materials can help children make sense of the links between different types of materials and to start to classify them as natural or manufactured.

Exploring materials using the senses is central to the activities within this part of the curriculum. Children can explore materials through:

- Sight – what does it look like?
- Smell – what does it smell like?
- Touch – what does it feel like?
- Hearing – what does it sound like?
- Taste – what does it taste like?

It is very important to help young children to recognise that not all materials can safely be explored through all the senses, and that safety warnings must be clear and repeated.

Physical processes

This part of the Key Stage 1 science curriculum is concerned with forces – push, pull and twist. Forces that are part of our everyday life include gravity, magnetism, muscular forces, mechanical propulsion, friction and electricity. At Key Stage 1, pupils learn mainly about the properties of electricity, through experiments with batteries, circuits and circuit breakers.

The role of the teaching assistant

There are some specific areas where teaching assistants can support the learning and teaching of Key Stage 1 science when working with groups and individual children. These can include finding out what children know about the topic already, clarifying the task and breaking it down into small steps. You may also help children formulate questions to be answered within the task and help them to predict what might happen. Supporting children in carrying out practical activities and maintaining and promoting safe behaviour and use of equipment are also key tasks for the teaching assistant.

It is important to help children to relate the task to the wider world, and ask, 'Why is this relevant to our lives?' This may include linking the activity in with other work the children are doing in other subjects or topics. Teaching assistants can provide a focus (often through questioning) through which children can draw conclusions about the outcomes of the activity. When working with children with different levels of ability, you can support individuals and groups by differentiating more complex tasks for some children. Finally, feeding back to teachers on the success of the activity and any confusions or gaps in knowledge identified can be a great help in the planning process.

There are other more general roles and responsibilities which teaching assistants may have in relation to the management of teaching and learning science. These may include supporting the teacher in planning how to organise the classroom for science activities, helping with displays of materials or children's work, and preparing, storing and maintaining equipment and materials. Teaching assistants also have a role in supporting the teacher to take groups out for trips, nature walks or other explorations of the environment. Supporting the use of IT in science, either through use of software to extend knowledge and understanding or through supporting children in information retrieval is another way in which you may work with children in Key Stage 1 science.

Conclusion

Supporting Key Stage 1 science can be very rewarding. In this subject, children can draw on a range of skills and abilities – literacy, numeracy, IT skills and their own creativity – to explore and make sense of the world around them. At the very least, sharing in these explorations can be great fun! But, children are also making important discoveries about their world and the objects and living things within it. Providing them with a safe and structured environment in which to do this is crucial. Children need to understand the ways in which scientific exploration is conducted and how we find out about the characteristics and properties of different materials or aspects of our world. It is important for you to be aware of and to convey to the children that science takes place as part of an ongoing process, and in the light of an existing body of scientific knowledge. Finding out more about science in the present and the past is an essential part of developing this awareness.

References

Bloomfield, P., de Boo, M. and Rawlings, B. (2000) 'Exploring our world', in: L. Drury, R. Campbell, and I. Miller (eds), *Looking at Early Years Education and Care*. London: David Fulton.

DfEE/QCA (1999) *National Curriculum for England*. Sudbury: QCA. www.nc.uk.net

Harlen, W. (2000) *The Teaching of Science in Primary Schools*, 3rd edn. London: David Fulton.

Holland, C. and Rowan, J. (1996) *The Really Practical Guide to Primary Science*, 2nd edn. Cheltenham: Stanley Thornes.

Newton, L. (2000) *Meeting the Standards in Primary Science – a Guide to the ITT NC*. London: RoutledgeFalmer.

O'Hara, M. (2000) *Teaching 3–8*. London: Continuum.

Riley, J. and Savage, J. (1994) 'Bulbs, buzzers and batteries – play and science', in: J. Moyles (ed), *The Excellence of Play*. Milton Keynes: Open University Press.

Siraj-Blatchford, J. and MacLeod Brudenell, I. (1999) *Supporting Science, Design and Technology in the Early Years*. Milton Keynes: Open University Press.

Wynn, C.M. and Wiggins, A.C. (1997) *The Five Biggest Ideas in Science*. New York: John Wiley and Sons.

Chapter 10

Learning science

Joan Solomon with Stephen Lunn

'Science should be everybody's favourite subject in primary school', says the distinguished academic and authority on science education, Joan Solomon, here in conversation with Stephen Lunn, a researcher at the Open University. A delight in using their senses and a natural propensity to play prepare children perfectly for the role of scientist, but they also need adults to guide their learning, for example by offering vocabulary and asking questions. Teaching assistants, working with small groups or individuals, are often best placed to take part in these scientific conversations.

Children learning science

I think we know very little about how children learn, in spite of years of looking at them. As far as teaching assistants are concerned, you need to know whether almost everybody in a class of thirty children, or the group of six, is really hanging on your every word, or simply very busy in some way. It doesn't do just to keep the pupils quiet, which is what I sometimes see happening. There are all sorts of 'withdrawal' things that children do which make a total barrier to any ideas coming in, like, for instance, chewing their nails and fiddling with bits of paper. So, making sure that children are absolutely quiet can be detrimental to learning. If on the other hand you have an idea that you genuinely believe will be of great interest, then don't try and get them quiet, try and get them excited, even if it's a bit noisy. You will of course have to say, 'You won't hear what I've got to say about baby elephants or whatever unless you do keep really quiet', but I've seen so many lessons recently in which even well-established teachers have managed to keep the children quiet, but where they haven't really been listening at all.

I think science is the most wonderful context for learning. Children are fascinated by animals, we all know that, but not just small furry ones. I've seen children, even babies, pointing a chubby finger at an ant going across the table. You know, they are absolutely fascinated. Once, when the National

Curriculum first came in, I went round lots of places on the edge of Oxford, asking the children what was their favourite subject. At First School they all said 'science', and in Middle School, quite a lot of them said 'science'. They didn't, however, in the upper schools. Children like science, because of the things that it deals with. When it's snowing, you can take them out to look at the snowflakes as they fall on their jerseys, and they're fascinated by that. If an animal is warm and furry they hold it and they feel this tiny heart going terribly fast, and it's astonishing to them. Then of course they will try and find out if their own hearts are going fast and you can try and introduce them to pulses and things like that.

I have no doubt that, with reasonably good teaching, science should be everybody's favourite subject in primary schools. One of the reasons is that it's closely connected with children's senses. Now if there's one thing small children excel in, it is the acuity of their senses. A tremendous number of little children can 'feel' tremendously well and so holding an animal is marvellous for them. They can actually hear much better than we can, much higher frequencies. When my grandchildren from London come to see me, the first thing they do when they come out of the car is look around. It's the first time they've met granny for a while, but they're not interested in granny at all, of course. I think what they are looking at is birds, and then I suddenly realise there are birds calling everywhere. It's like an orchestra for them. They're absolutely astonished. Much of this I cannot hear.

Mostly children have all five senses and they love using them. A little boy came out on our nature walk and he sniffed and said, 'I can smell nature already, Miss.' I'm sure a lot of their enjoyment of science is to do with the straight use of the senses, and they get a great joy out of this because it's natural to them. It doesn't need any effort. When they discover that grown-ups can't hear as well as they can, they get thrilled to bits because grown-ups are usually better at absolutely everything than they are. It was recently discovered that elephants have a mating call which is too low for most adults to hear. I'm actually frightfully fascinated by elephants, but then so are a lot of children. It was a woman who was exploring elephants somewhere in some national park in Africa who remembered that when she was little she used to sing in the church choir. She leant up against the organ and the low pipes of the organ gave a note so low that she could feel it in the air, rather than hear it – a sort of throbbing. I have a little CD which has got all the noises that elephants make. I got it from writing to the BBC because they'd done a programme about elephants. And there they were, the five different calls. But the interesting thing is that that was a discovery that could have been made by any eight-year-old child, and it was made by a woman remembering what it was like when she was eight, not by an adult, because adults can't really hear it. It is interesting, isn't it, because this is what we have to do if we're working with primary school children. We must know something about what life is like for them. You won't find many books on primary education which tell you anything like that.

Finding the words

When doing science children can find themselves at a loss for the right word. I saw a lesson once which started off with a piece of plastic, fairly thick plastic, and some drops of water on it, big ones and little ones. I've subsequently written about a lesson called 'gobbling drops' because when the two drops touch each other, they go 'woomph' and coalesce to form a big drop. This is a function of surface tension which I don't teach them anything about of course. They need words to describe it, so the teacher said, 'What are the drops like?' Various things came out: 'They're round', 'They're circles', 'They're drops', 'They are little balls'. Somebody said they're like an ice cream, which I thought was incredibly silly at first. But it wasn't really them being silly, it was me if you think about it. In a cornet, that's exactly what you have, that round bit, or almost exactly. So the teacher said: 'Those shapes, they aren't completely round, are they? They're flat underneath. That shape we call a dome.' And all these little children went round saying 'dome', because it's a particularly nice word to say because if you practise it in the corner with nobody looking, you'll find that you use your lips rather curiously. There was a little girl, who was a bit bumptious but very clever, and she said to her teacher, 'Well, they aren't all, they're flat on top.' And the teacher said 'Would you put your hand up if you've got something to say?' And I thought 'Oh dear', because the child had actually finished off the explanation. It was a communal discussion activity with the teacher coming in every now and then – 'Yes, it's not quite like a ball, yes, it's not actually a flat circle is it', and so on. Then this little girl, whose name I think was Anne, got it in the neck for saying they're flattened on top! But in fact she had brought it to a conclusion. So they now had new words and they had a new observation, and both of those went together.

When you're trying to describe things in science, you'll need more vocabulary, but it won't necessarily be the technical vocabulary that makes people say: 'Oh science has so many technical words.' The word 'dome' will be used again if you were looking at architecture, for example. If you watch children learning science, where they give answers to the teacher or teaching assistant who is carefully bringing out new vocabulary, you'll see that you couldn't tell whether it was an English lesson or a science lesson really. Of course, numeracy comes into science as well. People seem to see that numeracy comes in, but are not so good at seeing that vocabulary comes in all the time. Listening to elephants, you've got to be able to describe what you hear. You might say 'throb', and you have a little child who might say 'when I hurt myself, I can feel it sort of throbbing in my finger'. So, in this way, we can bring these words together and it's very important to talk it over.

Feelings about science

The first thing that teachers and teaching assistants have to do is to make sure that they never say, 'Now, we're going to do something about electricity. Now you pay attention because this is very difficult.' I've heard that so many times. If children find that adults find science very difficult, very shortly they will find science very difficult because they base themselves on what adults do. This country has always assumed that teachers (and teaching assistants) will teach with almost no training. At the beginning of the National Curriculum, there was the 'cascade' method of training people. America was giving a ten-year introductory period to introducing science into their elementary schools. It seemed we weren't giving any time at all. We were just saying, 'During your ordinary lesson times or after school or in your INSET days you will learn all these things.' So people had to learn them in a hurry, which reinforced them in their view that it was too difficult. 'It must be difficult because I don't understand it' – and that is dreadful. You really must feel that turning on an electric bulb is just play. Right at the beginning of the National Curriculum many primary teachers assumed that science and technology would be at the bottom of the things that they could teach, and about three years later they found it near the top, and that's the play part of it.

With regard to play, there are those who've written about this like Jerome Bruner and also Suzanne Miller who said one of the things about play is that there's a sort of 'moratorium on failure'. You can't fail if you're playing because in play there's no objective except the fun of finding out something. If it isn't fun, children discontinue the play and go on to something else. In most primary schools, all the way through Key Stage 1, there's quite a lot of activity which you could call play. For instance, nature walks are like play, and you can't go wrong. That's the difference between play and study. In study, there is a straight line and you're trying to achieve something, but in play children do a number of things, but can stop and change direction at any point – 'I'm just playing,' as they say.

Adults who didn't relate to science teaching at school are the ones who ought to be playing, the same as the children. They should take science home and do it on their kitchen table or on a windowsill. I learned all the things I know about transistors on a kitchen table, because I had very small children at that time. I hadn't got time to go to any courses and it was great fun actually. There I was, a physics graduate. I suppose it must have been in the 70s, so I suppose I was 40. I didn't know how you could make circuits and what sort of resistances we were talking about, and what were the most likely mistakes. The likely mistakes, of course, in all electrical experiments are that you haven't taken the insulation off something, you know, something absolutely simple like that.

People talk about feelings and values in relation to, for example, experiments on animals. I don't know, but I think children will feel very passionately about animals. When talking to children, it's important to bring out their values, find out what they actually think, and give them some credibility. Of course now there are so many people changing to being vegetarians – well that comes out too. Adults and children may have very strongly held beliefs that you shouldn't harm animals.

Supporting children's learning in science

I think that it would be a good idea, when the teaching assistant is in class supporting individuals, supporting groups, to get the children to talk. For example: 'I didn't understand about that. What did you think about those flowers? Have you seen them before?' I would have thought that it involved putting themselves on the conversational level of the children. Some children can engage in discussion at the whole class level, but a lot find speaking up in front of the whole class a big challenge, whereas in a small group around the table it's much easier to engage in a dialogue. And when you have 30 children, and there still are 30 children in classrooms I notice, often, it's awfully difficult to engage them all from the front, so obviously what you need to do is to have groups.

I think teaching assistants have very much to contribute to children's independent working. If, as a teacher, you think that you'll be able to have everybody doing autonomous things in the classroom, the answer probably is that first of all you have five people on each table and try and get them to work in small groups. But if you're teaching from the front it's really quite difficult to do that if you've got a difficult group that insist on quarrelling with each other – and some do. But then if you're a teaching assistant, and you've got a group of six children, you have really a golden opportunity. You could come in a bit, and say, 'Gosh that was interesting', and then keeping the train of thought going, 'What would happen if . . . ?' You're in a marvellous position, I would have thought, as a teaching assistant working with just one group, of getting them going. If you're the teaching assistant, you could do very well by little self-effacing questions like: 'I wonder if it would be true in such and such a case?'

Looking to the future

My thoughts about a future curriculum follow on from what I've been saying. I'd like to give children lots of things which stimulate them, their senses, their interest, and I would like to receive descriptions from them. I wouldn't want a massive amount of writing. Perhaps say to them: 'Just words that you could use if you were telling your mum about what you saw or felt.' So the science curriculum would be connected with the natural world and sometimes, as with electricity, not with the natural world. So there are a whole lot of things that can be linked to science, but I think I'd always go back to the senses. I think it's very valuable for primary aged children to do painting, music and dance. I don't believe that all experiment is about controlling variables and fair tests, and so there should be very little of that I think. Science should be in the child's lived world and also their imagined world.

Section 2
Contexts for learning

Ian Eyres and Carrie Cable

How do you separate a curriculum from its context? We have included the chapter *Learning at Coombes School* (Chapter 11) in this section because, in its embracing of creativity, the school's approach to teaching and learning supplies a special context to all the learning undertaken. This context includes the values, expectations, styles of teaching and support and resourcing which the staff believe contribute to a creative education. In a similar way, in Chapter 12, Sheilagh Crowther uses ICT and other resources to provide a supportive context for two children learning English as an additional language. Where context is so influential on learning we cannot escape the conclusion that it is part of the curriculum.

One frequently overlooked learning context, and one which teaching assistants often know well, is the school playground. In Chapter 13, Sarah Thomson offers a critique of what schools offer children in their free time, urging them to develop a context in which children can be more adventurous. In Chapter 14, Elizabeth Grugeon looks at the playground as a social environment created by the language practices of the children themselves. The importance of school buildings cannot be overstated and the influence of architecture on children's learning experiences is considered by Catherine Burke and Ian Grosvenor in Chapter 15.

Finally the section considers some out-of-school learning contexts. The context for learning which Kayte Brimacombe has created for her son, and which she describes in Chapter 16 includes both a physical context and 'rules of engagement'. We feel this must, as in the case of the Coombes School environment, be considered a de facto curriculum. A child's family can be considered a learning context in a number of ways. For many children much of the period of their most rapid learning, their first five years, is largely experienced in their own home, and they take the knowledge and learning strategies they develop in that context into school with them, to become part of the context of their school learning. Parents are not the only family members who support children's learning, and in Chapter 17 Charmian Kenner and her colleagues examine the role played by grandparents in a number of families. For cultural and other reasons, some parents choose to send their children to supplementary schools. In Chapter 18 John Bastiani identifies some of the benefits these complementary contexts offer children and parents.

Chapter 11

Learning at Coombes School

Bob Jeffrey and Peter Woods

> Coombes County Infants and Nursery School, in Arborfield, Berkshire, England, has been the focus of numerous research studies. Well known for its highly creative approaches to teaching and learning, the creative learning practices of learners and staff are recorded in this chapter, an edited version of one first published by Jeffrey and Woods in 2003 in a book documenting the work and life of the school.

> Pupils have excellent attitudes to learning . . . Pupils are keen to take ownership of their own learning.
>
> (OfSTED, 1997: para. 2, p. 1)

In this chapter, we focus on the ways in which Coombes establishes authenticity, supports learners' transformation of knowledge and encourages co-operative learning.

Establishing authenticity

> The main strength of the teaching is the use of real world experiences and the quality of resources used to stimulate enthusiasm amongst pupils.
>
> (OfSTED 1997: para. 3, p. 1)

> One thing we do is to put children into contact with reality. I think a lot of educational institutions are not authentic, not real world, and what we are aiming for here is to set children's learning in real life. . . . The key element of it is how they actually relate to each other and to adults. . . . We are interested in equipping kids to live life to the full in the future and the present.
>
> (Sue Rowe, Teacher)

The Coombes approach also encourages children to develop and own their own knowledge. Learning at Coombes is not done just for the sake of educational tests or for pleasing teachers and parents. Children are encouraged to reconstruct new knowledge and processes to make them meaningful in the children's own terms:

> You have to work at your own level, and you've got to be constantly open to the children's ideas, because education only becomes genuine when they put in a very strong input. If they don't, it somehow never sits within them as a part of themselves; they have to make that movement towards it all the time. Otherwise it's being layered on them superficially.
>
> (Sue Rowe, Teacher)

Coombes' teachers focus, in particular, on active learning and encouraging positive feelings.

Active learning

Play and active learning have been acknowledged as crucial to the cognitive and other developmental processes of children (Moyles 1997). Coombes promotes these principles through:

> hands-on, real experiences. That's why we keep sheep, and why we use the grounds so that they can actually get out there and do these things, not just look at pictures in a book or read about them or be told about them. They see the sheep being washed and sheared, they see the lambs being born, they go out and do pond dipping. They don't have to make an excursion . . . it's part of the ongoing curriculum and through that the children get a broad outlook on life.
>
> (Carole, Teacher)

The active approach makes learning meaningful; being mobile and active enhances engagement:

> We are learning about life and electricity at the moment. [. . .] You join the light clips up to the wire to make the light work or the fan work. We enjoy it because of the way that we are doing it. We don't sit down all the time.
>
> (David, Year 2)

Theresa (parent) had benefited from the school's 'open-door' policy; she was impressed with the children's application:

> The children were all busy . . . there was no misbehaving. There seemed to be adults with them on each table. . . . And my child's very active. I just knew that if he went to a school where he had to sit his bottom on that chair and copy what was on the board or wait for the teacher's attention, his mind would be gone. So he's come here, and he's just flourished.

Combining active learning and the replication of practices can heighten authenticity and bring a sense of individuality:

> I painted the ceiling in the classroom like Michelangelo did. . . . It was exciting because I was doing something different to the other children.
>
> (Alison, Year 2)

Active learning engages the senses:

> It is interesting being with the sheep because you can feel the warm wool and texture, and it is soft like my hair. It is interesting feeling things. It feels lovely when you get your hands in the mixing bowl when we do cooking.
>
> (Michelle, Year 2)

Any opportunity to include a sense of taste was always included in any investigation. 'When we did our Spanish topic we made paella. It had octopus and mussels' (Gigi, Year 2).

Active learning involves role play, particularly appropriate for young children who use narrative as an organising tool (Fox 1989). Rachel had been discussing the paintings of Mary Cassatt with her class, which portrayed tender moments between mothers and daughters, but looking at the paintings was not enough. She arranged for the class to observe a mother bathing her baby, with the children gathered round in a circle:

> We feel that it's really important to give them a really exciting stimulus so they can actually see a tender moment, see the mother looking lovingly at the child, helping wash the child, brushing her daughter's hair or washing the child's toes or the child just sitting with her mother as she's sewing.

> The children would then do a 'writers' workshop', some encouraging others, some sitting quietly and reflecting, the teacher also supporting, trying to get them to feel themselves as writers, believing in themselves and building up their confidence. Once that has taken hold, you can start to correct their work in a constructive way – but not until.
>
> (Sue Humphries, Headteacher)

Authentic learning contexts allow learners the opportunity to transform learning into a problem-solving experience:

> I look forward to doing experiments like the lights and batteries. It is like testing things. I don't care if it goes wrong. If I was a witch and I had to make a new potion in my cauldron I would experiment.
>
> (Craig, Year 2)

This kind of role play is empowering:

> It's having that curiosity of mind and of spirit, of wanting to know because it's interesting for itself. It's realising that you, too, can do it; you, too, can be a scientist, a true researcher.
>
> (Sue Rowe, teacher)

It increases the fun of learning:

> Amy was pretending to be a baby for Miss Rowe when we were talking about bones and growing. I like it when Miss Rowe encourages us to pretend. She does things interestingly with her voice as she plays a part. We did a play of the three pigs. We had a really bad wolf and we all joined in. It was fun.
>
> (Michelle, Year 2)

Role play also allows experimentation with one's self and an opportunity to see things from other perspectives, a critical feature in being creative:

> In the RE lesson we had to play a part and then think about that person's life. You get a chance to be somebody else. [. . .] It is enjoyable because we are being things we don't normally do. It was good pretending to be angry.
>
> (Simon, Year 1)

Generating positive feelings

Feeling positively about learning combines the emotional and the cognitive in an experience that draws the learner inside the activity. Feelings hold the key to cognition. At Coombes, there is much talk of excitement, joy, fun, happiness, confidence. The Headteacher, Sue Humphries, says:

> It really has something to do with a confident personality. If the setting is right it's going to help you to fulfil yourself as a person. So that all those qualities that make you fun to be with are burnished. They're going to be brought to the fore and emphasised. You might be a clever barrister, or a brilliant author or painter or road-sweeper or waitress but it's going to be the personal qualities that you bring to the job and the way that you relate to other people that's going to mean that you're happy in your life and filled with a sense of achievement and purpose. Education can foster those qualities, and education goes on and on.

Dee's daughter was 'a very bright and receptive child, but she was crippled by her lack of confidence'. She might easily have 'become very intimidated at a very early age' in the current pressurised National Curriculum environment. But at Coombes, 'everything is just fostered and encouraged. Because there is no regimentation, the children find it very easy to find their own level and just pick everything up. Some don't get left miles behind because of an attitude difference.' Celebrating achievement enhances feelings of well-being:

> It was good because Mrs Daniels was proud of me. It made me happy because . . . I like standing up and people saying 'Well done!'

This confidence, once established, seems to stay with them. James, a parent, felt:

> They are confident in the world as they go out today as six or even five-year-olds. They're holding an adult conversation. [. . .] If they've been to Coombes, children really are different. They're constantly surprising you.

With confidence comes the competence to be critical, rather than simply desiring to please the teacher. Lynn (parent) felt:

> They question every single thing: if you tell a child something, they're going to test it out; if they prove it for themselves they learn it.

The generation of positive feelings is encouraged by the development of an 'adventure culture' of learning through providing opportunities to experiment, play, be innovative and exercise control.

A constant stream of novel encounters maintains the adventure culture; open-ended possibilities are important for stimulating anticipation and excitement:

> We had to collect together twigs and leaves and make a nest and then we drew them. It was exciting because nobody knew what they were going to do. We could choose what we used. We didn't know what it would look like before we started.
>
> (Maria, Year 1)

The teachers have created challenges taking into account children's fears and desires for risk-taking. Risk-taking is part of learning. Anticipation is an emotion that draws on past experiences of risk-taking and challenge, 'When we go in the dark house it is dark and we can't see. We have to find some toys. We have a torch. It was fun because you keep on bumping into people (Hannah, Nursery). As Sue Humphries puts it:

> As you grow, you are making up your own story inside yourself and that story has to be filled with happiness – it will be filled with unhappiness quite naturally – but its construct, together with the intellectual abilities that are being developed, has to be happy, glad, anticipatory, so that you come to school filled with curiosity and a sense of 'I want to be here and I want to join in'.

Transforming knowledge

Learners interpret knowledge according to their experience and interests and express it in their own terms. They thus 'impose order on chaos' (Edwards and Forman 1993). McGuiness (1999: 1) notes that

> Developing thinking skills is supported by theories of cognition which see learners as active creators of their knowledge and frameworks of interpretation. Learning is about searching out meaning and imposing structure.

Young children generate meaning by filtering and then transforming knowledge through their imaginations. Children experiment with imaginative constructions and play with ideas (Craft 2002).

Narrative is a common mode of children using their imaginations to transform knowledge. This is, in fact, their main form of cognitive activity (Fox 1989). Children are given time and support to enable them to filter learning experiences through their preferred media. Curriculum objectives are then realised by encouraging the learners to show their knowledge through a narrative. When asked, after a history activity, by the researcher, 'What have you learnt this morning?' the children's responses were very limited, but when asked to 'Tell me the story of beating the bounds', they gave much richer answers.

Encouraging imaginative responses was a strategy used by the teachers to enhance learning, for example by encouraging children to make up number stories:

> There were two monkeys up a tree and the ground began to shake and two more monkeys climbed up the tree to join them.

. . . The little girl saw five fairies but one was so scared it had to go back to fairyland.

(Reception children, field note)

Similarly, when Sue asked the children to imagine what it would be like if their muscles grew faster than their bones and vice versa, the children used their imaginations to develop their knowledge of the body:

I'd be all floppy if my bones didn't grow.
My skin would be hanging down off the end of my fingers . . .
My bones would be stretching my body so I would be very thin. . . .
My brain would be getting squashed.

The extensive focus on language development and discussion enables children to develop a disposition for analysing learning experiences metaphorically:

I felt the harp vibrating and I listened to the music. When I felt the vibrations it made me think of a nail pricking my finger very gently.

Taking ownership of knowledge through the imagination is to make it meaningful in terms of the self. The knowledge then becomes valuable to the learner as an expression of the self and any encouragement of this process is extending the worth of the particular knowledge the teacher is exploring. Knowledge augments the extensions of self (Edwards and Forman 1993).

Learning co-operatively

Ownership of knowledge and control over learning are also gained in interactive social contexts. Participation among and between teachers, pupils, parents and others is a big feature of the learning experience at Coombes. Everyone who passes through the doors at Coombes is included in the pedagogic experience. Celebrating innovative suggestions from learners helps create a co-participative climate for learning,

Jude asks the Year 2 group how many they need to get from 75 to 100. She then commends a girl who offers a solution as to how to make the calculation: add on or take off the five and count in tens and then remember the five.

(Field note)

In this creative climate, learners feel free to make suggestions to improve the quality of lessons:

Miss Rowe said we were going to collect some greenery for an Irish display and I went up to Miss Rowe and said, 'Shall I sit on top of a chair on the table?' And then the class went outside and got lots of green leaves and they settled it around me.

(Rachael, Year 2)

Co-participation (Edwards and Forman 1993) brings learners into the learning process as contributors:

A Year 1 girl in Carol's class reminds all the children that the task they are being asked to do – wax relief – has been done before and she points to an example on the wall.

This is not seen as a criticism on her part, but a contribution to remind others that they have previous experience of the practice.

(Field note)

Co-participation spreads to peer participation:

> Sophie (Year 2) asks another child if she can use her hands to help with doubling numbers and the pair of them use this strategy to complete the task.

(Field note)

Another form of co-participation valued at Coombes is that of reversing teacher and learner roles. In some cases children take over teaching roles, as when three Year 2 children were instructed to assist the researcher in the art of making a 'smudged picture' with pastels:

> 'Then you get a white for the sky and rub it on. Do it dead gently and smudge it in.' 'With your fingers like Miss Davis taught us.' 'It makes a good effect, it makes it a better picture.' . . . 'Do it very lightly. Leave a space for the sun. Use pinks and oranges and yellows.' 'You have to use all these colours because the sky changes when it gets dark.' . . . 'Now leave it. That's good, that. Now you need to get the black and do little dotted lines where you have smudged the colours in.'

(Field note)

Taking on a teaching role gives children a measure of control and an opportunity to be creative. In this case the children mix their teacher's expressions with their experience to describe the process of smudge painting. In doing so they are also developing their understanding of the teaching and learning process.

There are also dialogues that develop between learners:

> Sue asks her mixed 5–7-year-old children how they would fill up an alien's empty brain and the children not only use their imagination but they confront each other's contributions.
> 'I would do it in a laboratory.'
> 'I would do it by telling.'
> 'You can't. Because it hasn't got anything in its brain to think with.'
> 'He wouldn't be able to remember anything.'
> 'You could make him go to sleep and then open his head a little to put the right information on his brain.'

Creative co-participation in teaching and learning involving the whole community was exemplified by the annual Fire of London topic. The children were told the story and a form of 'common knowledge' (Edwards and Mercer 1987) with teachers and peers was developed as they retold it verbally and in writing:

> The houses were too close and so the fire spread quickly. They had to run away quickly down to the river and get away by boat. The wind was blowing quickly and it was too strong to get across the river. When they caught a fish they didn't need to cook them because they were all boiled by the warm water of the London fire. Nine people died. One man told them to pull down the places where they stored things and the fire couldn't go any further:

(Susan, Year 1)

Figure 1.1

Families were then invited in to be co-participants by asking them to assist their children in constructing a model of a Tudor building. All the metre-high houses, churches and warehouses were installed in the hall on a street plan. This was then used for a week as a resource for maths work in mapping, direction, measurement, shape recognition and tessellation. The children used the 'roads' frequently, often on their own to traverse the hall to other parts of the building. Then on Thursday afternoon all the children gathered up their houses and, along with parents, grandparents and friends, the whole school troops out to the field and lays out the houses on the street map for the last time:

> We set fire to them. We smile at how much time we spent on them and then we burn them. For one of my children it became a real problem. She just did not want to burn it after she had made it. At the very last moment she decided not to let it be burnt and it still lies in the loft at home. But both of them can remember the key facts.
>
> (Parent governor)

While taking care to observe safety regulations, the headteacher then sets light to the 'baker's shop' and the children, staff and parents collectively engage in a learning experience never to be forgotten.

Conclusion

Coombes creates an authentic learning experience that recognises children's active dynamism and combines it with an openness to the way learners make experiences meaningful. Longitudinal research into the effects of the 1990s reforms carried out in primary schools found that pedagogies that minimised consideration of the learners' capacities and interests and the involvement of the learner in the objectives and the processes of teaching and learning resulted in 'a sense of children in flight from an experience of learning that they found unsatisfying, unmotivating and uncomfortable' (Pollard *et al.* 2000: 103). Teaching and learning programmes that do not strive for authenticity and support learners' control and ownership of knowledge may well result in disengaged learning (ibid.).

Children start off being creative (Beetlestone 1998), prefer some control over their learning and welcome opportunities to fantasise and to use their imagination (Pollard 1999). Children are equipped with the capacities and perceptual tools for organising and reacting to senses, for seeking exchange – embodying the actions of the semiologist and detective – to hypothesise, to deal with missing explanations and to reconstruct facts (Edwards and Forman 1993). To be creative, learners often have to tear things down and build them up again by transforming them (Beetlestone 1998). It is argued that it is not possible to teach creativity, only to set the conditions (Smith *et al.* 1999), a task Coombes sees as essential.

The Government report into creativity and culture (NACCCE 1999) sug-gested that there were three tasks for creativity in education: encouraging positive identities; fostering a language for the twenty-first century that included playfulness, flexibility and innovation; and generating a habit of learning and being creative. Coombes has provided a learning model for these objectives.

References

Beetlestone, F. (1998) *Creative Children, Imaginative Teaching.* Buckingham: Open University Press.

Craft, A. (2002) *Creativity and Early Years Education.* London: Continuum.

Edwards, C. and Forman, G.F. (eds) (1993) *The Hundred Languages of Children: The Reggio Emilia approach to early childhood education.* Greenwich: Ablex Publishing.

Edwards, D. and Mercer, N. (1987) *Common Knowledge: The Development of Understanding in Classrooms.* London: Methuen.

Fox, C. (1989) 'Children Thinking through Story'. *English in Education,* **23** (2), 33–42.

McGuinness, C. (1999) 'From thinking skills to thinking classrooms'. London: DfEE.

Moyles, J. (1997) 'Just for Fun? The Child as Active Learner and Meaning Maker', in: N. Kitson and R. Merry (eds), *Teaching in the Primary School: A Learning Relationship.* London: Routledge.

NACCCE (1999) *All our Futures: Creativity, Culture and Education.* London: DfEE.

OfSTED (1997) *OfSTED Inspection of Coombes First School.* London: OfSTED.

Pollard, A. (1999) 'Towards a New Perspective on Children's Learning'. *Education, 3–13,* **27** (3), 56–60.

Pollard, A. and Triggs, P., with Broadfoot, P., McNess, E. and Osborn, M. (2000) *What Pupils Say: Changing Policy and Practice in Primary Education.* London: Continuum.

Smith, F., Hardman, F. and Mroz, M. (1999) 'Devaluating the Effectiveness of the National Literacy Strategy: Identifying Indicators of Success'. European Conference of Educational Research, 22–25 September, Lahti, Finland.

Woods, P. and Jeffrey, B. (2003) *The Creative School. A framework for success, quality and effectiveness.* London: Routledge Falmer.

Chapter 12

Making sense of it all: using ICT to support older bilingual new arrivals

Sheilagh Crowther with Ian Eyres

Sheilagh Crowther is a teacher working for Gloucestershire's Ethnic Minorities Achievement Service, supporting children with English as an additional language in their own classrooms. She has developed special expertise in the use of ICT and in this chapter she describes how she, a class teacher and a teaching assistant worked together to use technology to help two Polish children play a full part in the life of their class while developing their English.

Two Polish ten-year-old twins, Bartek and Wyktoria arrived in their new Year 6 class in Tring Primary School at the end of September. All newly arrived children whatever their age or first language, need to feel welcome and they need to have their past achievements and experiences recognised. Bartek and Wyktoria had been confident, successful pupils in Poland and found a classroom environment in which they were unable to communicate easily with adults and children frustrating.

Although the long-term aim was for the two children to play a full part in every aspect of the life of the class, initially additional support strategies were essential. Without these, lessons would be difficult, if not impossible for the children to understand. The pace would often be too fast, and there would often be no visual or concrete material or action to support what teachers, teaching assistants and children were saying. Unfamiliar subjects and the style and format of the lesson itself could compound the problem. Children could also experience difficulties in following instructions and suggestions, and they may not be able to attempt set tasks on their own.

Making sense through ICT

Newly arrived children like Bartek and Wyktoria are seeking to make sense of the experiences, and especially the language they encounter in their new classroom environment. Many of the things ICT can do are of potential benefit to pupils who are learning English. Even in their first few days, pupils will be able to make some sense of what they are seeing and hearing, and computers, for instance, can help them gain additional information with which to build up a more comprehensible picture. A computer will allow them to work at their own pace, listening or reading as many times as they need to. Children can record and listen to their own voice, use on-line translation facilities and find pictures to explain words. ICT can enable children to work independently and initiate activity, and can also support interactive ways of working which promote children's communication skills.

Older new arrivals, like Bartek and Wyktoria, will be used to performing at a relatively high level in their first language, and a computer will permit them to continue to do this. ICT resources in many languages are readily available, as are websites in pupils' first languages. Email, which allows rapid and even instantaneous responses ('real time chat'), permits the setting up of links with overseas schools and pupils.

Besides being an essential continuing connection with family and culture, the use of their first language allows children to continue to develop a full range of concepts and thinking skills without the hindrance of having to do everything with the limited vocabulary and grammar of an unfamiliar language.

The maintenance of their first language will also benefit children's English development: oral and literacy skills are transferable, so that what pupils learn in their first language will assist them in learning in English.

Classroom interactions

When Bartek and Wyktoria started at Tring, the first concern of the teaching assistant based in their class was to make the pupils feel as welcome as possible. She used an internet translation site to produce labels for classroom equipment, and learn greetings, and useful nouns. The class were then able to say 'Hello' 'Welcome' and 'My name is . . .' 'What's your name?' in Polish. She taught the new arrivals to say these things in English.

Later, she worked with the pupils to translate key words for class topics, displaying this vocabulary around the classroom. Working together at the computer, the two children were able to practise English pronunciation of words. They also taught Polish words to the class, so that practising repetition was a purposeful two-way process. These initial activities encouraged monolingual English peers to use the translation tool collaboratively with the Polish pupils, which assisted communication and collaborative work.

A six-week 'study-buddy' scheme was set up for the class. During independent reading time, two children (different each day) took part in an interactive activity with the twins. Often pupils chose to use the computer to translate some words they needed. Turn-taking games tend to repeat certain phrases and Bartek and Wyktoria gradually began to use these.

The two children were introduced to a reading scheme – they were competent and fluent readers in Polish, and this presented a problem in finding age appropriate texts in English. They were quickly 'reading' (i.e. decoding) texts which were beyond their level of comprehension. Bartek and Wyktoria preferred not to read aloud. The difference between the ways Polish and English use the same alphabet to represent sounds – for example written 'w' in Polish is pronounced like an English 'v' – and the difficulty of pronouncing consonant blends not found in Polish made this a trial, even though they were able to interpret the gist of a text. Instead, they used the computer with headphones to listen to talking books related to their reading scheme. This provided modelling for pronunciation, and visual support for reading comprehension through the visual animations. The talking books also encouraged the children to use a variety of skills in their reading – for example using picture clues, and provided exercises to check comprehension, such as sequencing text and pictures.

ICT thus offered opportunities for Bartek and Wyktoria to become familiar with a topic before it was presented to the whole class. A talking book on 'The Solar System' supported their comprehension in the term's science topic on 'The earth and beyond'. The language of Macbeth was not accessible, but watching a video animation version beforehand allowed them to follow the story. The class worked in groups to present dramatisations, and this gave the children the opportunity (working in different groups) to participate with their peers. They were actively involved in making costumes and props, and they began to communicate using gestures and short two- or three- word utterances, e.g. 'Nathan hat big' with gesture to indicate that the hat was going to be too big.

Bartek and Wyktoria had good numeracy skills, which they could express well in their first language, but were not initially able to access much of the content of the numeracy hour lessons. They were placed for an initial period in a different group where the class teacher used an interactive whiteboard. In this group, teaching concentrated on mathematical language, reinforced with visuals on the whiteboard. This helped the pupils gain some mathematical language in English, and they were given differentiated numeracy work which took account of their abilities.

Conclusion

Arriving in an established class which uses a different language is likely to be a bewildering experience, and Bartek and Wyktoria needed to find ways to communicate and make sense of their new environment as quickly as possible. Along with the support of the class teacher, teaching assistant and the children's new classmates, ICT through its interactive potential, its ability to support purposeful activity and help make meaning, offered many powerful resources to support Bartek and Wyktoria's learning.

Chapter 13

A well-equipped hamster cage: the rationalisation of primary school playtime

Sarah Thomson

Is children's school playtime being over-managed by adults? Sarah Thomson, a researcher, describes her study into the nature of playtime in four primary schools. She suggests that health and safety regulations and a 'culture of blame and compensation' have led to playtimes being carefully monitored and organised to the detriment of children's creativity, originality and spontaneity. She believes playtime should provide children with considerable freedom of choice about what to play.

Defining play

Playtime, as defined by the National Playing Fields Association (NPFA) (1998), is 'a period of time when activities are undertaken by children in their leisure time … these activities are spontaneous and freely chosen'. In addition, Huizinga (1950) maintains that play 'first and foremost is a voluntary activity' and that 'play to order is no longer play'. Moreover he suggests that the 'charm of play' is that it is for '*us* not for "others"' (Huizinga 1950: 5–7). More recently, Hall and Abbott (1991: 36) note that 'play should be in the control of the player and the spirit of playfulness which is the essence of play cannot be imposed or demanded'. However, comments made by Blatchford (1996, 1998, 1999) in the UK and Evans (1990, 1994, 1997) in Australia suggest that children's playtime activities are at risk of being constrained for one reason or another. Blatchford maintains that 'current developments are moving us more toward an interventionalist approach' (Blatchford 1998: 9). So, where within these definitions of play do the activities of the contemporary primary school playground lie? In this chapter, drawing on qualitative data, I will investigate the possible reasons behind current developments and explore how these developments have influenced the nature of today's primary school playground activities. Additionally, I will discuss whether the activity of the contemporary school playground reflects the definition of play.

The study

The group of schools in which the investigation was based is limited in size. However, the findings of this study may be indicative of a similar trend in other schools. I visited four primary schools within the same county school system in England. The data was obtained from a series of visits to these schools over the whole school year and is based on field notes collected from a number of playtime observation sessions, and from informal interviews with headteachers, teachers and midday assistants. The four schools comprise of a rural village school, a newly built school serving a new housing estate, an established suburban school whose pupil ratio consisted of children from private and local authority housing, and a school close to the town centre. These four schools contained pupils from a wide cross-section of socio-economic backgrounds.

Current developments

At the end of the 1960s, the Opies (1969) detected a tendency for adults to intervene in playground activities and cautioned against this interventionist approach. Later Blatchford (1996, 1998, 1999) and Evans (1990, 1994, 1997) also acknowledge that the 'interventionist stance is gaining dominance, and risks overrunning pupils freedom' (Blatchford 1998: 172). Blatchford links this interventionist approach with 'the understandable wish of schools to ensure control over behaviour and learning' (1999: 65). Therefore, is it possible that embedded in contemporary school children's playtime is a culture that sets out to constrain and manipulate children's playtime activities?

In the process of identifying some of the influences that affected the type of games forbidden or encouraged in the primary school playground, I uncovered a number of underlying current developments that surrounded breaktime activities. My research revealed that far from playtime being the most 'forgotten part of the school day' (Blatchford 1989), it was apparent that many members of staff (in particular the headteachers) were very concerned with the minutiae of playtime and the plethora of concerns that surrounded its management.

Their concerns fell into two categories; one where the staff were following official statutory controls or commands placed upon them by prescriptive agencies. These agencies comprised of the Office for Standards in Education (OfSTED), the Health and Safety Executive (HSE), the Local Education Authority (LEA), the Local Health Education Authority, teachers' unions and school governors. The other category embraced issues such as parental pressure and the culture of blame and compensation. Uppermost, in the minds of those responsible for the supervision of playtime, was the impact that particular bureaucratic and legislative processes had on breaktime events and vice versa. In several cases, the dictates of prescriptive agencies and parental reaction appeared to be big obstacles to a play-friendly school playtime.

Health and safety

The origins of current developments are traceable to a number of significant events in school legislation. One of which is the Health and Safety at Work Act 1974. 'Section 3 requires employers to ensure so far as is reasonably practicable, the health and safety of persons not in their employment. Pupils at school are protected by this duty' (Graham 2001). The responses to questions such as 'why certain games were not played' always provoked a member of staff into comments on safety. The health and safety regulations and its administration seem to dominate the minds and practices of some of the heads of the schools I visited. An enquiry about what specific school health and safety regulations the local education authority concerned had for its children revealed that there was no specific outline for children. Heads use their own common sense over concerns about playground equipment. 'This of course leads to an onerous responsibility for the safety of each individual pupil of the school being laid at that particular Head's door' (Frith 1985: 102). Several teachers discussed with me fears about accidents and the completion of numerous accident books and accident reports. Accident books were divided into 'bumps, bruises and minor injuries' or 'serious' accidents. At the end of playtime, it was quite normal to see ancillary helpers entering the school and meticulously completing the accident books. Somewhat bizarrely, the outcome of all this diligent recording means that in the desire to fill in an accident book correctly and accurately, the midday assistant (MDA) occasionally leaves the injured child uncomforted and unattended.

'Spontaneous and freely chosen'?

It became clear throughout the research that in the desire to reduce accidents and limit the number of children injured, head teachers resorted to banning some games. Games such as bulldog, conkers, skipping and the then current craze of 'world-wide wrestling' were forbidden because of fears about injuries to children. Other games quite often forbidden were games such as football, Pokemon and yo-yos. These latter games were banned for a number of reasons, mostly because of the amount of time taken by the teacher with the '*management*' of loss of items and the arbitration of disputes. Football because it caused '*world war three*' and because it was considered antisocial and took a lot of management in class before and after break because of disputes about who had scored and team allocation. Pokemon because of the '*hassle*' caused by arguments and the loss of highly prized cards; the game of Yo-yos, another craze at the time of the study, was also banned at some of the schools for much the same reasons. One of the schools studied took the view that children taking the initiative about play and bringing in games from home caused more trouble than it was worth.

All of these games and crazes were 'freely chosen' by the children but discouraged at school playtime.

Parental concern

Allied with the concern for health and safety was the school staff's concern with parental complaint. When I asked one head why she did not allow the game of British bulldogs, she replied that she was obliged to protect the children from injuring themselves and that games such as these meant that parents took issue with the school about their child being hurt or their clothing being ripped. Certainly, parents are exhibiting a greater awareness of their legal rights, and evidence suggests that more and more parents are exercising those rights within the educational arena.

OfSTED

Comments from OfSTED are another reason for focusing teachers' attention on playtime activities. Since the first OfSTED inspections of primary schools in September 1994, headteachers and their staff have had to concentrate their attention on what was previously a place of little consequence. The OfSTED Handbook for Inspecting Primary Schools makes it clear in their guideline examples that inspection of the behaviour in the playground is part of the Inspectors' remit. The Inspectors will 'evaluate behaviour throughout the school day, in classrooms and when they play or lunch', they will look to see 'if youngest children are confident in the playground' (OfSTED 2000). OfSTED Inspectors' remarks about playtimes range from comments on behaviour to the uninspiring nature of the playground. An example of how OfSTED inspections can effect playground protocol is illustrated in a Southampton primary school OfSTED Report on playground behaviour. This report pointed out that one of 'the key issues for action' was 'the implementation of a plan for dealing with challenging behaviour in the playground'. The Inspectors' report said that the school should 'consider in particular, a policy of dealing with incidents in the playground, that there should be a consistency in dealing with playground boisterousness' (OfSTED 1997/8). A member of staff informed me that because of this report the school had set up a system of 'effective sanctions and referrals' in response to the Inspectors' comments. He had also provided an in-service training programme for his lunch-time staff. He did make the impromptu comment 'that one person's "boisterous" child was another's friendly, confident, high-spirited child'.

Imminent visits from OfSTED often have the effect of turning the playground from an empty area of tarmac into a space decorated with furniture such as playhouses and colourful plastic seating areas. These initiatives combined with the drive to market the school premises means that the overall effect of school playgrounds with their jolly dustbins and colourful plastic seating is one of a well-equipped hamster cage.

The 'charm of play is for us not for "others"'

There is the 'general perception that children are not as constructive in their play as they once were' (Blatchford 1999: 61). Therefore, initiatives are brought in to develop the quality of children's play. For instance South Somerset Museum is running a project in conjunction with Ash Primary School, Somerset, which involves a playtime scheme where they teach the children old traditional games, such as skipping and hopscotch. In addition, headteacher Nigel Johnson of Grange Primary School, Stoke-on-Trent, proclaimed that 'children are being taught the time-honoured playground games because the games are there to make sure children do not idly waste away their time. Rather than having everybody chasing around, it is good to have them playing together' (Russell 1999). This transformation of spontaneous play into purposeful and productive activity is at the heart of these initiatives. Sutton-Smith (1981, 1990) suggests that this type of control is part of 'the experimental manipulations of childhood' (1990: 3). He discusses whether the contemporary children's playground lacks true spontaneity and whether it reflects children's 'freedom, inventiveness and vigour', or their 'curiosity, imagination and play' because 'adults organise children's sports, recreation, playgrounds, consumer preferences and educational play' (Sutton-Smith 1990: 3).

Furthermore, when initiatives such as these had been instigated in one of the schools in the study, the MDAs declared that the children had lost interest. Initiatives such as these do not succeed because the 'charm of play is no longer for us' (the children) but for 'others' (Huizinga 1950). These types of games perhaps often have very little to do with spontaneous creative play that children would like to indulge in. It takes away their element of ownership of these games. The ownership of traditional games has passed from the children to the adults. In the drive to improve the quality of children's play, adults are removing the ownership of children's games and transferring its control to 'others'. Games encouraged in the school playground are quite often instigated and monitored by the adults, who govern, process, and organise these games into packages. These are then reintroduced to the children in an artificial format. The mastery of these games by children is then instrumental to the teacher's goals and the institution's desired outcome rather than for the enjoyment of the children.

Fear of litigation

One of the major factors in restricting children's spontaneous play was the teachers' anxiety about institutional and individual accountability. Teachers and midday supervisors were concerned that the outcome of some playtime activities would lead to incidents and accidents that would then lead to litigation. Therefore, staff quite often took an 'if in doubt ban it' approach (Thomson 2002). Any games or play activities that were considered potentially dangerous were banned. During my research, I found that the legal department of the relevant local education authority was quite secretive about its affairs. This does nothing to allay the fears of teachers. However, teachers and teaching assistants should realise the fear of risk is out of proportion to the reality of the number of serious accidents that occur in the playground. Teachers should take comfort from the words of one judge pronouncing on a case of playground negligence: 'life is full of physical dangers which children must learn to recognise, and develop the ability to avoid. The playground is one of the places to learn.' In another case, the judge remarked: 'it is wrong to protect (children) against minor injuries by forbidding them the ordinary pleasures which school children so much enjoy' (Lowe 2000).

'Play to order is no longer play'

Playtime is part of the school timetable and the children do not select when they have their break. Certainly, playtime at school is 'play to order'. Children are told to go out and play, whatever the weather or their fears; quite often there is little alternative to going out into the playground. Playtime at school in the UK is a compulsory activity scheduled for specific periods of the day. Blatchford *et al.* (1990: 166) note that at playtime 48 per cent of children 'expressed a desire to stay in, either to work or to do something else'. Certainly having a flexible playtime at school is hardly a 'voluntary activity', at best is a 'forcible imitation of it' (Huizinga 1950).

Discussion

The primary school playground is symbolic of children's time and there is the understanding that the space has been provided specifically for the children and their activities. It signifies an acknowledgement of their 'culture'. The notion then of school breaktime is that it provides children with a time and a place for 'non-serious' (Huizinga 1950) activity. In essence, it offers them a place where they make choices about their activities. Therefore, the playground space should offer an arena for behaviour that is fundamentally different from the context of adult behaviour. Arguably, the playground is one of the sacrosanct areas for children at school. However, rules and regulations that now surround playtime at school mean that playtime at school is no longer a benign experience and its current framework of organisation has resulted in a series of unfortunate consequences. Overall, this can be summarised as an increasing attempt to organise children's lives down to the last millisecond. I feel that this continual intervention and monitoring of playtime activities has a deleterious affect on children because it limits their play experiences and de-skills them in the general characteristics of spontaneous play.

Whilst I do not advocate that children play in the playground without any supervision or the occasional adult intervention, breaktime in school should allow the child a greater freedom of choice about what to play. There appears to be little scope left for creativity, originality or spontaneity in the playground. When pupils do bring their toys or crazes into school, these are, as previously mentioned, banned. Yet, the toys that children bring in from home are important to them. For young children it can be a positive bridge between home and school.

During the observation period, it was clear that confiscation of footballs in the playground quite often led to the Year 5 and 6 boys becoming a nuisance to those around them because they had nothing else to occupy them. Therefore, perhaps a game of football is the lesser of the two evils. If staff were to allow all those who want to stay in at playtime to do so, then those who go outside will have more room. Research shows that girls, given the choice, would stay in and chat and younger children do not like the cold. If fewer children occupied the playground then the boys might have more room for games of football. However, I appreciate that there are issues of supervision here. Perhaps parents can be encouraged to volunteer to supervise children indoors.

Summer playtimes seemed to be the time when the children's playtime activities were at their most relaxed and peaceful, when the children seemed most contented. The biggest changes affecting this state of play were the weather and the use of space. Use of space is a significant factor in children's enjoyment of playtime. The teachers' fear of mud, dirty clothes and mess brought into the school appeared to be the driving force behind limiting children (other than summer time) playing on any fields attached to the playground. If the school had a supply of wellingtons, this would increase the amount of play space. Once a central stock was established, the financial outlay to maintain the level would be small. At the end of many school playtimes an extraordinary amount of time seemed to be spent in getting children into straight lines, 'tidy lines of twos' before going into school. Therefore, why not use this time to take off wellingtons and clean up. If nothing else, the time might be spent more constructively asking the children what they thought about their playtime experiences.

It remains to be seen if the demands of external prescriptive agencies and the culture of accountability will eventually form a framework of control, in which the freedom of play has no part, because the demands of both create a 'straitjacket of compulsion and direction' (Hall and Abbott 1991: 36). As the current director of the Health and Safety points out 'it is impractical to expect schools to be risk-free zones, if they were where would children learn the skills necessary to face the hazards and risks they will encounter through life' (Graham 2001). There will always be certain necessary constraints surrounding playtime protocol but currently these seem to supersede the objective of playtime. If we are going to rationalise playtime, then it needs to be done in such a way that promotes the freedom of choice for children. So that for the child, playtime does stand outside of 'ordinary life' and really does act as an 'interlude' in the daily life of academic study (Huizinga 1950: 5).

References

Blatchford, P. (1989) *Playtime in the Primary School: Problems and Improvements.* Windsor: NFER-Nelson.

Blatchford, P., Creeser, R. and Mooney, A. (1990) 'Playground games and playtime: the children's view'. *Educational Research,* **32** (3), 163–74.

Blatchford, P. (1996) 'Taking Pupils Seriously: Recent Research and Initiatives on Breaktime in Schools'. *Education 3– 13,* **24** (3).

Blatchford, P. (1998) *Social Life in School; Pupils' experience of the breaktime and recess from 7– 16 years.* London: Falmer Press.

Blatchford, P. (1999) 'Friendships at school: the role of breaktimes'. *Education 3– 13,* **27** (1).

Department for Education and Science (DES) (1989) *Elton Report:* Discipline in Schools: Report of the Committee of Enquiry, chaired by Lord Elton. London: HMSO.

Evans, J. (1990) 'The Teacher Role in Playground Supervision'. *Play and Culture,* **33,** 219–34.

Evans, J. (1994) 'Problems in the Playground'. *Education 3– 13,* **22** (2), 34–40.

Evans, J. (1997) 'Children's attitudes to recess and the changes taking place in Australian primary schools' *Research in Education,* **56,** 49–61.

Frith, D. (1985) *School Management in Practice.* London: Longman Group.

Graham, P. (Director of Health and Safety Executive) (2001) 'Educating society to calculate hazards'. *Times Educational Supplement,* 05.01.2001.

Hall, N. and Abbott, L. (eds) (1991) *Play in the Primary Curriculum.* London: Hodder & Stoughton.

Huizinga, J. (1950) 'A Study of the Play Element in Culture', in: *Homo Ludens.* London: Routledge Kegan.

Lowe, C. (2000) 'Legal Issues'. *Times Educational Supplement,* 22.12.2000.

National Playing Fields Association (NPFA) (1998).

Opie, I. and Opie, P. (1969) *Children's Games in Street and Playground.* London: Oxford University Press.

OfSTED (2000) *Handbook for Inspecting Primary and Nursery Schools.* London: HMSO.

OfSTED (1997/8) *St Marks C of E Controlled Junior School, Southampton.*

Russell, B. (1999) 'Old Games are more than child's play'. *The Independent,* 06.03.1999.

Sutton-Smith, B. (1981) *A History of Children's Play: New Zealand 1840– 1950.* Philadelphia: University of Pennsylvania Press.

Sutton-Smith, B. (1990) 'School playground as festival'. *Children's Environments Quarterly,* **7** (2) 3–7.

Thomson, S.J. (2002) 'Harmless Fun Can Kill Someone'. *Entertainment Law,* **1** (1), Spring.

Chapter 14

The articulate playground: trainee teachers meet pocket monsters

Elizabeth Grugeon

Speaking and listening have an established role within primary classrooms, but it is easy to forget that much of children's oral language use and learning takes place outside the classroom. The playground is a domain that teaching assistants often know well; in this chapter Liz Grugeon draws together the observations of a number of trainee teachers to show children using language for many purposes. It helps them organise their games and fantasy play, allows 'business' to be conducted and reinforces the social order, for example. Some children who appear quiet in the classroom are shown to be perfectly articulate and able to command an audience when the context is right for them.

'Not in front of the grown-ups' – jokes and traditional games

Tracy was not alone when she observed that traditional playground games frequently included a forbidden word or two: 'bum', 'knickers', 'arse'. This was particularly the case with games which included songs and rhymes. She wondered whether this could be the reason

> why these games have a stage on the playground and not in the classroom or home, or not at least when teacher or mum can hear ... Adults do not always appreciate the subversiveness of these songs; they have grown up and forgotten them and the pleasure and excitement of singing them.

As David Crystal says, 'Being naughty with language seems innately attractive' (Crystal 1998: 169). In his book *Language Play* he is dismayed that so little attention is paid to children's informal language, believing that 'language play ... is a prerequisite for successful reading and spelling' (Crystal 1998: 181).

Many students noticed how children in the playground loved to tell jokes. Other students observed and remarked on gender differences; girls often playing games which involved verbal interaction in small, cohesive groups, while boys tended to take up more space with games involving running and chasing: football, Power Rangers and stylised fighting routines. Students were surprised to discover how much language was involved in these very active games.

Football

'Come on, pass it here. Here, here! Do it like this . . . Pass it to me. NO, NO, NO! YEP here!' (Kulbir Bansal, large multi-ethnic urban lower school, March 2000).

On a large urban middle school playground, Tom observed that the Year 5 and 6 boys

> virtually all played football throughout their playtime. During the game most of the talk could be split into two categories which were either instruction, like 'kick the ball' or criticism, 'why do you always shoot, can't you pass the ball for a change?' Both categories of interaction involved short sentences and even shorter responses. The four boys who talked most, held high status positions within the group and were all good footballers. They adopted the role of unofficial captains and vice-captains between them. They had the football skills to dominate the game which made it easier for them to dominate the other boys who lacked their confidence.
>
> (Tom Bush, March 2000)

Lara also watched a group of Year 6 boys, in a large junior school on the outskirts of a town, who were also dominating the playground space. She observed that:

> the verbal communication on the pitch was loud. The boys shouted short comments to each other. . . . However, the game also required the involvement of cooperative skills in order to function effectively.

Like Tom, she noticed that 'certain boys tended to give commands concerning players' position on the pitch, most of which were accepted' and that 'the rules governing who played where . . . were obviously clear to the pupils' (Blatchford 1998: 69). When she talked to the boys afterwards she found that they were articulate and knowledgeable and that their talk was characterised by a humorous sparring repartee. They also had an impressive knowledge about the game and the linguistic conventions of the football commentator.

> S: *Rivaldo*
> B: *What Rinaldo?*
> S: *No, Rivaldo, you ponce*
> B: *I say Rinaldo, he's right quick with his feet and pings the ball*
> G: *I say Carno*
> J: *'Juninho', or Zola, 'And he's taking the ball down the field, and he's tackled, will he make it . . . yes, he scores. It's a goal!'*
>
> (Lara Smith, March 2000)

For boys, it was evidently important to be 'hard' and good at football. It was one of the ways in which they were negotiating their masculine identity. At the same time, the girls were excluded and marginalised by these games.

Girls on the edge

Many students explored gender issues. Louise was interested by a game called 'Go-Gos' which was played by both boys and girls in Year 5 in her rural middle school. A girl explained, 'We don't play with boys 'cos they're better at, erm . . . throwing and stuff, aren't they?' And Louise noted that the boys 'bagsied' the best positions for playing Go-Gos, 'leaving the girls to play in areas where interruptions were more likely'. The boys' confident behaviour in the playground was reflected in their language; girls were more passive in their conversations with her, while the boys tended to interrupt and speak over each other. She also noted that football, played only by boys,

> involves the use of exclusive language with expressions such as 'down the line' and other specialist vocabulary . . . vernacular language, including swearing, was also evident. . . . The boys often play football in role and 'become' Michael Owen or Alan Shearer, changing to Tony Adams or Sol Campbell if they are defending.
>
> (Louise Bundy, March 2000)

Examples from many of the students showed that the media was exerting a powerful influence on children's play; they noted ways in which this emerged in role play games when television 'brings new words into the language' (Keaney and Lucas 1994: 43).

Playing Pokemon

On the playground of a large urban multi-ethnic infant school, Anne's interview with Year 2 boys also explains how children are coping with the Pokemon (collectible cards, portraying monsters) phenomenon in the face of disapproval by the adult world. Wherever the cards are banned the children seem to compensate by absorbing the language and conventions of Pokemon in their imaginative play.

> Child A: *Um, well we don't normally have adventures. Er, Ash goes off with all his Pokemons and then he normally comes back with the, er . . . medals, and does stuff like that . . . and my made-up Pokemon was Bulbasaur's umbrella and what I need to do is to get my arms in here . . . like Bulbasaur's got them on his back . . . he's got guns that come out of his back but my made-up Pokemon . . . he's got guns instead of hands.*
>
> (Year 2 boys. Anne Lees, March 2000)

Swapping and bartering

Jonathan recorded two Year 6 boys actually swapping cards at an urban middle school:

> The swapping process uses a varied amount of bartering . . . they take the strengths of the Pokemon very seriously as they negotiate fiercely.

Child A: *I'm not giving you that for only one Squirtle. It's not worth it. He's only got three power points to Charmander's five. No way, nah . . . what else?*

Child B: *That's stupid, 'cos Rychu can have up to seven blast power points if you put him with Squirtle . . . yeah?*

Child A: *No way, it takes too long for them to evolve . . . I'm not giving that.*

These older boys have a good grasp of the linguistic conventions of bartering.

On the playground children played a chasing game based on Pokemon, where they took on a role and acted out a narrative based on confrontation between the characters.

> As the children's narrative game based on Pokemon was not a traditional game with established rules it incorporated not only a discussion about rules but an attempt on the children's part to make up their own rules (Moyles 1994: 7). This involved a discussion which required them to explain the reasons behind certain rules. For example, one boy aged six, decided there should be somewhere you could go when you 'retreat' in order to show that you were 'retreating' and also because it would enable children to rest if they were tired without fear of being 'attacked'.
>
> (Sarah-Jane Simmons, March 2000)

Clare observed that while the girls were largely engaged in skipping and clapping games,

> the boys' entrance to the playground was very different. . . . After a couple of loops round the playground they tended to come to a standstill in small groups and take out their Pokemon cards for swaps and battles.

Clare felt that this influx of cartoon-related products was not a bad thing; through watching television, often alongside their play, children were developing specific skills (Simatos and Spencer 1992: 115).

> There was one child who was obviously very knowledgeable about Pokemon and how the battles were decided. This meant that he appeared to take on the role of adjudicator and dominate in this way, with many of the children approaching him to clear up disputes they had over who had won the battle and arguments about 'fair swaps'. He is a child who is quiet in the classroom; often refraining from raising his hand because he lacks confidence in his own ability. However, when dealing with a subject he is confident with, he is more than able to express himself clearly to others.
>
> (Clare Drake, March 2000)

Clare recorded girls participating in Pokemon games, 'either with each other or with boys' and she reflected, 'I think this may be to do with the fact that Pokemon games are played statically and do not involve a high level of aggression or competitiveness.'

Other media influences

The Pokemon games reflect the latest media craze but there was much evidence of other media influences. Claire, in a small village school, observed six Year

1 children, four boys and two girls, playing a game of what she thought was the traditional chasing game 'It':

> *Claire:* What do you call this game?
> *Child A:* Croc.
> *Claire:* Who taught you to play this game?
> *Child A:* I don't know. I've got Croc on my Playstation.

(Claire Pearson, March 2000)

On a multi-ethnic, urban infant school playground WWF (World Wrestling Federation) was a particularly popular game. Five Year 4 boys discussed how they were going to re-enact scenes from WWF.

> The boys would come up with ideas only to have them challenged and discarded by others. There were numerous interruptions when someone was desperate to have their idea heard and sometimes another member of the group would carry these ideas forward. I noticed that the boys would help each other with the technical vocabulary such as the names of wrestlers and their trademark wrestling moves. . . . The names and trademark moves of the wrestlers provided a focus for the discussion. Many of the wrestlers have alliterative names, such as 'Scotty Too Hotty' and 'Big Boss Man'. This led to a member of the group suggesting that they should make up their own names and trademark moves. One pupil invented the name 'Stinkin' Steven' and the trademark move 'Stinkin' Steven Slammer'.

(Clare Fawcett, March 2000)

Bringing the playground into the classroom?

What implications does this evidence of children's spontaneous informal language outside the classroom offer to teachers of literacy? The students who contributed to this discussion had discovered a rich source of language in the rhymes, jokes and narrative of the playground. They had demonstrated that children's traditional games are alive and well at the start of the twenty-first century and that newer influences were continuing to be absorbed and creatively subverted as they always have been; Popeye the Sailor Man and Pokemon, Shirley Temple and the Spice Girls comfortably co-exist. The student teachers' assignment was to analyse the evidence they had collected and discuss ways in which it would influence their work in the classroom. But that is material for another chapter!

References

Blatchford, P. (1998) *Social Life in School – pupils' experience of breaktime and recess from 7–16 years.* London: Falmer Press.

Crystal, D. (1998) *Language Play.* London: Penguin.

Keaney, B. and Lucas, B. (1994) *Looking at Language.* Cambridge: Cambridge University Press.

Moyles, J. (1994) (ed) *The Excellence of Play*. Buckingham: The Open University Press.

Simatos, A. and Spencer, K. (1992) *Children and Media*. Liverpool: Manutius Press.

Widdowson, J. (2000) 'Childlore: Gateway to language skills', in: J. Bishop, and M. Curtis (eds), *Play Today in the Primary School Playground: Life, learning and creativity*. Buckingham: The Open University Press.

Chapter 15

School buildings: 'A safe haven, not a prison . . .'

Catherine Burke and Ian Grosvenor

In 1967 *The Observer* newspaper ran a competition entitled 'The School I'd Like'. Just over 30 years later, in 2001, *The Guardian* newspaper repeated that competition. In this chapter, Catherine Burke, a lecturer at University of Leeds, and Ian Grosvenor, the director of Learning and Teaching, University of Birmingham, report on one aspect of the second competition. They describe children's responses related to the design and the quality of school buildings and they urge educators, designers and architects to take note of what children have to say in order that stimulating 'spaces for learning' might be better constructed.

The School We'd Like is:
A beautiful school
A comfortable school
A safe school
A listening school
A flexible school
A relevant school
A respectful school
A school without walls
A school for everybody.

The school building, the landscape of the school, the spaces and places within, the décor, furnishing and features have been called 'the third teacher' (Edwards, Gandini and Forman 1998). A beautiful, comfortable, safe and inclusive environment has, throughout the history of school architecture, generally been compromised by more pressing concerns, usually associated with cost and discipline. The material history of schooling, as conveyed in school buildings, is evident still in the villages, towns and cities of any nation. In the UK, one need not look far to locate, still functioning as schools, stone-built 'voluntary' schools of the mid-nineteenth century. The 'Board' schools of the late nineteenth century still stand, as red brick emblems of the cities in which they were built in an era which placed enormous faith in 'direct works' and 'municipalisation'. The schools built in the 1920s and 1930s reflected changes in educational policy indicating the beginning of a recognition of the diverse needs of children and consideration of health and hygiene. These decades saw the building of looser groupings of units, classrooms with larger windows and with removable walls being capable of being thrown almost entirely open. Architects worked to precise standards of lighting and ventilation as set out by the Ministry of Education. The post-war building plans saw the erection of buildings utilising modern prefabricated materials. Schools were built in large numbers, quickly and cheaply with the view that they would provide a stop gap until greater resources were available. 'Finger plan' schools, featuring one-storey classrooms set in parallel rows with a wide corridor to one side were popular. Thus started, for children, the long journey to toilets, hall and dining room as the buildings sprawled over large plots.

Already in the late 1960s, it was estimated that nearly 750,000 primary school children in England were being educated in schools of which the main buildings were built before 1875 (Department of Education and Science 1967: 389). Standards were poor in general but there were particular problems, such as the 65 per cent of schools whose toilets were located in school playgrounds.

The new buildings erected in the 1960s and 1970s were needed to accommodate the swelling numbers on the school roll, the adoption of comprehensive secondary education and the extension of the school leaving age after 1973. Architects often used prefabricated assembly systems to help reduce costs and most new schools tended to resemble factories in their construction and style. Design aesthetics and comfort were usually given less importance than economy. However, many of the ideas about the flexible use of school buildings, first voiced by Henry Morris in the inter-war years, were revisited during this period. It was argued:

> Society is no longer prepared to make available a set of valuable buildings and resources for the exclusive use of a small, arbitrarily defined sector of the community, to be used seven hours a day for two-thirds of the year. School buildings have to be regarded therefore as a resource for the total community available to many different groups, used for many different purposes and open if necessary twenty four hours a day.
>
> (Michael Hacker of the Architects and Buildings Branch,
> Ministry of Education, cited in Saint 1987: 196)

Open-plan arrangements reflecting child-centred pedagogy were criticised during the late 1970s and early 1980s. Educational policy under successive Conservative governments emphasised the importance of traditional methods of instruction and whole-class teaching rather than group collaboration and teacher facilitation. A recently concluded research study of classroom arrangements in the UK suggests, however, that for the majority, tradition overcame fashion (Comber and Wall 2001: 100).

After decades of having to meet the enormous costs of refurbishment and repairs, the UK government in 1992 adopted the policy of financing public services including the building and refurbishment of schools via the public–private finance initiative (PFI). The first privately financed state primary school was opened in Hull in January 1999. At the time of writing, 20 public–private finance initiative contracts are already operational, a total of 30 new, rebuilt, or extensively refurbished schools are now open and another 500 are planned (*Guardian*, 30 September 2002). However, there is some disquiet among the teaching profession about the standards and quality of buildings that have recently emerged and concern that the design of schools today will rapidly become outdated as the organisation of learning changes in the future. The UK government's own watchdog on architectural matters, the Commission for Architecture and the Built Environment (CABE) has recently voiced concern over design standards of new schools built under the initiative. Their chief executive, Jon Rouse has stated, of the 30 PFI schools already built, many are like 'sheds without windows', and fail to comply with best-practice standards of natural light (Rouse 2002).

CABE has warned that there is insufficient effort being made to consult the users of school buildings. 'Schools need to get involved in that process and be specific about what they need. The whole process has got to be led by the curriculum' (CABE 2002). However, CABE does not advise that children and young people should be involved in the design process.

It is remarkable, in view of the fact that architectural education is very rarely provided within compulsory schooling, that there was such a wealth of ideas from children (in both the 1967 and 2001 competitions) about the shape and design of schools. However, some have argued that children are 'natural builders' or 'have a natural talent as planners and designers' (Hart 1987; Gallagher 1998) and that the school curriculum might be better organised to recognise this. Writing in the USA, architecture and design educator Claire Gallagher has noted, 'The typical means of instruction in our educational culture is either linguistic and/or mathematical. Rarely is any attention paid to visual or spatial thinking or problem-solving' (1998: 109). Her work with 'at risk' elementary school children in designing and planning their own neighbourhoods has illuminated how children have a distinctive knowledge and understanding of spatial environments that policy-makers rarely tap.

The 'School I'd Like' competition spontaneously produced dozens of models, hundreds of plans and thousands of implied designs of ideal sites for learning. In addition there was produced a remarkable collection of drawings and paintings through which children have expressed their ideas on curriculum, use of time, role of teachers and form of school. These design ideas address more than the shape of building and the ordering of spaces; they tell of a vision of education that reaches beyond the strict mechanics of building science.

The 1967 competition had also produced entries which were architectural in approach. Indeed, one of the winners at that time was a detailed plan produced by a 17-year-old pupil, said to want to become an architect. Like many of the plans and models contributed in 2001, this plan featured domes and pyramidal structures, circular spaces and a lot of glass.

Blishen was compelled to comment on the number of circular designs suggested by the 1967 competition entries. He noted that the young designers, having none of the problems of an actual architect . . . let themselves go and there can't for a very long time have been such a lavish decreeing of pleasure domes.

(Blishen, 1969: 43)

He suggested that such a quantity of circular schemes were, in fact,

reactions against a quality in school buildings that many inveigh against: their squareness. . . . Most were tired of squareness: where an actual shape was suggested, nine times out of ten it was a round one.

(ibid.)

The 1967 cohort wanted schools not to resemble schools at all, but to resemble the adult world where individual privacy, comfort and relaxation were permitted. And it was not only the classrooms and building shell which were subject to the circuitous but also the organisation of bodies in spaces more generally:

There would have to be a school with rooms, but furnished with soft chairs in a circle.

(Richard, 15)

Within a circular school with circular classrooms and spiral staircases, what becomes challenged is the institutional: the regulation and ordering of bodies in precise spaces; the processing of children as in a factory; the rehabilitation of individuals as in a prison. An alternative regularity found in nature is envisaged in schools as colonies of life and development. The outer membrane, as in a cell, is penetrable, filled with light, transparent and attracts public view.

Jerome Bruner has proposed that the curriculum should be conceived of as a spiral to suggest how learning is achieved through a series of ever deeper encounters 'in the processes of meaning making and our constructions of reality'. The object of instruction should not be 'coverage' but rather 'depth', and the teacher is a collaborative learner and guide to understanding which begins with an intuitive impulse, 'circling back to represent the domain more powerfully or formally as needed' (Bruner 1996: xii). When describing the spaces for learning as 'caves' and the corridors as 'spirals', the children here could be seen to be expressing their instinctive cultural understanding of how learning occurs.

We could argue that the preference for dome-like features in the recently collected archive can be explained simply through acknowledgement of the fact that domes are features of leisure environments that children and young people frequent. These features are representative of enjoyment, freedom, play and excitement. Perhaps it could be argued, however, that we have here in this collection of material, responding to the same question over time, evidence of constancy in childhood. Traditionally the school room is square, has corners and contains rows of bodies in disciplined rank. The comments of children about the significance of this in contrast to their preferred spherical arrangements betray an understanding that a shift occurs in the organisation of authority and control in moving from the rectangular to the circular.

A recurring theme of likening school to a prison is found in competition entries, both past and present, suggesting that, from the point of view of those compelled to attend, little has altered in the basic character of school in spite of the vast extent of policy intervention over the intervening period. Blishen said of the contributions to the 1967 competition, 'When I was reading these essays, the image of the prison returned to me again and again' (1969: 14): '. . . we're like caged animals!' is a remark which speaks for many in the more recent collection.

Comfort, privacy, space for social activity and rest, and colourful, softly textured, inviting interiors are called for by countless numbers of participants in the 2001 Archive. Once again there is continuity with the demands from the past. 'They cry out for colour, and are very conscious of the drab uniformity of many of the walls within which they sit' (Blishen 1969: 43).

Toilets continue to be an appalling problem in many schools, over 30 years after the Plowden committee recognised the severity of the problem, and there were very few ideal schools, whether in essay, design, photographic or video format, that did not feature strongly a major criticism of the school toilets. Many suggest practical ways they can be improved but most wanted them to be less institutional, more comfortable and accessible. For many children, not being able to lock the toilet door safely causes distress.

Many children are still compelled to attend school buildings designed and built half a century ago. Distressed about the poor state of the fabric of their schools, most want more space and recognise the limitations of school design in relation to inclusive school policies. Young people in special schools who have difficulty just getting around the inadequately designed school spaces, take the opportunity to recommend change. Some argue convincingly that if the overall appearance of the school were improved then children would be more likely to want to attend and not to truant.

What emerges from the material is evidence that children have the capacity to examine critically the normal and everyday spaces in which they learn and can articulate their future in previously unimagined ways. They want to feel proud of the school to which they belong but many feel embarrassed by their surroundings. Children seem to regard the built environment as 'the third teacher'. To listen to these voices past and present is instructive to all educators, architects, designers and policy-makers who have responsibility for conceiving and constructing the spaces for learning which children inhabit. Seeming to understand the perspective voiced here, Paulo Freire once argued:

> One of our challenges as educators is to discover what historically is possible in the sense of contributing toward the transformation of the world, giving rise to a world that is rounder, less angular, more humane.
>
> (Freire, in Macedo 1996: 397)

References

Blishen, E. (1969) *The School That I'd Like*. London: Penguin.
Bruner, J. (1996) *The Culture of Education*. Cambridge, MA: Harvard University Press.

CABE (2002) *Client Guide: Achieving Well Designed Schools Through PFI.* September. London: CABE.

Comber, C. and Wall, D. (2001) 'The classroom environment: a framework for learning', in: C.F. Paechter, R. Edwards, R. Harrison and P. Twining (eds), *Learning, Space and Identity (Learning Matters).* London: Paul Chapman Publishers.

Department of Education and Science (1967) *Children and their Primary Schools. A Report of the Central Advisory Council for Education (England). Vol. 1: The Report. (Plowden Report).* London: HMSO.

Edwards, C., Gandini, L. and Forman, G. (eds) (1998) *The Hundred Languages of Children*, 2nd edn. Greenwich, CT: Ablex.

Gallagher, C. (1998) 'The "Our Town" Project: a case for reform in urban design and classroom practice', in: *Emergent Paradigms in Design Education: Sustainability, Collaboration & Community*, Sydney, NSW: University of New South Wales.

Hart, R.A. (1987) 'Children's participation in planning and design. Theory, research and practice', in: C.S. Weinstein and T.G. David (eds), *Spaces for Children. The Built Environment and Child Development.* New York: Plenum Press.

Macedo, D. (1996) 'A dialogue: culture, language, and race'. *The Harvard Educational Review,* **42**, 383–98.

Rouse, J. (Chief Executive of CABE) (2002) Interview for the BBC *Newsnight* programme, 16.10.2002.

Saint, A. (1987) *Towards a Social Architecture. The Role of School-Building in Post-War England.* London: Yale University Press.

Chapter 16

Joining Gabriel's play

Kayte Brimacombe with Roger Hancock

Kayte Brimacombe lives in North London and is the mother of three children. Kayte talked with Roger Hancock, a lecturer at the Open University, about her experience of helping her son Gabriel to play in order to stimulate his wish to communicate with others. Kayte's involvement in setting up play opportunities within the context of her home raises a number of considerations related to parental involvement in children's education, schools learning from parents, and particularly, what it is for adults to become truly involved in children's play.

My son Gabriel is nine and he has Down's syndrome and autism. Children with Down's syndrome have an extra, critical portion of the number 21 chromosome present in some or all of their cells. This can alter the rate of different aspects of their physical, cognitive, social and linguistic development, often resulting in learning difficulties. Children with autism typically experience difficulties with social interaction, social communication and imagination. They often resist changes in their routines. They also show repetitive behaviour patterns and can get stuck in such movements, usually called 'stimming'. For them, getting stuck might be important or pleasurable – flapping their hands is a common example. It could be said to be their way of playing. However, because it's repetitive it seems to be of limited value developmentally.

A place to play

We have set up in our home a play-based programme for Gabriel based on the Son-Rise Program® (see, ATCA 2004). This sees a child with autism as the teacher and suggests that parents and carers 'join' with them instead of taking an approach that goes against what they might wish to do.

There is a room in our house which is dedicated to play and fun. It's an ordinary sized bedroom with plain walls and the window is covered to minimise distractions. It's got a very soft floor covering because a lot of play takes place on the floor. The shelves are high so that Gabriel needs to communicate in order to choose something to play with. One of the main difficulties with autism is children can't select out stimuli – the radiator humming or the clock ticking can draw their attention as much as a face. When distractions are minimised adults become much more interesting and this increases the likelihood of communication. This is difficult for Gabriel in a normal family environment where there are many things happening.

Interestingly, limiting the number of distractions has a positive effect on adults too. When we go into the playroom no one else enters, so this allows us to really focus on Gabriel and keep our minds on play.

In the playroom we adults need to be very energetic and enthusiastic, have fun, and stretch ourselves in terms of building up our ability to play. Gabriel then becomes motivated to say 'more' or 'again' or 'up' or 'down'. These are very simple communications but he's stimulated to make those sounds and words because he's in on what is happening. In this way he is encouraged to share in the experiences of others.

Enlisting others

In addition to playing with members of his family, including his five-year-old sister, Gabriel also plays with trained volunteers. This gives him additional experience of communicating with other people and it also helps us if we can share what is a challenging family involvement. We recently went to the United States to receive further training from the programme's originators and this has given us more confidence when working with volunteers.

Currently, three volunteers are involved. They are given in-house training to help them build up their play skills, and taught how to be 'present' with Gabriel. The play room has an observation panel so sessions can be observed and feedback can be given on what is effective.

Gabriel's sister is the best person to play with him. She's quite happy to spin round and round in circles with him for ages and ages. Adults can't do this without feeling dizzy. She's also very good at linking with his body language so that there can be times when she truly connects with his experience.

Learning to play

The central message of the Son-Rise Program® is, therefore, that children with autism should be 'joined' in whatever they are doing. This is so even if they are engaged in something that might not normally be seen by adults as play. To some extent joining involves mirroring Gabriel's play. However, it's not just mimicking him but getting into his experience and understanding what he might be getting from what he's doing. For example, the way in which he's moving an object might provide interest for him because the light is bouncing off it in a certain way. So, an adult needs to discover what lies behind his involvement. It's a way of learning about his way of experiencing things and also being very understanding and accepting of him. This acceptance helps him to become interested in others. In this way, a bridge can be built which facilitates shared interests, communication and pleasure.

Time in the playroom has successfully built up Gabriel's communication skills. Sometimes, however, he's not in the mood and this has to be accepted. But mostly he realises that when he's in the play room he's in for a lot of fun. He can't really do anything wrong in there – anything goes, so it's known as the 'Yes' room.

A lot starts off through rough and tumble play, play that might also be appropriate with a toddler – swinging around, up and down games, for example. There's a big mirror that helps eye-contact with Gabriel. There's a great big ball and a rocker and a little trampoline. Physical games help build up his initial interest, get a smile from him and help him to want to play. He then might indicate that he wants more of something. On the shelf there are different things like big cars, skittles and huge bricks and he might indicate that he wants to go up and choose something to play with. It's a positive cycle of him getting what he wants and then him wanting more of it.

At the moment the focus is on eye contact and this has improved dramatically in the last four months. Very simple vocalisations are developing – like 'up', 'down', 'more', 'ball', 'push', and 'jump'. Gabriel makes approximations for these words so they're not that clear. However, he is a nine-year old child who hasn't spoken since he was two so it's a very dramatic effect for the family.

The key to success with Gabriel is to genuinely have fun and not to fake this. The people who are best at playing with him are those who can really enjoy it themselves. Lots of different people have, over time, become involved and this includes teachers and teaching assistants at his school. Often, there is a nervousness about being with a child with autism. Inexperienced people tend to 'flatten out'. They seem to lose a lot of their energy and their enthusiasm. It seems as though they're picking up on the perceived lack of feeling coming from Gabriel. So they tend to get stuck as well and unintentionally they can reinforce his 'stuck' situation. The secret is to work at successfully joining him and then try to change whatever's happening ever so slightly.

Given Gabriel's progress at home, the staff at the school are now adapting how they work with him to incorporate the principles of joining. The approaches they have been using to date have not enabled him to make very much progress. Gabriel is a little more sociable than many children with autism so this has helped his progress with the Son-Rise approach. The school have created a play room for him where he can go for short sessions. They have observed Gabriel's home programme and seen a video of him at play with different volunteers. Although there's some carry over of the family's approach to school, Gabriel's main programme continues to take place at home during evenings and weekends.

Conclusion

The Son-Rise approach has proved to be effective for Gabriel. To a large extent its principles are basically common sense, however. It is about removing the distractions which children with autism can't screen out easily for themselves, joining them in whatever they are doing, and then using enthusiasm, engagement and fun to help them to be drawn into social interaction.

For many adults, the process of joining can be very hard at first because grown-ups tend to have many things on their minds. However, once the skill of being 'present' in play has been acquired, then new ideas, creativity and playfulness can seem like very natural things. A lot of the qualities that people would wish to develop in themselves are valuable when people play together – like being authentic with someone and being 'alongside' them.

Working with Gabriel has done much to increase family and school understanding about the nature of play and about the act of playing. Those closely involved feel they have not only learnt to join him when playing but that this skill has a wider significance for the way in which adults collaborate with children to support their play and their education more generally.

Reference

ATCA (Autism Treatment Center of America) (2004) See: http://www.autismtreatmentcenter.org/contents/other_sections/index.php

Chapter 17

The role of grandparents in children's learning

Charmian Kenner, Tahera Arju, Eve Gregory, John Jessel and Mahera Ruby

The role of grandparents in children's learning is a neglected area of research, but as the authors of this chapter, members of a research team at Goldsmith's College, University of London, discovered, their contribution is worth further consideration. Grandparents often have a close and special relationship with their grandchildren and the research team found many examples of them involved in a range of learning events in the home, where the grandparents sensitively joined with children in a process of discovery or shared their knowledge and experience. Schools may wish to consider how they could extend their notions of partnership to include grandparents and other family members.

Setting the scene

Sumayah, her cousin and her grandmother are showing our research team how they work together in the small garden of their terraced house in Tower Hamlets, London's East End. First there are leaves to be swept up. Five-year-old Sumayah is determined to do the job and begins pushing the broom. After letting Sumayah sweep for a while, her grandmother takes over and demonstrates the firm strokes needed, then leaves Sumayah to finish the task. Next there are trees and plants to be watered. In this tiny space, Sumayah's family grow apples, pears, lemons, pumpkins, tomatoes and herbs, using the agricultural knowledge brought by the grandparents from Bangladesh. This knowledge is now being passed on to Sumayah and her cousin; it is they who are left in charge of the garden when their grandparents are away on visits to Bangladesh.

Learning from experience

What do the children learn from this experience? As they do the watering with three sets of hands grasping the watering-can handle – Sumayah's, her cousin's and her grandmother's – they find out how much water to give each tree or plant. They also know that not every plant is watered on every occasion; some need more water than others.

Sumayah points to the growing tip of a lemon tree seedling, commenting that the leaves are a different colour from the others because they are new. Her cousin shows three plants in a line of pots and explains while pointing to each one that two of them are his uncle's and one is Sumayah's. Sumayah is responsible for her own particular plant and she will thus find out in detail how to nurture it. For example, she knows whereabouts in the garden the plant has to be placed to receive the right amount of light. Her knowledge goes beyond the classic primary school experiment of growing cress under different conditions in order to discover that plants need light and water to thrive. As well as being aware that these elements are essential, Sumayah also knows what quantities are necessary for each plant.

The project

Our research project with grandparents and grandchildren in English-speaking and Bengali-speaking families in East London revealed a wealth of such learning events taking place between the older and younger generations. We had suspected that this little-investigated inter-generational relationship was of special importance to children's learning, but we were surprised by the wide range of activities going on.

An initial questionnaire, answered by eleven Bangladeshi British families and three Anglo (English-speaking) families, offered a list of 20 activities and asked grandparents whether they engaged in any of these with their three- to six-year-old grandchildren. Figure 17.1 shows the spread of activities.

Firstly, the questionnaire demonstrated that Bangladeshi British as well as Anglo families took children on outings to the park, played and read with them, involved them in cooking and gardening, told them stories and recited rhymes together. This finding challenges the assumption often made that ethnic minority families do not offer their children these kinds of learning experiences.

Secondly, the Bangladeshi British families placed a high priority on 'visiting others' and 'talking about members of the family and family history'. These were categories which the Anglo members of our research team had not originally thought of including, until two of the researchers – themselves from Bangladeshi backgrounds – made the suggestion. They explained that family visits are of considerable importance in Bangladeshi culture. When children go to see relatives, often accompanying their grandparents, they learn how to greet each person appropriately and how to behave within the social group. They gain knowledge of each relative's place in the complex kinship network and where they themselves fit in, giving them a sense of their own identity. Conversations with grandparents enhance their understanding of family history. These are important types of learning experience often overlooked by mainstream educators, and largely absent from the National Curriculum. We need a wider definition of the term 'learning' in order to encompass the rich variety of knowledge children gain from spending time in family settings.

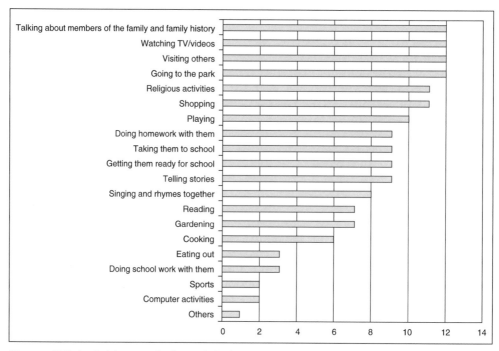

Figure 17.1 Activities carried out jointly by children and their grandparents, showing the number of grandparents reporting each activity.

The study

Having gained an initial idea of the kinds of learning experiences happening between grandparents and grandchildren, we approached 12 families who agreed to participate further in the project. Six were Sylheti/Bengali-speaking of Bangladeshi origin and six were monolingual English-speaking. Four families had children in the nursery class, four in Reception and four in Year 1. In interviews with grandparents and video recordings of learning events at home such as cooking, gardening, storytelling and computer activities, we examined the following questions:

- In what ways do grandparents and grandchildren take the lead in the learning interactions?
- In what ways are the learning interactions co-constructed by the participants?
- What kinds of knowledge are exchanged between the younger and older learners?
- What is the role of the computer in the cultural, linguistic and technical aspects of learning?

A special relationship

Children's relationship with their grandparents involved a sense of mutual vulnerability. Grandparents were recognised as needing care due to age and a certain amount of frailty. Sitting at the computer with his grandmother Hazel and observing her hand as she held the mouse in front of him, three-year-old Sam suddenly raised his own hands and declared: 'I'm not getting old . . . I've not got old skin.' Hazel agreed with amusement, noting that she indeed had wrinkles while Sam did not.

The grandparents in the project were keen to take care of their young grandchildren, and expressed this through a supportive use of touch. The close physical relationship between the generations was noticeable in the events we video recorded: Sahil's grandmother Razia linking her arm through her grandson's as they talked about the books they read together, Hazel patting Sam's tummy while talking about the computer game they were playing. The children's response showed a reciprocal use of touch: Sahil's younger siblings climbed on their grandmother's lap as she and Sahil read a poetry book, while Sam rested his head against his grandmother's shoulder as he listened to her comments on the computer game.

Guidance through touch

Touch was an important means of communication between young children and grandparents. As well as building children's sense of security and self-confidence, it was used by grandparents to guide kinaesthetic learning. The example was given above of Sumayah's grandmother helping her grandchildren to water plants in the garden. Through her touch, she indicated at what angle to hold the watering-can and how much water to give. We also observed Sahil's grandmother guiding his hand as he wrote in Bengali, enabling him to experience the flow of the pen on the page to inscribe the pattern of each letter. Once again, guidance through touch could be reciprocal. Moments later, Sahil placed his hand over his grandmother's to show her how to operate the mouse on the computer.

Learning exchanges around language

Grandparents often considered themselves responsible for particular areas of their grandchildren's learning. In the case of the Bengali-speaking families, one of these areas was language. For example, Sahil's grandmother Razia was seen by the family as responsible for maintaining the children's knowledge of Bengali. Sahil's mother, having grown up in Britain, tended to speak English as well as Bengali to her children, but wanted them to develop their family language in order to retain a link with their heritage and culture. Razia entered into her task with considerable energy. She used books brought by the children's mother from

Bangladesh, including stories such as 'Snow White' in Bengali which she knew the children would enjoy.

Sahil was able to identify different categories of Bengali book – alphabet primers, 'chora' (poetry) books, and the 'Snow White' storybook – realising that each had a different purpose. When reading the 'chora' book with his grandmother, he closely followed her lead. The oral recitation of poetry was enjoyed by Sahil and also by his younger sisters, who ran into the room to join in when they heard the rhythm of their grandmother's voice. As well as developing their vocabulary and expression in Bengali, the children were receiving an introduction to rhyme – a skill considered very important by early years educators.

Meanwhile, Razia was learning English from her grandchildren, in an inter-generational language exchange. Along with other grandparents in the study, Razia mentioned that contact with her grandson added to her knowledge of English. When Sahil was asked by the researchers whether his grandmother knew English, Razia (understanding the question perfectly) told her grandson in Bengali 'say Granny doesn't speak English'. She was maintaining her role as the resource person for Bengali within the family, but throughout the video recorded event her knowledge of English was evident. When Sahil was asked what he most enjoyed doing with his grandmother, he thought for a few moments and then replied in English 'I enjoy she telling me what the word means in Bangla' ('Bangla' is the term often used for Bengali). Contented, Razia smiled and kissed him, once again showing her understanding.

Several of the Bengali-speaking grandparents were also introducing their grandchildren to Arabic for the purposes of reading the Qur'an. Sumayah and her grandmother spread out a prayer mat on the carpet and sat together on the mat, with Sumayah reciting verses of the Qur'an after her grandmother. This early introduction to the sounds and intonation of classical Arabic was a prelude to a gradual understanding of the content of the verses, just as children participating in hymn-singing or prayers in an Anglican church would be inducted into the richness of language which they would later comprehend more fully.

Learning exchanges around computers

It can be seen from the questionnaire results that few grandparents engaged in computer activities with their grandchildren. For the Bangladeshi grandparents particularly, computers were unfamiliar and there were language constraints – computers operate in English script unless special software is obtained.

The potential for learning from computer activities was emphasised by our video observation of Hazel with her grand-daughter Lizzie. Hazel and Lizzie frequently used the Internet at Hazel's house to search for information to enhance the other learning activities they did together. For example, they often looked at wildlife in the garden and once discovered an unusual moth which they could not then find in Hazel's reference book. Via the Internet, they identified its picture, with the name 'Quercus' and information about the male and female moths and egg-laying habits. They then printed out this page and glued it into Lizzie's scrapbook.

Hazel's support for Lizzie's learning was sensitively given, allowing Lizzie to take the lead when doing the typing or clicking the mouse on the appropriate spots. At some moments, Lizzie's responses preceded those of her grandmother. While Hazel was working out what step to take next on the search engine 'Google', Lizzie had already pulled out the keyboard ready to type the search word. Hazel stated that she was less confident about word processing than her grandchildren, 'but now that Lizzie is learning at school, hopefully she'll teach me'.

In this exchange of competencies, Hazel helped to structure the stages of the learning event for Lizzie and supplied alphabet letters to complete the word 'moths' when Lizzie was unsure. Lizzie's eager confidence in using the word processing commands suggested that she would indeed soon be instructing her grandmother in this area. Her desire to go beyond the limits of this particular investigation by printing out information about another moth on the same website (despite her grandmother's attempts to keep to the original task) would exploit the possibilities of hypertext and introduce new areas of learning for them both.

A different form of support

In comparison, the activities conducted by Bangladeshi grandparents (when the research team supplied a laptop computer for them to use with their grandchildren) at first seemed more basic. The children were unfamiliar with a laptop although they had used other types of computer at school, and for most of the grandparents it was their first chance to use the technology. The children mostly typed their names, working out how to use the different form of mouse incorporated in the laptop keyboard.

However, a closer examination of these events reveals that the grandparents, sitting quietly beside their grandchildren, were playing an important role similar to that of Lizzie's grandmother. Through their presence they helped to structure the event, for example by ensuring that the child was the main actor and an older cousin did not take over, or by suggesting the activity of typing the child's name and supporting the child's efforts through their own knowledge of English letters. By giving their attention through gaze or pointing, even though they did not touch the computer, they helped the child maintain concentration and accomplish the task.

Furthermore, the grandparents showed a growing interest in what was happening on the screen. Their curiosity indicated a potential to develop knowledge and expertise if they were to have access to software or websites, which operated in their own language, as Lizzie's grandmother did. One aim of the research project is to increase family involvement with computers at our partner school in the study, Hermitage Primary School in Tower Hamlets. If

Bangladeshi grandparents can attend family workshops with tutoring and resources in Bengali, this could lead to positive outcomes for their own learning and that of their grandchildren.

Grandparents may need special encouragement to come into school and share their wisdom and experience. When invitations were issued to a 'Grandparents' Coffee Morning' at Hermitage School, a number of grandparents attended, some having dressed in their best clothes for the occasion. The grandparents were proud that the school had acknowledged their importance in their grandchildren's education – and the children were delighted to bring to school these key figures in their learning lives.

Conclusion

This research project has begun to open up a fascinating world of learning between grandchildren and grandparents, hitherto little-known to schools, particularly with regard to ethnic minority families. Our findings suggest the potential benefits if teachers widen their links with 'parents and carers' to ensure that the significant role of grandparents is recognised and built upon in home–school interactions.

Chapter 18

Supplementary schools and their parents: an overlooked resource?

John Bastiani

In this chapter, John Bastiani, visiting professor in Education at Nottingham Trent University, writes about the growth of supplementary school provision and the need for a greater understanding of its aims and nature. He draws upon a study of three Saturday Schools in South London, which was informed by the views of parents and children. He suggests that supplementary schools offer much that enable the educational progress of black and bilingual pupils and that these schools are therefore in a strong position to inform mainstream thinking if it is willing to listen.

There are clear educational benefits for children attending supplementary school. We're not working in competition with the mainstream school. We are effectively all working towards the same end – educated, more rounded, more independent, more aware children . . .

(Parent)

. . . it's because we all have the same interest in the children here. We're working with the children; the system is working *for* the children. It's the other way round in mainstream schools . . . the children are working *for the system* . . . They need to work more for the children.

(Parent)

I'd like to see mainstream schools become more child-centred. We pay our taxes; our taxes pay to provide an education for our children and I'd like to see more fighting on behalf of our children's needs and less pandering to central government's targets and numbers games . . .

(Parent)

There are at least one thousand supplementary and mother-tongue schools in Britain – probably many more. A significant number of these, especially those catering for Black communities, have long and often chequered histories. However, there is little systematic knowledge and information available about what Saturday Schools – as they are popularly known – are like, how they are viewed by those who support them and what their impact is upon the lives of the children who attend them.

This article draws upon a longer study, which I carried out, on behalf of The Institute for Public Policy and Research (IPPR), 'Supplementary Schooling in the Lambeth Education Action Zone'. The study was commissioned by the Centre for British Teachers and Lambeth Education Action Zone from IPPR to look at what parents felt supplementary schools in the Zone had to offer and what, if anything, could be done to utilise their experience and develop links with the Zone's mainstream schools. It is based upon a study of three Saturday Schools that have served the Black communities of Brixton and Stockwell, in South London, for many years, in spite of recurring problems of funding, accommodation and support. Like many other inner-city LEAs, Lambeth has increasingly recognised the need to provide and maintain additional forms of educational activity as a necessary ingredient in their overall plans for tackling underachievement and improving their results.

The wider study gives particular emphasis to the views of parents (and to the views of pupils themselves). There is now an extensive and convincing body of evidence which underlines the crucial importance of parental involvement and family support to children's progress and development (see Wolfendale and Bastiani 2000).

Although difficult to disentangle in the everyday world, there seem to be three overlapping elements, each of which has important implications

First, parents are, and continue to be, the most important influence on children's attitudes, behaviour and achievement – by far. Secondly, when schools and families can learn to work productively together, children benefit in tangible and lasting ways. Lastly, being a parent of school-aged children can be both a catalyst of, and platform for, parents' own education and development. It is also parents, of course, who get a clear view of their children in both supplementary and mainstream school settings.

Supplementary schools have attempted to tackle the combined effects of low expectations and continuing underachievement that are characteristic of much school provision in urban settings. They have provided a means for transmitting and reinforcing much cultural and linguistic learning that is precious to ethnic minorities and which is often undervalued in the wider society. They also have much currently unrecognised potential as a focus for alternative and complementary forms of provision and experience, whose positive achievements contrast sharply with the government's short-term and short-sighted obsession with narrowly focused targets and crude outcomes, so clearly identified by the parents quoted at the beginning of this article.

Saturday Schools are very popular among parents and pupils respectively, although they are, however, virtually ignored by mainstream schools. They seem to be very effective in catering for a wide range of ages and abilities – from pupils with statements of special educational need to the very able children, both of whom can be said to have special needs that are not adequately met in mainstream schools.

Saturday Schools have a special ethos and identity, which stems from a combination of:

- an approach to learning and teaching that is based upon a mix of formal and informal pedagogy and flexible use of time
- a great deal of individual attention, encouragement and support, from volunteers and mentoring schemes of different kinds
- strong parental involvement – in the day-to-day running of centres, in their management and in supporting children's work at home
- more of a family atmosphere than an institutional climate; many parents were formerly pupils themselves; older brothers and sisters continue to help out on a voluntary basis and co-operative rather than competitive values are stressed
- a grass-roots approach that has strong neighbourhood links with individuals and organisations that have relevant knowledge, skill and experience and are willing to share it, on a voluntary basis, for the common good.

Black (and mother-tongue) supplementary schools recognise the importance of shared culture and identity. Black staff aim to provide positive role models of successful learners; they have an experience and understanding of racism in schools and on the streets; and they can often draw upon their knowledge of black history and culture in their teaching.

But none of this is news. We have known for many years that children's learning is more likely to thrive in small-scale, pupil-friendly communities, characterised by flexible approaches to teaching and learning and underpinned by active family support.

What *is* new, however, is a recognition of the potential of such experience, largely unrecognised and unacknowledged at present in contributing to, and being supported by, the work of hard-pressed schools in our cities. And, especially, in making a positive contribution to the progress and development of black and bilingual pupils, many of whom do not get the education to which they are entitled and which they deserve.

In spite of the many and continuing difficulties that supplementary schools experience at the margins of the educational service, they remain confident about their role, upbeat about their achievements and distinctly optimistic about their futures.

In this, the non-compulsory nature of the educational enterprise, the mixture of paid and voluntary effort and the underlying commitment to what they are doing contributes to, and benefits from, the enthusiasm of all those involved. They represent an untapped educational alternative which has wider application and much to teach us.

References

Abdelrazak, M. and Kempadoo, M. (eds) (1999) *Directory of Supplementary and Mother-Tongue Classes (1999–2000).* London: Resource Unit for Supplementary and Mother-Tongue Schools.

Bastiani, J. (2004) *Supplementary Schooling in the Lambeth Education Action Zone.* IPPR: London. Available at: http://www.ippr.org.uk/research/teams/project.asp?id=896&pid=896

Bastiani, J. (ed) (1997) *Home-School Work in Multicultural Settings.* London: David Fulton.

Wolfendale, S. and Bastiani, J. (eds) (2000) *The Contribution of Parents to School Effectiveness.* David Fulton: London.

Section 3
Working together

Carrie Cable and Ian Eyres

This section explores some of the different ways in which teachers, teaching assistants and parents work together to support children's learning. Teaching assistants draw on a wide range of skills and experience, knowledge and understanding in carrying out a range of roles. In Chapter 19 Hilary Cremin, Gary Thomas and Karen Vincett describe their research into approaches to teamwork in the classroom. They discuss three different approaches and how effective teachers and teaching assistants thought they were in supporting their work and children's learning. Jenny Houssart worked in the role of a learning support assistant in a number of primary classrooms. In Chapter 20 she describes the knowledge, skills and understandings that learning support assistants bring to the task of supporting children's mathematical thinking and reflects on the important contribution that their observations can make to children's learning.

Some teaching assistants are bilingual and speak the languages of children and parents in their schools. They often draw on their knowledge and understanding of other languages and cultures in facilitating the learning of bilingual pupils and home–school relationships. In Chapter 21 Carrie Cable discusses the particular contribution these staff can make to children's learning. In Chapter 22 Lindsey Haynes, a teaching assistant, describes how she works in close collaboration with her class teacher to develop children's creativity through encouraging children to be active participants in their own learning and in the creation of their learning environment.

In Chapter 23, Janet Atkin and John Bastiani describe a research project that looked at parental involvement in their children's learning. They were interested to find out what role parents took and how they would describe what they did. The wide variation in parental practice they found led them to advise against generalisations or narrow definitions of teaching.

Many schools establish effective links between children's homes and school but as Suzanne Brown found out there can be a variety of practice. In Chapter 24 she describes the findings of a survey she carried out in one LEA.

The final chapter in this section looks at pupil involvement in their learning. In Chapter 25, Ruth Dann argues that pupil self-assessment should be an essential component in formative assessment because it will provide valuable insights into children's thinking and understanding and tell us what children consider to be important about their own learning.

Chapter 19

Winning teams

Hilary Cremin, Gary Thomas and Karen Vincett

How best can teachers and teaching assistants work together in classrooms? Given the continuing increase in the numbers of teaching assistants to be found in schools, there would seem to be a need to better understand what is in fact a new form of team teaching. In this article Hilary Cremin (senior lecturer at Oxford Brookes University), Gary Thomas (professor of education Birmingham University), and Karen Vincett (senior educational psychologist, Essex LEA) report on research that examined three approaches to classroom teamwork. These are termed 'room management', 'zoning' and 'reflective teamwork'.

The number of teaching assistants in schools has mushroomed in recent years. Everyone is certain this is a good thing, but there is less certainty about the best way for assistants to support the teacher. Who should do what? And how should they do it?

These questions led Essex County Council Special Educational Needs and Psychology Service to set up a research project in 2001 with Oxford Brookes University Institute of Education. The project sought ways of organising the work of assistants – particularly where they were helping children experiencing difficulty at school.

We began by searching the literature for information on methods of working with assistants. We had to go back to the 1970s, to the US and to special education, to find useful research.

We located two models – *room management* and *zoning* – that we felt could be adapted to help organise the work of assistants in today's mainstream schools. To these we added another method, *reflective teamwork*, which is based in team psychology.

Room management

Room management works by ensuring that every adult in the class has a clear role. The roles are determined by important functions that teachers without assistants normally have to undertake on their own: managing the large group and providing individual help.

With an extra person available, or so the argument behind room management goes, these activities, which are difficult to fulfil simultaneously, can be separated. The two adults become the activity manager and the individual helper. The activity manager will concentrate on the group, while the individual helper will work exclusively with individuals, providing intensive help in a timetabled way to a predefined list of children.

The teacher remains in overall charge, but teacher or assistant can take on either of the roles, depending on the needs of the class and the activity planned.

Zoning the classroom

Zoning is a simple system that works by organising the class into learning zones, structured by the placement of the groups in a class. For example, six groups may be split into: a zone of five groups and a zone with a single group; a zone of four groups and one with a pair of groups; or into two zones of three groups. Each zone is then allocated to teacher or assistant, under the overall direction of the teacher. While making the allocation, thought is given to how the children are placed, and how the adults will work.

Reflective teamwork

Reflective teamwork is a method of improving the planning, organisation and general teamwork of teacher and teaching assistant. It does this through teamwork games and exercises, and through planning and reflection meetings.

Testing the theories

For the first phase of the project we worked with six teachers and their assistants, who had all volunteered to take part. We divided the strategies among them: two used room management, two used zoning and two used reflective teamwork.

We observed each class on video, examining each child in turn under baseline conditions (i.e., before the new method was tried) and then under each new method of organisation to see how far they were engaged (i.e., how far they were doing what they were supposed to be doing). We also asked staff to take diaries and to tell us about their experiences and feelings.

The results were fascinating. In all of the classes and with all of the systems there were significant improvements in the children's engagement. Room management made the most marked difference, with zoning and reflective teamwork also effecting worthwhile improvements.

However, staff varied in their attitudes to the programmes. One teacher who was using room management, for example, found the model took a lot of time to plan, and was difficult to mesh with the expectations of the Literacy Hour. Zoning and reflective teamwork were accepted more easily, and some useful ideas for adapting and improving the systems came forward.

Developing strategies

With these new ideas and with the success of the first project, we came to the second phase, begun last year and again funded by Essex LEA. Here, we asked for volunteers from a broader range of schools, including secondary schools. Interest was high, and we worked with a mixture of 12 primary and secondary schools.

Using the detailed feedback provided by the teachers and teaching assistants in the first phase of the project, we used an action research framework to enable participants in the programme to develop their own models from the best elements of room management, zoning and reflective teamwork.

The aim was no longer to see whether the methods were effective or which method was best, because each had been shown to have strengths. What we did now, in a training seminar for all staff, was say, 'This method seems to be good for this reason and that for that reason – mix and match to develop a system that meets your needs in your circumstances.'

The teachers and assistants went about this task with gusto and tried out their own adaptations, taking what they saw as the best of these various models to make their own. The results are still coming in, but early indications are that the new methods they have developed are highly effective, again enabling strong improvements in children's engagement. It also seems that the improved teamwork may be effecting improvements in children's self-esteem, and enabling teaching assistants to feel fully involved in the education of the children.

Chapter 20

Supporting primary mathematics

Jenny Houssart

> To gather material for this chapter, Jenny Houssart, a Research Fellow at the Open University's Centre for Mathematics Education, worked in the role of a learning support assistant in a number of primary classrooms. Her observations show teaching assistants bringing considerable knowledge and expertise to bear as they work with children developing their mathematical thinking. She concludes that the most successful partnerships are those where the teacher values and makes use of the observations teaching assistants make.

This chapter is based on research carried out in primary mathematics classrooms in which I adopted a role similar to that of a Learning Support Assistant (LSA). The main issue considered is what action LSAs might take as a result of what they see and hear. This is introduced by considering possible scenarios, which are then followed by a case study of positive practice. This is followed by a discussion of how LSAs' actions influenced the children's learning of mathematics.

The literature stresses the importance of teamwork. For example, Balshaw (1999) suggests that where practice is effective, assistants are seen as partners in the classroom rather than merely helpers. A similar view is put forward by Farell *et al.* (1999) who make points about communication and teamwork between teachers and assistants. Fox (1998) suggests that assistants and teachers should establish ground rules for working together. A question assistants might ask teachers is therefore 'Can I contribute or ask questions during the lesson?' A variant of this question is considered in more detail here. My question is 'What interventions are possible and appropriate as a result of what LSAs see or hear in a mathematics lesson?' The next section explores some possible scenarios.

Possible scenarios

The following scenarios are suggested to prompt questions about what an LSA might do in particular situations. Suppose the LSA feels that one of the following is happening:

- A child is struggling with the work being explained by the teacher.
- A particular activity is not working well for several children.
- The work is too easy for one or several of the children.
- The teacher is saying something confusing, or even incorrect.
- The amount of time allowed for a task is inappropriate for some children.

How might the LSA react in these scenarios? Some possibilities are:

- Do and say nothing.
- Raise the issue with the teacher tactfully, after the lesson.
- Raise the issue openly when it occurs and in the hearing of the children.
- Take action to deal with the issue without consulting the teacher.

The scenarios suggested may provoke different reactions. These may range from feeling these things only happen in 'bad' classrooms, through an acknowledgement that they can sometimes happen to most people, to the view that they represent the complexities of teaching and learning and are ever present. Another key issue is that all the scenarios hinge on the LSA's opinion of what is happening. How seriously this is taken will depend on how the LSA's view is valued, especially if it potentially contradicts the teacher's view. One approach is that teachers are highly trained experts, so their view is paramount. Certainly the training and knowledge of the LSA is a closely related issue and this varies widely.

However there are other points to consider. First, the LSA is in an excellent position to observe individual children, partly because they do not normally have to maintain a teacher's awareness of the whole room, delivering the lesson and considering what changes to make. Second, some LSAs work closely with individual children, sometimes across several years. They develop pictures of strengths and difficulties that a teacher might not have.

My experience of working alongside teachers and LSAs in bottom mathematics sets, containing high proportions of children with special needs, is that very different approaches can be taken to the scenarios listed above. In one classroom, for example, LSAs often took no action, though they occasionally shared their observations quietly with each other. The view was that other adults were not expected to speak when the teacher was teaching the class. There was also a feeling that making suggestions or pointing out problems, even tactfully and outside the childrens' hearing, was an unacceptable threat to the teacher's authority. In another classroom, however, LSAs commonly raised issues with the teacher as they occurred. They also sometimes discussed issues afterwards, or occasionally took action themselves. In the following section, this classroom is taken as a case study of good practice.

Case study

Context

The following incidents occurred in a small bottom mathematics set in a large primary school. The children were mixed Year 3 and Year 4. All were considered to have special needs in mathematics and some had statements. The teacher was supported by two LSAs, Mrs Taylor and Mrs Carrington. The latter was assigned to work mainly with one child, James.

> I was present at lessons once a week as part of my research into mathematical tasks. I adopted a role similar to that of the LSAs, working alongside children as directed by the teacher. When possible, I made notes about childrens' responses to mathematical tasks. The following incidents from my notes all show that an LSA noticed something about the child's response.

Open discussion

In these incidents the LSAs raised issues as they arose and in the teacher's hearing.

Coins in a jar

> The children were sitting on the mat, working on counting activities. One activity involved 2p coins being dropped in a glass jar. The children had to close their eyes and count in twos in their heads, using the sound of the coins dropping in the jar. When 12p was dropped in the jar, Neil said it was 22p and Claire said 10p. Most others seemed to get the correct answer.
>
> The next example was 20p. Only three hands went up at the end, two of them offering the correct answer. The next example was 14p. Several incorrect answers were offered, for example 12p, 16p, 22p, 31p. The next example was 18p and this again led to several incorrect answers.
>
> At this point the teacher and Mrs Taylor started to discuss the activity. They seemed surprised at the difficulty the children had with this compared to similar activities. They talked about the fact that the children did better with numbers up to 10 and concluded that they needed to concentrate on counting in 2s between 10 and 20 in future activities.

The end of the adults' discussion suggests that they were trying to work out on the spot what was proving difficult for the children. Similar short discussions occurred on other occasions, often amounting to a comparison of two activities. One example of this was counting alone rather than as a group. Another was counting in fives starting from a number higher than zero or five. The discussion above also suggests that an idea arose about possible future activities. Incidents where the adults talked about possible next steps occurred in other lessons; sometimes immediate changes were made as a result.

In all the examples above, the adult discussion was about the responses of the group in general to an activity. The example given below concerns an individual child's response.

Spider

> The children were on the mat and the teacher was leading an activity using a large hundred square and a plastic spider which she moved around the square. The children started by being asked the number 10 more than the one the spider was on. Later questions included 20 and 30, more and less.
>
> At one point the spider was on 64. The teacher said that his dinner was on '20 more' and the children had to say which number this was. Douglas was asked but said he was not sure and didn't give a number. Other children then answered correctly.
>
> The activity continued with different examples and Mrs Carrington helped Douglas, who was sitting near her. A little later she told the teacher that she thought Douglas was 'struggling' and asked if he could move nearer to the hundred square so he could touch it. The teacher initially agreed, but then had the idea of giving Douglas a smaller hundred square to work with. She handed the hundred square to Mrs Carrington, who worked with Douglas on the next examples using it. Neil, who was sitting nearby, also made some use of it.
>
> The next example was 20 less than 55. Douglas continued to have problems. He seemed to moving in ones rather than tens and said to Mrs Carrington, 'I'm looking at the next door neighbour numbers.' After further examples, Douglas was getting correct answers and was encouraged by Mrs Carrington to put his hand up and answer.

Looking back at this incident, I wonder whether Mrs Carrington started watching Douglas when he didn't give an answer to the teacher's earlier question. Because her intervention was immediate, Douglas was given something to help him with subsequent examples. Raising the matter afterwards would not have had this effect. However, provision of the hundred square did not enable Douglas to answer the questions straight away. What it did was to give the adults more information about his difficulty, enabling him to be helped further. After more help and encouragement from Mrs Carrington, Douglas answered the questions correctly. Provision of the hundred square was also helpful to Neil.

This suggests a particularly significant point of more general use: that what appears to be a difficulty confined to one child may in fact be more widespread in the group. In other words, an 'individual difficulty' reveals a more widespread one.

This incident also suggests shared values between the teacher and Mrs Carrington in wanting to help the children understand the mathematics, rather than just giving correct answers. A potential problem with this example however is that it involves an individual child's difficulty being discussed very openly. Perhaps for this reason, individuals were sometimes discussed before or after the lesson when the children weren't there – something considered in the next section.

Discussion outside lessons

Before-lesson discussions sometimes arose when the teacher told other adults what was planned for the lesson and speculation followed about possible outcomes and possible changes. Individual rather than apparently 'whole group' problems were more commonly raised in this way. After-lesson discussions occurred when adults informed each other about children they had worked with individually or in small groups, as shown below.

Smartie graphs

The lesson had just finished. The main activity had been to draw a graph of colours from a tube of Smarties. The children had gone to play, taking their Smarties with them. The adults were putting the graphs in the children's folders.

Mrs Taylor, who had worked on the same table as James, talked about how well he had done today. She said he needed less help than expected with the graph and she thought he really understood what he was doing.

This led to a discussion of James and how much he can do by himself. Mrs Carrington, who usually works with James, talked about some other incidents. She said that although she was there to work with him, she wanted to encourage his independence rather than sit with him every minute.

The after-lesson discussions lacked the immediate impact of 'on the spot' discussions, but they nevertheless had advantages. One was that there was more time for discussion. Confidentiality was another.

The discussion about James and the Smartie graphs moved on from reporting back on his work to discussing a key issue, that of how LSAs assigned to individual children maintain the balance between helping them and encouraging their independence. Major issues were also sometimes discussed as a result of reflecting on how a particular task went, or talking about what would be done next. One such discussion was about how much time should be spent on consolidation and whether children should still be moved forward if they seemed to have difficulties with current work. Also discussed was the difficulty children had when activities were varied, for example from counting in twos to counting in fives or from adding to subtracting. The teacher and the LSAs talked about whether it was legitimate to keep the activity the same in the hopes that children might keep getting correct answers. They contrasted this with the hope that children should be able to respond to variations in the task rather than just repeating the same thing. None of these discussions were apparently planned, they arose naturally from a situation where the adults talked openly to each other about the children's responses to the work.

Other issues

In the examples above, LSAs suggested changes to the teacher and hence I was aware of their suggestions. It is obviously harder to know whether they made any changes to tasks without saying anything. On the occasions when I worked close to another adult, I sensed that it was considered acceptable to make minor changes according to how the activity was going. Often these were mentioned in casual discussion afterwards.

There were also occasions when LSAs suggested that children got pieces of equipment to help them, without asking the teacher. It seemed to be accepted practice for LSAs to provide support or extension for tasks, albeit in small ways, without necessarily asking or telling the teacher. Sometimes the issue of time needed for a task arose. There was some flexibility here, with LSAs occasionally judging that a child needed more time to complete a task as the others returned to the mat, and this was usually agreed with the teacher.

It will be clear from the incidents above that there was a good working relationship between the adults in the classroom. There was also a certain amount of shared humour, helping to diffuse potentially embarrassing situations. If a mistake was made or an answer forgotten by the adults, one of the others was usually able to step in under the shared joke that we were having a bad day or had forgotten where we were up to.

Discussion

Impact on mathematics

The incidents above suggest that the way this classroom team worked together had some impact on the mathematics. Sometimes the impact was fairly direct and obvious, as in the 'Spider' example, where adult intervention enabled Douglas' difficulties to be considered more closely. As a result Douglas succeeded with a task which he had originally not seemed able to do.

Sometimes the effect of intervention was more subtle. In the 'coins in the jar' incident, the combined views of the adults were used to inform decisions about what might be done next. The combined views of the adults were also sometimes used to consider the strengths and difficulties of individuals, usually in discussions outside the lesson. The success of this team in considering and acting on pupil difficulties is notable as these areas are highlighted in recent reports as things teachers are finding difficult (e.g. OfSTED 2001). It seems that teamwork may be a way of addressing this.

Finally, the climate of open discussion and sharing of views often led the team of adults to reflect on and consider important and complex questions. Issues such as how much help LSAs should give children they are assigned to and how much children with learning difficulties should be encouraged to move forward, seemed to flow naturally from discussions about incidents during lessons.

Factors influencing approaches

It is worth speculating a little on the factors that enabled this team to work in the way described. Certainly the LSAs had the mathematical knowledge and understanding to make useful contributions. Perhaps more importantly the teacher was aware of this knowledge and understanding and valued it. This may be because she took time to talk to the LSAs and got to know their strengths. It is also worth noting that the LSAs were involved in numeracy training within the school, meaning that all the teachers had some awareness of the knowledge of the LSAs and also meaning that LSAs and teachers were likely to share some understanding of issues and approaches. Matters were helped by the teacher's openness to ideas and by the fact that the adults appeared to get on well socially and to value each other's views and experiences.

Conclusions

The case study outlined above supports the view that children's learning is enhanced if use is made of the observations of LSAs. In this case study classroom, an atmosphere had been established where LSAs felt free to comment on or act upon their observations. As a result, the adults worked effectively as a team, doing their best to diagnose and act on children's difficulties. Their teamwork was also evident in their discussion of complex issues related to teaching, supporting and assessing pupils with learning difficulties. LSAs views were not just rhetorically 'valued' by the teacher in an abstract sense, they were welcomed and turned to positive effect to assist learning. This was especially valuable where 'individual' problems were shown to affect many more children, and teaching was consequently improved for the whole class.

The team described here had established a way of working together which meant that LSAs sometimes contributed when the teacher was talking to the class and it was not seen as disrespectful or undermining to the teacher for them to do so. In contrasting cases, opportunities were missed when LSAs held back, perhaps out of respect for the teacher's authority. My findings suggest that what is needed is for teachers also to respect the views of LSAs. If their views are sought and valued, children's learning is likely to be enhanced.

Note: Further findings are reported in Houssart, J. (2004) *Low Attainers in Primary Mathematics. The whisperers and the maths fairy.* London: Routledge.

References

Balshaw, M. (1999) *Help in the Classroom,* 2nd edn. London: David Fulton.

Farell, P., Balshaw, M. and Polat, F. (1999) *The Management, Role and Training of Learning Support Assistants.* Nottingham: DfEE.

Fox, G. (1998) *A Handbook for Learning Support Assistants: Teachers and Assistants Working Together.* London: David Fulton.

OfSTED (2001) *The National Numeracy Strategy: The second year, An evaluation by HMI.* London: Office for Standard in Education.

Chapter 21

Reflections on practice: three bilingual teaching assistants/instructors reflect on their roles

Carrie Cable

The job descriptions for teaching assistants do not always reflect the myriad complexity of their roles. In interviews with Carrie Cable, a lecturer at the Open University, three bilingual teaching assistants/instructors reflected on the similarities and differences between their roles and those of monolingual staff. These staff were working in different education authorities in England but shared many similar views on the special contribution they make to children's learning, teachers' understandings and effective home–school relationships.

The bilingual teaching assistants/instructors

Surinder works as a bilingual instructor, and as a member of a centralised team of bilingual staff, for a large, mainly rural county where her work involves her in supporting isolated learners in different primary schools on a peripatetic basis. She speaks Punjabi and some Urdu and Gujerati. Margaret worked as a bilingual instructor for a centralised team but was deployed full-time to one primary school with a large number of children learning English as an additional language. She speaks Twi, Ga and some Arabic and was educated and qualified as a teacher in Ghana. Amina is employed full-time as a bilingual assistant by an inner-city primary school. She works across a number of classes spending half a day in each class, mainly supporting literacy and numeracy activities, but also other areas of the curriculum. She speaks Bengali and Sylheti. In semi-structured interviews they reflected on how they utilised their knowledge and understanding of other languages and cultures to support bilingual pupils in their schools.

Utilising their cultural knowledge and understanding

All three bilingual staff felt that knowledge and understanding of the cultural backgrounds of the children and their families was one of the important contributions that they made to the education and care of the children they worked with. They were able to communicate these understandings to teachers and help them gain valuable insights into children's skills and behaviour, especially when they first started school or nursery.

Surinder outlined some of the cultural differences that she felt it was important for teachers to understand, including sleeping, eating and routines.

Surinder: It's quite a norm to wait till the parents go to bed and then turn in. There are few parents who will actually be very firm about it ... It's much easier, rather than having to coax them, so it's a way children don't cry, you don't want them to cry, so they normally sleep with the parents in their bed. There is a cot but the child is quite good at manipulating, jumping out of the cot – they work that one out at a very young age and milk it to the full ... They eat later – they eat their meals later – so it's a totally different pattern to life compared to what we traditionally do in the UK, and then people brought up that way, I think, have those life-long habits which they don't see there's anything wrong with because why? It's not wrong, that's the way it has always worked and their children fit into that pattern as well.

Although they acknowledged that practices in different communities varied, they all felt that it was the knowledge that there could be differences which was important, and that their explanations helped monolingual and monocultural staff to better understand parents and children's needs. As well as helping teachers to understand important elements of children's home backgrounds, they also, when necessary, helped parents to become familiar with the customs and practices in UK nurseries and schools. They saw their role as supporting children's social integration, well-being and self-esteem, and fostering their independence so that they would be able to thrive in the nursery or school.

Mediating communication between home and school

All the bilingual staff were involved in working closely with parents, including those parents who did not share one of their other languages. Although many teaching assistants are involved in informal contact with parents at the school gate before and after school; few of them have formal contact or are asked to specifically make contact with parents.

Margaret: When the children come in, I do a home visit, talk to them about their backgrounds – so at first I develop that relationship, that special relationship with the parents from the home. That, you know, brings them to the school and when they come to the school, I take them round the school to familiarise them with the school surroundings and I tell them how the school functions, about the timetable and the things that the children require.

Sometimes when the school is on a visit, outing, I make sure, you know, I get one of the parents to come along so they will know more about the school.

As well as having a role in helping parents to understand the educational system, the curriculum and the demands of the school, they were involved in providing workshop sessions about the curriculum for parents. They also talked about the importance of involving parents in the life of the school and inviting them in to share stories or prepare and cook food with the children.

Sometimes contact involved 'trouble-shooting' or 'problem-solving'.

Surinder: I had one child who transferred from another school and he had an appalling attendance record. I worked out that one of the days he wouldn't be in school was the day that we went swimming. So I stopped and called the mum one day and said: 'He's missing a lot of school, which means he's missing a lot of lessons, can you find ways of working with me on this one? Is there a problem?' I said to the boy: 'Are you afraid of going under water? How come I wear my swimming costume?' He smiled at me. You say to the child: 'It's fun, don't miss out on swimming.' So he'll go home and say: 'I'd like to swim, can I have my towel?' And then say to his mum that swimming is really good. Maybe mum was thinking he would be wet and he wouldn't dry himself and catch a cold so the day of swimming he didn't go to school. Anyway this mum was absolutely brilliant, she was one hundred per cent supportive. He was really struggling in Year 1 and not getting very far in Year 2, now he's in the top end of the class results. It's the little things you know.

On occasions they were also approached, sometimes confidentially, by parents who wanted to share a concern or obtain information.

Margaret: If there was a problem they would always come to me first, always come to me first – because of my background I understand them better. They felt more comfortable if they complained to me, that I won't go back and tell the teacher and she won't be angry with the children. And maybe I'll be able to explain it to them in their language better, better to them because I understand them better. In a language they will understand, you know the vocabulary I use, the vocabulary they will understand.

Both Margaret and Amina described how they would attend interviews at the parents' request with staff and parents even though they did not share the parents' first language and the parents spoke some English. They both said that staff also felt that this 'interpreting' role was valuable in communicating with parents. Margaret thought that parents were happy to approach her because, even when they did not share the same first language, there were elements of their backgrounds and experiences that were similar and she was not white and monolingual. Parents, they felt, saw them as people they could trust and as people who would represent their views.

Amina and Surinder, and to a lesser extent, Margaret, were involved in interpreting for parents through the medium of their first language and Amina was also involved in translating some information to be sent home to parents. This was not a major part of her role however, and she felt that drawing parents' attention to and discussing the information that was sent home in English was more helpful for parents and ensured that they understood what was intended. These discussions usually took place informally before and after school.

However, they all felt that having bilingual staff wasn't enough on its own for effective communication to take place.

Amina: To be able to do that, you need a couple of things: one of the things you need is support from the school which needs to be quite proactive about it, not to sit on the back burner; two, you need to feel perhaps a certain amount of standing or power to be able to do that, you need to have a certain amount of confidence to say: 'Let's do that.'

They felt that they could communicate with parents – whether or not they spoke the same first language – and represent parents' views. They empathised with parents and wanted the schools to understand and take account of their concerns and perspectives. At the same time they saw themselves firmly as members of the school staff and used the 'language' of school. At times they moved backwards and forward between the two 'languages', but did not find this difficult.

Margaret: Perhaps it's because I understand that English is not the master language; there are other languages through which we can communicate.

Contributing to assessment

All the staff were usually involved in making some kind of assessment of children new to the school. They felt that schools did not automatically seek out this information as part of their procedures and relied on them to do this through informal contacts with parents or with siblings.

Surinder: It means you have to stop at the gate and say can you provide me with information on your child . . . for example, asking siblings about literacy levels, etc.

They were not involved in carrying out assessments in the mother tongue except on an ad hoc basis. Only in instances where the child was perceived to have a difficulty in learning did the possibility of a mother tongue assessment arise and only then in some cases. Cline (1998) has identified clear omissions in guidance relating to the assessment of bilingual children who may have learning difficulties and recommends the involvement of bilingual staff at every stage.

They felt that teachers had a better understanding of the distinction between the needs of children learning English as an additional language and those with a learning difficulty than in the past. However, Surinder said that there were still schools in her area who 'put children on the special needs register'. She spoke of the long-term effects this could have on children's learning and self-esteem when it also meant they were assigned to groups labelled as 'low ability' and provided with inappropriate support.

Surinder: And once you are in there, it's very hard to break away – very, very hard. You have to really fight to bring a child out of SEN [Special Education Needs] and by that point they've usually a few friendships.

Supporting and mediating children's learning

Margaret and Amina spent most of their time supporting children in classroom activities. They usually worked with mixed groups of bilingual and monolingual learners. The nature of Surinder's role meant that she was more inclined to work for short, intensive periods with an individual child once or twice a week. Amina and Margaret were more fully involved in planning and attended after-school planning sessions. Margaret also usually planned her own activities to do with the groups she worked with. Amina worked with groups especially during the designated group times in literacy and mathematics lessons, but she was also involved in working alongside the class teacher – sometimes role switching and sometimes using Bengali with the whole class. They were all involved in feeding back their observations of children's achievements and areas for further development to teachers and for monitoring the progress of the bilingual children they worked with. Supporting children's learning prior to Key Stage 1 and 2 SATs was something they had all been involved in and their help in preparing children for these tests was sought by the schools.

Margaret commented on the importance of the groups that children were in and her role in selecting monolingual children to join her groups who would provide good language role models for children.

Margaret: I always selected a few monolingual children, so as we did the activity they'd pick up the language from their peers ... children learn more from their peers – it's always better to have a mixed group, especially [for] very confident ones to be with them, and usually they pick up the language from them. It's also easier when they work with their friends, because, you know, they pick up language from their friends.

Socio-cultural perspectives on learning emphasise the social and cultural contexts for learning and the role of adults in supporting learning. The assistants emphasised the importance of drawing on children's knowledge and experience and enabling them to make links with their prior experiences and learning.

Amina described how she would utilise a variety of measuring instruments to introduce children new to UK schooling to measuring activities and ensure that they developed a clear understanding of the concept before using rulers or measuring tapes. She would use Bengali or Sylheti to support children's learning in these situations.

Amina: In other countries, when we are doing measuring, we would use different measuring devices, like the feet, because some of them, you know, might not have seen a ruler or a measuring tape before, you know, they use the palm or the arm and they are familiar more with these devices – so starting from what they know and what they are already aware of makes the lesson more interesting to them.

Margaret described a lesson when she was working with a child who had recently joined the school:

Margaret: There was this lesson on water and I took him and two other friends and I started off on how you use water and I started telling them about my childhood and how we used to go and have our bath in the river, wash our clothes and hang them by the river and these boys started saying: 'Yes.' 'Yes.' 'Yes, back home my mother used to do that, we used to do that.' So after the lesson I told him to make a picture of himself at the riverside and the activities that go on there back home in India. He produced a nice picture, and when I took that picture to the teacher she was really surprised and said: 'Oh this boy has all this in him and he never speaks to me in the class.' She put it on the board. It made that child very proud, and after two terms this boy was among the best three children in the class because of the support he received from the beginning, that got out the confidence in him.

She felt that there were experiences common to people from both an African and Asian background and the fact that she could use examples in her teaching that children would be able to relate to gave them starting points into developing both their linguistic and curriculum knowledge. In the above example she was also acting as an advocate for the child, ensuring that his understanding was communicated to and acknowledged by the teacher.

They were also involved in giving advice with respect to the curriculum. Amina was involved in selecting bilingual resources and in preparing some of these herself. She was in charge of the 'multicultural resources', which included toys, games and musical instruments, and for ensuring that they were available in different classrooms to support role-play, themes and practical activities.

They also all talked about the additional and non-verbal ways of communicating meaning, including drawing, signs, symbolic representations, drama, and role play, as well as gestures, actions and facial expressions. They felt that, because they were used to communicating with other people who did not share their languages, they utilised these devices both consciously and unconsciously in working with children.

A key element of their role was supporting children's learning and language development. However, although they were all committed to children maintaining and developing their skills and competence in their first languages, they did not see this as primarily their role in school.

The importance of bilingual staff

Surinder: My perception of this is they relate to you, you are possibly somebody who is one of them, especially if you are an only child coming into school. It [school] is very much monolingual, very much white – culturally, linguistically, in every way. I think they probably feel a sense of belonging – that's OK. Like saying to this child – I'm going to bring my sense of identity to this; it's normalised something for them. I think that's important.

They felt that constructing a 'normal' experience for children, one in which they could see and have access to people who they could perceive, not necessarily as speaking the same language or coming from the same cultural background as themselves, but who they could perceive as not white and not monolingual, was very important.

Margaret: So long as they know that there is someone else whose language is not only English, you know, but who has a different language or who understands them. Because, usually, if I don't understand the language at all, it is possible they come from a country where we have similarities in doing things – so the fact that there is another person whose first language is not English brings confidence to them, they talk to you.

Concluding thoughts

My aim in talking to these three bilingual teaching assistants/instructors was to find out more about their perceptions of their role and contribution to children's learning. They all felt that they made significant contributions to children's learning that could not be provided by monolingual staff. These were related to fostering the social conditions necessary for learning as well as to supporting language development in the classroom.

The knowledge and understanding of children's cultural backgrounds and home experiences, other languages and parents' concerns enabled these teaching assistants/instructors to facilitate and enhance communication between home and school in ways that would otherwise not have happened, or at least not to the same extent. They acted as 'Funds of Knowledge' (Moll *et al.* 1992) by providing information for staff, mediating communication, and facilitating children's understanding of and engagement with the school curriculum. They also helped to give children a sense of identity through their sense of their own identities as bicultural and bilingual people living and working in the UK.

References

Cline, T. (1998) 'The assessment of special educational needs for bilingual children'. *British Journal of Special Education*, **25** (4), 159–63.

Moll, L.C., Amanti, C., Neff, D. and Gonzalez, N. (1992) 'Funds of knowledge for teaching: Using a qualitative approach to connect homes and classrooms'. *Theory into Practice*, **31** (2), 132–41.

Chapter 22

Enabling children's creativity

Lindsey Haynes with Anna Craft

Lindsey Haynes, a teaching assistant, and Anna Craft, a lecturer at the Open University, collaborated in the writing of this chapter. Anna worked as a researcher with Lindsey and Jean Keene, the class teacher, between 2003 and 2005, exploring how they worked together to develop children's creativity and their own creative practice.

I am a full-time teaching assistant in a Reception class at Cunningham Hill Infant School in Hertfordshire, England. There is a close working relationship between all staff and the teaching assistants are encouraged to take a proactive role within the school. All teaching assistants are included in the weekly staff meetings and have the opportunity to contribute ideas. Teachers and teaching assistants also have regular opportunities to plan together: in my case the teacher asks for my suggestions at a very early stage and we develop ideas together.

Each year group has parallel classes and all of them have a full-time teaching assistant. I have my own clearly defined areas of responsibility: helping with administrative functions, ensuring materials are adequately stocked, dealing with injuries and the occasional accident, but most importantly I support the teacher and the children in the classroom. I work with the children in all aspects of the curriculum, either with individual children, small groups or on occasion the whole class. I also have regular contact with the parents.

Setting the context for developing our children's creativity

The school does not have its own nursery so the children enter Reception with a wide range of pre-school experience. During the first few weeks the class teacher and I introduce the children to each other, the classroom and the school. We go as slowly as necessary at this stage to ensure the children feel safe and begin to gel together as a unit. We set clear and consistent boundaries and have high expectations of the children. We share information and observations throughout the day and in that way are able to adapt quickly to the children's needs and interests. The ability to work in this way has developed during the five years we have worked together. It is from this foundation that we develop the children's creativity, and we do this as a partnership.

From the very beginning the teacher made it clear to the children and their parents that we would both be important to their children's education. At first this seemed somewhat daunting, as I had little experience, but knowing I was trusted was a source of encouragement and as my skills and knowledge of the class routines developed I began to offer suggestions and take on more responsibility for working independently. Working together in this way means that the teacher is able to delegate tasks while retaining overall responsibility, and I am very positive about my role. I feel that this relationship has been made because I work with the same teacher on a full-time basis. Over time, she has learned about how best to use the skills that I have. These include art and craft, listening skills, and the capacity to stimulate and record children's own ideas, both individual and collective. She expects us to share our perceptions of the children's creative learning on a regular basis and offers me opportunities to suggest activities that might extend the children's ideas. I feel highly valued and a vital part of the team in this class and in the school.

The building blocks of creativity in the Reception class

While in Reception the children are taught basic skills and techniques: we see it as essential to make firm foundations. We endeavour to make these sessions as interesting as possible. The children may use flashcards within the classroom or we may go to the library and use the labelling on the shelves. The children count the numbers for lunch each day and find the corresponding figure on a numberline and then we might practise further by playing hopscotch outside. These types of activity are available for the children to choose during child-initiated sessions and the children often report finding a particular number or letter in a new setting.

From only a few weeks into being in the class, we then encourage all children to develop their skills and knowledge creatively, often through a whole class project. Any project of this sort is planned by the teacher with my input. All projects will include cross-curricular elements, with a clear set of learning objectives, which include developing children's creativity. We aim to develop the children's ability to:

• ask questions
• make connections
• envisage what might be
• explore options
• reflect critically.

These are the five areas of the creativity framework developed by the Qualifications and Curriculum Authority (QCA 2005a, 2005b). On the basis of the way that we work on creativity, we were chosen by QCA to be one of five focus classrooms for a training video made for other practitioners, produced in 2005.

Each of these creative processes are developed across the physical space – indoors and outdoors – as well as right across the curriculum. The children's own ideas inform the ways that we develop and engage with our learning environment. The display boards are often used for large interactive displays deeply influenced by the children, and very much 'owned' by them, whilst the role-play area has, again at the children's suggestion, been converted into many things including a café, a castle and a ferry. The outdoor classroom has housed a garage and a film studio. The children suggest ways that we might develop a particular part of the classroom, and together we make the transformation. The children have powerful ownership and control over how they develop play in these areas, and we encourage diversity in both what they do and how they reflect on it later, encouraging children to give each other feedback.

This type of work may take days to complete and will be used for several weeks so it is important that alterations can be made to extend the children's learning.

So how exactly do we get the children to share their ideas, and how do we facilitate the expression of these in our classroom? Many of our class projects are focused through the collaborative construction of interactive displays, which involve many ideas proposed and developed by the children. These displays then become a learning resource for them to use and play with at many points in each day. The displays form such an important part of the way we work that when our new intake joins us in September we always retain some displays made by the previous year group, for the new children to play with, learn from and, hopefully, be inspired by. We feel that making and using interactive displays stimulates children's curiosity and creativity and this is what I will focus on in the rest of this chapter.

Developing creativity through the use of display

Asking questions, making connections

We try to engage in creative practice throughout any project, as well as nurturing the children's creativity. We encourage the children to generate both questions and connections, right at the start.

Each new project is introduced by the teacher to the whole class, and a theme is suggested for the display which will symbolise the project.

Everybody is encouraged to offer ideas for both the project and the display, which may include what they know already, and also suggestions for what we could find out next, and what we might proceed together with for the project. All of the ideas are valued and recorded.

I take part in this introductory session by supporting children who have specific needs. We feel that it is important to be seen to value all the ideas as

Figure 22.1 Listening carefully to children is an important part of creative practice

this encourages the children to think creatively rather than being restricted to ideas they think will be accepted. So, by arrangement with the class teacher, I often sit close to children who might otherwise be shy of suggesting their ideas in the whole class group, and I can either voice ideas that the children may share with me, or encourage such children to talk to the whole class themselves about their idea.

Once the class has had a go at generating some initial ideas, I will then work with small, mixed-ability groups to discuss ideas for the project in more detail. I encourage them to think about how their knowledge and skills can be used, I help them plan achievable targets and I ensure that the equipment they require is available.

A recent project and display were based upon a discussion of 'the seasons'. The teacher had encouraged the children to consider how our display might include the changes that occur in the natural environment during the autumn and to watch how this changed over time. Straight after the whole-class discussion, we took the class outside to look at the changes as they were occurring. The children collected leaves, seeds and berries. They studied the hedge very closely and when we returned to the classroom the children themselves began, excitedly, to explore the possibility of this forming the basis of the display. They generated ideas about the background to their autumn scene, ways that they could represent the hedge itself, as well as objects that they could show in, under, next to and above it.

Listening carefully to the children's enthusiasm for their hedge idea, the children chose which aspect of the display to work on. Having decided as a whole class that paint was their chosen medium, I supported the children in making the display. I encouraged each group to focus on the colours and shapes of the objects they wanted to represent.

Some of the groups chose to paint large sections of the hedge, while others painted individual fruits and seeds. At one stage there was a long discussion about the difference in colour between a blackberry and an elderberry. We had purple available to use but one child asked if we could make a new colour, as the berries were 'not the same sort of purple'. All of the group then studied the fruit more closely and decided the elderberries were a much darker colour. I was then able to use this opportunity to show the children how to mix colours, encouraging them to explore the possibilities. We are very aware that although we are encouraging the children to have and express ideas, we need to build their knowledge and skill all the time, and this will mean that some sessions will be adult-led – in this case mixing colours – but the children are always given the opportunity to return to an activity and explore further themselves. The work that is produced during these independent sessions is used to inform future planning. In this case I reminded subsequent groups of the need to look very closely before they started their pictures, they responded by including the red colour on the elderberry stems and different shades on the leaves.

Envisaging what might be, exploring options and reflecting critically

Imagining possibilities, taking ideas further and reflecting on these are all integral to our class practice in developing creativity through our projects.

In this case, the children, who were in their first term in Reception, drew on their previous knowledge and skills, to develop the display further over the weeks that followed. They often brought objects from home.

The first change was the addition of leaves, nuts and berries they found. One child brought a sweet chestnut in its case. She thought that it looked like a hedgehog and asked me if she could stick on some berries to make eyes. 'Henry', as our hedgehog become known, stimulated a great deal of class discussion: What did he eat? Where did he live? What other animals might live in the hedge? Such questions arose in all kinds of interactions, including when the class were sitting together on the carpet. During different lessons and using resources such as our class and school library, and the Internet, children were encouraged to research their questions.

Eventually a house for Henry was added along with mice, birds, badgers, insects and their homes. The house was made by covering a box with natural materials, grass, leaves, etc. The insects were drawn using a computer package; the mice and owls were made using collage.

Through the representation of an autumn scene, the children were learning about animals, their habitats, the changes that occur and some of the reasons for these. They were also developing early research skills and improving their mouse control skills. Individuals and groups then shared their learning with the whole class, giving us the opportunity to celebrate their achievements.

My role in supporting and enabling the interactive displays

We feel strongly that creativity should be at the heart of teaching and learning in our classroom. This means motivating the children to feel what they are doing has both relevance to them and can be shaped by them. Therefore it is important to us that the ideas for any project should come from the children.

My role is to listen and by asking questions encourage them to explore these ideas within the broad framework, which is suggested by the class teacher, rather than offer my own. I try to ask questions that allow the children to move forward themselves. During the hedgerow discussion the animal theme became extremely popular and ideas ranged from owls to zebras. I then asked the children to think about where these animals lived and together we refined their choice to the animals that may actually be found in that environment. I want the children to learn to share their own ideas and by opening a discussion allow them the space to reflect on these to refine their ideas.

The time spent with the children at this stage is extremely important as it is their opportunity to envisage what might be and with my support work out which materials and techniques they will need to bring their ideas to fruition. We feel that resources are vital. We have a cupboard full of collected and found objects as well as standard art and craft materials, which support our work on interactive displays. Although I always provide a range of materials to start a project as soon as the ideas have crystallised, I allow time to enable the children and myself to collect any additional material that we may need.

The displays are a tool for the children to use independently and as such I need to ensure that they are accessible, robust and wherever possible interactive. The children are shown how to use the display; for example, the animals in the autumn project were all free standing. The children were able to move them within the display and then to other areas in the classroom making links and extending their learning through play. In this display, the children were able to weave long 'leaves' in and out of the static and three-dimensional leaves of the hedge. The children returned to this display for many weeks during their free choice time. The interest in Henry continued for the whole year, and he became part of several subsequent displays, having a holiday home in a display based on the nursery rhyme, 'One, two, three, four, five, Once I caught a fish alive'.

As the children begin to work with an interactive display they often come up with new ideas to extend it. Part of my role is to be available and listen to these while the ideas are fresh in their minds and plan a time for the children to make the necessary changes. The ability to be flexible and to develop a project in line with the children's interests is something that is encouraged throughout the school. However it is made possible by the teaching of basic skills and by developing the children's ability to work independently. As the children's confidence grows they are more willing to offer ideas and are able to support them. When the autumn project took place the children were new to the class and the school and were only just beginning to make sense of this new environment. The framework for this type of work is still decided by the teacher but with each subsequent project their involvement grows. In a display later in the year the children were asked to think how we might record our memories of the school year. Most of the children wanted to offer suggestions and the most popular was a memory quilt. They wanted it to be made of material like a patchwork quilt. I worked with this and found material and fabric pens, which the children used to record the things they had enjoyed the most during the year. I joined the pieces together and then the children helped to display it. The children want to be involved in all aspects of a display and enjoy sharing their knowledge with others in the class and visitors, parents, etc.

As the children move through Reception their ability to think creatively and to make links across the curriculum, coupled with a grasp of new techniques, allows quite complex displays to be undertaken. The children have increasing ownership over this complexity, being encouraged to consider how the display might be used, its aesthetic dimensions, as well as its robustness. I will be told where to put particular items in a display, be asked to move things if they are insufficiently accessible and recently was asked not to cut out as this was something that they could do for themselves!

Final reflections: Valuing creativity in the classroom and school

I really enjoy working in reception and being allowed to take such an active part in the class is very satisfying. I am fortunate to work in a school where class teachers and their assistants work as a team, where the role of the teaching assistant is valued and where thinking and working creatively is promoted.

Creativity in our class is developed through all parts of the curriculum, but in this chapter I have focused on demonstrating how the creative process is modelled and supported through concrete, often art-and-craft-based activity, while acknowledging that creativity is much broader than art. My role in the creative process is to act as facilitator, to help the children use the basic skills that they are taught to make connections and envisage what might be.

I have the time, which is not always available to the teacher, to listen when it is convenient to the child. I talk to the children, ask questions and encourage them in their thinking, making choices and connections. The skills I need and use during the making of a display are equally valuable throughout all activities.

Chapter 23

'Are they teaching'? An alternative perspective on parents as educators

Janet Atkin and John Bastiani

Parental involvement in children's school learning poses questions about the nature of their role and the extent to which they can be said to be teaching their children. In this chapter Janet Atkin, formerly a lecturer at the University of Nottingham, and John Bastiani, visiting professor in Education at Nottingham Trent University, provide insights into the various roles that parents can adopt when they provide learning support to their children. Their research leads them to suggest that parental practice can vary widely and they raise a note of caution with regard to the tendency for schools to see parents as a homogeneous group or to define teaching in narrow terms.

The enormous impact of parental and family influences on children's learning and development – both in and out of school – is now clearly documented (DfES 2003). This clear and wide-ranging evidence is also generally accepted by those who work in schools and support their work, even if this is not always reflected in responsive practice.

What is less clear, however, is *why* this should be so and how it comes about. Any exploration of this area quickly uncovers two important generalisations.

First, families and schools are increasingly expected to undertake a number of the responsibilities that were formerly the province of the other. These significant changes are currently being reinforced by key government educational and childcare policies, e.g. the Sure Start and Extended Schools Programmes.

Secondly, there is a cumulative body of mainly qualitative research which shows that just as educational professionals, of all kinds, have widely differing, deep-seated and even contradictory views about what children need to learn and how they can be best enabled to do this, so, too, do parents.

This article, which relocates a programme of earlier research and development, takes a close look at some of the ways in which parents think about their role in their children's learning and how they, as parents, can best support this.

The research

The research into parental perspectives grew out of a long-standing programme of in-service training and professional development linked to the home, school and community fields.

We had become increasingly aware that there was a lack of evidence about how parents develop understandings of educational processes in general, how they make sense of their children's schooling, and how they act as educators of their own children. In order to investigate this, a number of separate but linked studies were set up in which a broad range of parents from all backgrounds and with very different kinds of experience of schools were interviewed. The studies shared a common approach which we called 'listening to parents' (Atkin *et al.* 1988). We placed the emphasis on enabling parents to give accounts in which they could develop their own concerns and points of view, set within a loosely structured framework. The interview was therefore treated as an opportunity for extended description, reflective analysis and comment rather than seeking to give definite answers to pre-specified questions. We believe it is through a methodology such as this that a clearer picture is gained, not only about *what* parents experience and do in relation to their children's education, but *how* they think about it.

What is teaching?

What emerged is that the concepts of teaching held by parents consist of a collection of ideas and beliefs which can be described in relation to three dimensions. We have called these dimensions *teaching as ideology, teaching as pedagogy* and *teaching as context* (see Figure 23.1). These dimensions are not simply a matter of polar opposites (an act of behaviour is either 'teaching' or it is not), but rather each exists in the form of a continuum, with subtle shadings and distinctions along it. When these dimensions are put together, the result is a complex and dynamic concept of teaching which reflects different models of learning, pedagogical strategies and appropriate settings. In analysing our data with these dimensions in mind we have concluded that, rather than parents and teachers having *different* understandings, there is as much variety among parents in relation to concepts of teaching as there is in the teaching profession as a whole. Mismatches between parents and teachers are more likely to be mismatches between particular parents and individual teachers, with different notions of teaching.

Teaching as ideology

This dimension draws attention to the different values and beliefs that are held about education, particularly in relation to how children learn and to the nature of the adult's role in relation to learning. The continuum can be seen as moving from a *reactive* role for the adult, characterised by phrases like 'being a pair of

		REACTIVE TEACHING ←——→ PROACTIVE TEACHING	
IDEOLOGY	Beliefs and intentions	• Child-centred model of learning • Incidental activities • 'Teacher' support for child's initiatives	• Conscious planning • Systematic implementation • 'Teacher' direction and control
PEDAGOGY	Tasks and approaches	• Spontaneous approaches • Improvisation of task • 'Home-made techniques	• Structured tasks and materials • Regular, planned activity • Formal techniques
CONTEXT	Settings and circumstances	• Exploiting the educative potential of home settings and family experience	• Reproducing the essential features of classroom life and work

Figure 23.1 What is teaching?

ears', 'showing an interest', 'being available', to a *proactive* role described as 'deliberate', 'coaching', 'having a lesson', 'teaching them X, Y and Z'. Here is a 'reactive' mother reflecting on how she helps her child:

Mother: I think a lot of parents do it without realising that you're doing it. Just the fact that you show interest in what they're doing, and um, you know, sort of become involved. Not to take over – I think it's important that you don't take over . . . But I think by being interested, you make them want to find out even more. Not necessarily saying, 'Right, get your books out, we'll have so and so done', you know, I think you've got to be available . . . I think you can help in education, for your particular child, just by knowing what they're interested in, and by stimulating it, and just, as I say, just being a pair of ears, really . . . We do a lot of things together as well . . . things that aren't a bit educational in one way, um, we went to fetch the Christmas tree from the woods . . . Children learn, you know, they learn without realising they're learning . . . but I don't think you ever think, it, it must be educational to a degree . . . I don't think you ever set a time of day aside and think, 'Right, we'll do some clever stuff!' you know.

Many of our parents characterised teaching as a conscious, deliberate act which took place at a set time of day, in a set place with a particular aim and noticeably marked by the child 'sitting still' and used this construct to deny that they taught their children.

Father: In terms of actually *teaching* her anything, no, we avoided that really, I mean, we used any opportunities that were available, um, if she looked at a word and wanted to know what it was we'd tell her, she did pick up some words like that, but we didn't make any kind of formal attempt to teach her anything, it was all just incidental, the way it should be (laughs).

Other parents with a different set of values and beliefs did see themselves as teaching in deliberate, formal ways.

Mother: Oh no. I taught her her tables. I mean no one there taught her her tables . . . I'd taught him the alphabet before, you know, from these 'A' is for Apple, and just sat and taught him from there.

This dimension then reflects the theories about teaching and learning that underpin how parents see their own role in the educative process and we suggest that the differences between them relate to beliefs and values that can also differentiate the teaching profession.

Teaching as pedagogy

This dimension relates to the particular kinds of techniques and materials that are used by the parent to promote learning, in other words the 'how' of teaching. Here the continuum is seen to range from the indirect 'doing the things a mother would normally do' to the direct 'sitting them down formally to learn'.
    For many parents the circumstances of everyday living provide the opportunities to use the strategies they consider appropriate:

Mother: I like to think I prepared them as well as I could. It wasn't something I did consciously. I certainly didn't say, 'Well you've got to be able to read, and you've got to be able to write your name. You've got to be able to do X, Y and Z.' No, we didn't do that at all; it was a matter of being interested in the children, letting them take an interest in everything that was going on at home. They used to help me cook; they used to help me do the shopping; we used to go out as a family a lot – and still do incidentally – and, um, we talked to them all the time, tried to answer questions and just tried to bring them up as children, as normal children.

Others are slightly less indirect.

Father: We didn't go overboard at all; we did what we normally think most parents would do and just as they developed and came through, we read books to them, normal things, encourage them, play number games, and the other little games they play. But it wasn't consciously with school in mind.

Here is one parent, himself a teacher, making a clear distinction between his idea of indirect, but nevertheless conscious, teaching with a methodology characterised by testing and formality.

Father: Both my wife and I read to him a great deal, apart from the nightly spot. We generally tried to build up an interest . . . so if he happened to be looking, I'd show him the book I was reading – not that I very often got the opportunity to sit down and read in his presence (laughs) . . . um, or such things as records; if there was a record on, then we'd show him the record sleeve. In other words, what we were mainly concerned about doing was showing, or trying to show, a connection between the written word and actual happenings – at no time did I actually make a *formal* attempt to teach him to read. That is not to say how-ever, that he didn't look at it . . . to the extent that I would trace the lines when I was reading to him, so that again he would begin to make the connection. If he asked what a word was, then I would tell him – but there was no question of feedback, in as much as 'Come on, I told you that word ten minutes ago, what is it now?'

It is, perhaps, the different kinds of behaviour that this dimension indicates that leads us to question the phrase 'direct parental teaching' used in earlier research. For teachers the words may conjure up images of children being directed into drill-like alphabet work, counting activities or copy writing, with parents taking a didactic, instructional role. We found hardly any parents describing what they did in this way (the mother who taught the alphabet and tables was almost the only exception). Far more common were parents who capitalised on the stuff of family life, the 'going places, seeing things, looking at books', as their educative strategy. Moreover, many parents were often very alert to their children's reactions to what they saw as direct teaching.

Teaching as context

We have already referred to parents who saw teaching as happening anywhere and everywhere and others who conceived of it being located in a particular kind of setting, usually sitting down at a table. This dimension of the concept of teaching not only distinguished these kinds of differences but also highlighted the way parents compared home-based learning with learning in school. The continuum could be characterised as ranging from 'teaching happens in any environment' to 'teaching happens in a classroom, sitting still at a desk'. Parents who hold the latter concept of teaching can be particularly anxious about their children's behaviour in school.

Mother: I think if somebody sort of said to Jenny, 'Right,' you know, 'You've got to sort of sit and learn', then I think she would, but I think she lacks the discipline to learn at the moment because she thinks that, you know, you can sort of get up and have a little skip and then come back.

This dimension, then, also reveals the way context is seen as exercising various degrees of control over the child. The freedom to follow an activity for as long as one wishes, which is seen by most parents to characterise the home (and the nursery) setting, is contrasted with school where the child is directed by the teacher and the teaching assistant. Similarly, parents themselves exercise different forms of control in their teaching. They determine whether they will be in a particular place (for example, always sitting at the kitchen table), or use the setting where the child happens to be (for example, the floor, the bath, the garden); they decide whether to set aside a particular time of day, on a regular basis, or to use incidental opportunities, as they arise.

Parents as educators: a wider view

So parental notions of teaching and learning are by no means obvious or straightforward. Parents, like teachers and teaching assistants, have widely differing educational philosophies. As a result, their images of teaching range from behaviour that is intended to achieve particular outcomes – using specific materials, in a formal setting, where strict attention is required – through a continuum to incidental, supportive approaches in which motivation, the development of attitudes, interests and skills, together with the personal characteristics of the child, are all given as much, if not more, attention than teaching content. In a similar way the notion of 'teaching' can also be used to make, or to avoid making, distinctions between school-based learning, directed by classroom-based professionals and home-based learning with 'its own salient characteristics, located in the family setting'.

The range and variety of parental viewpoints can be summarised in the following way.

This alternative perspective, which stresses the range and diversity of parental viewpoints, offers information which is of potential value in the development of more effective communication, contact and involvement between families and schools, particularly where the learning of pupils is a central concern. Against this background, the present practice of most schools appears to be rather crude, limited and one-sided, assuming, as it does, that parents are a homogeneous group.

While we have given considerable emphasis to the uncovering of a fuller picture of parental beliefs about teaching and the behaviour thought to be appropriate to these views, this should not be seen as the basis of a *static* portrayal of the relationship between families and schools, along the lines of a classic demarcation dispute. Parental attitudes and behaviour will be responsive to, and influenced by, their actual *experience* of schools, teachers and teaching assistants, particularly in the early stages.

In summary, parental belief and experience leads to a variety of interpretation of educational roles and tasks in which the capacity and willingness of parents to see themselves as educators is complex, dynamic and, above all, problematic.

Such a perspective is important, not so much for its own sake, as for its capacity to inform practice and to identify important areas of growth and development. There are many important and relatively unexplored areas in the field of home–school relations. In our view, it is not enough to examine these as a series of ready-made issues. What is required is a searching examination of how such issues come to be regarded as important, together with a critical analysis of the assumptions incorporated in the key concepts, methods of inquiry and forms of evidence.

Against such a background, this account can be seen as a direct challenge to a view of teachers and parents having distinct approaches. Instead, we have tried to pinpoint the views of parents concerning the nature of 'teaching' and their roles in it, *as they see it themselves*. For we have found such an approach to be an important means of bringing research, policy and the development of practice together in a productive way.

References

Atkin, J. and Bastiani, J., with Goode, J. (1988) *Listening to Parents: An approach to the improvement of home–school relations.* London: Routledge.

DfES (2003) *The Impact of Parental Involvement on Children's Education.* London: DfES.

Chapter 24

Effective home–school links

Suzanne Brown

> The importance of close home–school collaboration is now widely accepted by all who work in and have an interest in schools, although this was not always the case. There continues to be debate, however, about what kind of practice best enables schools, parents and carers to work together for the benefit of children's learning. Suzanne Brown, headteacher of Queen's Church of England Primary School, Nuneaton, carried out a survey of all Warwickshire schools to get a clearer notion of 'effective' practice in this area. Her study was revealing of the range of practice that can be found in one LEA, but also stands to guide and inform more widely.

> The bond between the child and their parents is the most critical influence on a child's life. Parenting has a strong impact on a child's educational development, behaviour, and mental health (DfES 2003: 39).

Obvious it may seem, but there has not always been full acknowledgement of the importance of home and the powerful influence it has upon progress in school. Increasingly as all other options have been tried, one way of reaching those magic targets is through enlisting additional support from home. But what are effective home–school links? Last year I embarked on a secondment on behalf of Warwickshire LEA to discover just that.

The research

A survey was sent out to all Warwickshire schools asking them about partnerships with home and how they encouraged good relations. It was followed by a series of more in-depth interviews at selected schools across the county. A total of 176 responses were received and sixteen individual schools were visited and headteachers interviewed.

It was intended not only to find out more about what was happening and the views of schools but to produce a report that would give examples of good practice that schools might benefit from sharing. The response was positive and the variety of examples of good practice considerable.

What are effective home–school links?

It's not only the government that believes home–school partnerships are very important in raising standards. Of the schools responding, all the headteachers, irrespective of phase of education, stated that they thought home–school partnerships were either important or very important. When asked what they meant by 'effective links' responses included:

- trust
- having an open door policy
- parents feeling that they are listened to
- good communication
- absence of complaints
- staff not feeling threatened
- approachable staff
- parents feeling confident and welcome
- participation
- united efforts
- clear expectations of children
- celebrating success
- home feeling well-informed
- shared aims
- successful courses for adults
- accessibility
- flexibility
- freedom of speech
- professionalism
- happy children
- team work.

In particular, communication and accessibility were stressed. The headteachers recognised the importance of keeping parents informed, providing a welcome and the opportunity for parents to express their concerns and opinions. Frequently quoted by headteachers were the values of trust and respect and the idea that ultimately we want the best for the children. It is over what 'the best' might be that some differences may occur.

Heads recognised the need to genuinely engage and not patronise parents, acknowledging the variety of stakeholders involved in the partnership. Frequently mentioned, directly or by implication, was the pressure that schools are feeling as a result of the educational climate. Heads felt the pressure from agendas presented by both parents and the DfES. This underlined the multiplicity and complexity of roles that schools are expected to hold.

A particularly comprehensive definition of the home–school partnership was expressed by one headteacher:

> Where the parents know and understand what is happening at school, are involved (as much as they want to be) with activities; where they are pro-active in their

children's learning and would like to continue to learn themselves; where they contribute to the learning community and feel listened to; where they are seen to be part of the education of themselves, their child and the school.

Rating documents and events

Schools were asked how important they thought different documents aimed at parents were. The Governors' Annual Report to Parents (GARP) and the Home–School Agreement were considered to be less important than written reports, home–school link books and curriculum leaflets. Although less welcome, schools were still actively trying to do their best to enhance the validity of these documents.

Examples from schools demonstrated the number of ways in which they had tried to make the GARP relevant and accessible. Any number of innovative attempts at attracting parents to the governors meetings have been tried. Particularly popular is tagging the meeting on to another better attended meeting in the hope that parents will stay around long enough to participate. GARPs find themselves back-to-back with concerts, parents' evenings, adult helper buffets and PTA meetings.

Schools were asked for their opinions about a range of contact opportunities with parents. Parents' evenings were rated particularly highly with all schools, bar one, rating them as very important or important. An interesting development seems to be the use of call centres to act as liaison when reminding parents of events and evenings they need to attend. This seems to have been particularly effective in secondary schools where contact can take place at evenings and weekends.

Communicating

Schools seem to be in agreement: the sooner an issue is dealt with the better. Effective communication is vital but not always easy to achieve. Personal contact, 'face-to-face' is highly rated as the most effective. Many questionnaires included references to being out on the playground, greeting parents and generally being available both formally (through timetabled drop-in sessions and surgeries) and informally during events and 'tea parties'.

One way to encourage parents to attend activities and events is through 'personal' invitations. If children are involved in performing at an event, parents are more likely to attend to support. In addition, children writing out invitations themselves seems to be more successful than the standard issue letter.

Schools rate directly targeting parents as the best way of including them. Where parents are individually approached and their help requested, they are far more likely to respond than when a general invitation is issued. In some cases this might be through personalised phone calls or a visit by an outreach member of staff.

Schools are aware of the importance of making sure that communication is positive as often as possible. There can be a tendency for school to contact home only when there is a problem. Alert to the dangers in this, schools are increasingly trying to find opportunities when they can make contact to congratulate. 'Golden letters' home, phone calls for praise as well as for passing on difficulties are real attempts to develop relationships and trust.

Changing family life

Several schools commented on the drop in numbers of parents participating in parent–teacher association. Schools suggested that this may be because of increasing family commitments and working parents. This also had an effect on other aspects of liaison:

> Because more and more parents now leave pupils with out-of-school carers we don't have the face to face contact with them that we once had. Messages have to be given via notes or through carers. More parents want to have plays, etc. in the evening and at open evening all want late appointments.

As more out-of-school clubs become available and as 'wrap-around' provision extends there are issues for school in terms of adjusting to the changing level and type of contact. As part of the 'extended school' vision we may find that with some families there may be more contact and less with others.

The extended school

Provision of adult-learning opportunities was not a priority for many schools. Secondary 11–16 schools were most likely to provide adult learner courses and junior and special schools the least. There is an increasing range of literacy and numeracy programmes available which aim to help parents help their children while also improving their own skills.

One difficulty with many home–school projects is the transitory nature of funding. Schools reported on the length of time it takes to win the trust of a community. Short-term funding and support does not provide schools with the time to develop the necessary provision. In some cases, quickly drawn-up projects do not respond to community need.

As we move towards the 'one-stop shop' concept of provision it is worthwhile questioning its efficacy for some of our 'hard-to-reach' parents. Some projects acknowledge that their target audience may be deterred by the school building itself and would prefer a less institutionalised meeting point. Reaching out to parents in the community rather than expecting them to come in to school may be a necessary strategy in some cases.

Accessibility and safety

A very strong theme throughout was the importance of accessibility. An increasingly important issue for many schools is how to balance the need for security arrangements without discouraging parents from coming in to school. Many schools mentioned the importance of offering an 'open door'. Only three schools from the survey did not profess to have an open door policy. However, safety and security needs were meaning schools were encountering tensions:

> A slight hiccup was caused when we put security locks on the doors. We have now re-emphasised our open door policy via the newsletter and word of mouth.

There can be danger in referring to all parents as a homogeneous group. A recurring refrain during interviews and in the survey was the difficulty in accessing a certain group of parents:

> While we try to be all-inclusive some parents are reluctant to come to meetings in school. Maybe they have had unfortunate experiences from their own school days and feel threatened. Inevitably the parents we really need to contact do not turn up at meetings.

Central to school development

The survey showed that schools did not generally ask the LEA for help with developing home–school links. This was not an area in which support was being provided, mostly because schools had not asked for it. This did not mean that it was not included on the school development plan. Areas that schools were currently developing included improving communication, parental support for children's learning, consultation with parents and involvement of parents in PTAs.

In summary, schools are showing their commitment to the community in a range of ways. In some cases they are facing obstacles which they are inventively challenging. With more local and national support we could expect even greater successes in the name of effective home–school links.

Reference

DfES (2003) *Every Child Matters: The consultation and summary of questions.* London: DfES.

Chapter 25

Developing pupils' skills in self-assessment in the primary classroom

Ruth Dann

If assessment is to be meaningful for pupils they need to be involved in the process. If teachers and teaching assistants want to plan to support children's learning they need to know what pupils think about their own learning. Ruth Dann, a lecturer at Keele University, argues that pupil self-assessment should be an essential component in formative assessment and one that will provide valuable insights into children's thinking and understanding and what they consider to be important about their learning.

- Pupil self-assessment is an essential component of formative assessment.
- The assessment process involves critical thinking so as to make judgements based on evidence about achievements.
- Pupil self-assessment will relate to pupils' understanding of the tasks they are completing, perceived expectations and the importance they give to individual effort and enjoyment.

The self-assessment process requires pupils to engage in a process which requires a range of skills. Some of these skills may complement those required in other areas of the curriculum, whereas others may be additional ones.

Pupil self-assessment as a dimension of formative assessment

Our model of the National Curriculum and assessment requires teachers and teaching assistants to assess pupils' learning in relation to descriptors which are progressively structured by levels. For some parts of the core curriculum, assessment of pupil achievement will be carried out by standard tasks/tests; the remainder will require teachers' own assessments.

Progression through the levels of the National Curriculum is envisaged to be at an average rate of one level every two years. Accordingly, the amount of detail offered through these assessment levels will be suitable for highlighting pupils' learning needs in relation to fairly large learning steps, but not in relation to more specific learning targets. If teaching is to be appropriately matched to pupil needs then teachers must be more informed about pupils' achievements at a more specific level. Formative assessment linked to specific programmes of study and schemes of work is thus essential.

In accordance with Torrance (1993), development of formative assessment practice must be built on research which seeks to examine the complexities of teacher–pupil interactions at a classroom level. Furthermore, as Gipps (1994) maintains, a key aspect of formative assessment is that 'the student comes to hold a notion of the standard or desired quality similar to that of the teacher, is able to monitor the quality of what is being produced at the time of the production, and is able to regulate their work appropriately' (126).

In order to gain insight into pupils' learning teachers must continually seek to understand pupils' achievements. Clearly, this will involve considering some of the following: marking finished work; observing classroom process; questioning (oral and written); understanding learning context; establishing pupils' priorities and goals for their learning. Learning is a complex process which embraces more than cognitive learning and must be identified and examined within a context. If learning is to be realistically explored, and the achievements identified, a range of evidence will need to be reflected upon by the teacher. Involving pupils more directly in the assessment process offers a potential source of evidence which has received little detailed analysis. It is an area in which teachers and teaching assistants may have valuable insights and a wealth of experiences from which formative assessment can be further built and developed.

Self-assessment gives children the opportunity to judge their achievements for themselves. This allows (adults) to gain a greater understanding of children's own thinking about their learning. Additionally, and from the child's perspective, the self-assessment process communicates an important message – that teachers value pupils' opinion about their learning. The potential which pupil self-assessment may offer is highlighted by Holt (1974). He states that 'perhaps the greatest of all the wrongs we do children is to deprive them of the chance to judge the worth of their own work and thus destroy in them the power to make such judgements, or even the belief that they can (504).

The process of pupil self-assessment

The way in which pupils may be engaged in the assessment process will vary in relation to the age and experience of the children as well as in relation to the focus of assessment. It may be that pupils' judgements about their work are sought by teachers through questions as part of the marking process. Alternatively, pupils may be invited to complete a self-assessment sheet requiring their judgement to be recorded in a general or specific form.

> *Task:*
> Creative Writing
>
> *Aims:*
> To develop skills in story structure – beginnings
> To develop imagination
>
> *Objectives:*
> Pupils will develop the beginning of the story by: setting the scene describing location and atmosphere; describing characters
>
> Pupils will demonstrate their imagination by building into their story four stated objects, so that these objects form important parts of the story. The objects' are:
>
> - a fox
> - a precious vase
> - a knitted hat
> - a tree house.

Pupil self-assessment can be encouraged by dialogue with the teacher, as in the example below.

> TEACHER: Tell me – what do you think is the best part of this work you have done?
> CHILD: I think it was the bit I wrote about the vase. It was hard to put it into the story, but then I got an idea.
> TEACHER: Yes, that was a good idea; I thought it was going to get smashed at first, but it didn't – I was glad. Was that the hardest part of the writing?
> CHILD: Well . . . sort of. It took me a long time to think of my story – trying to fit the four things in.

Example 1 Pupil self-assessment through teacher–pupil discussion

This, however, is time consuming. For it to be adequately adopted in the classroom, only a small number of children can participate on each occasion. Giving every pupil an opportunity will require careful planning over a half-term or termly period.

Opportunities in which all pupils can play a part demand a written prompt for pupils to think about and record their achievements. These prompts may use a specifically task-focused proforma or could be in a more general outline form.

The type of self-assessment used must be matched to pupils' skills as well as to the task being considered. The purpose which pupils' perceive for the process will greatly influence the way in which it is carried out.

Self-assessment may be aimed at encouraging pupils to make judgements about their work in relation to specific criteria. Alternatively its aim may be to ascertain pupils' own priorities for and interpretations of their own work, which can offer useful information to the teacher when making assessments. Both are useful; each, however, demands different skills.

Pupil self-assessment using criteria

Criterion-referenced assessment may well be the focus for teacher assessment. It may also form the focus for pupil self-assessment. For consideration, however, is the way in which criteria are both shared and communicated. The National Curriculum offers statements grouped into level descriptions which form the focus for assessment, but these are not designed as criteria for assessing individual lessons. The focus for such criteria needs to be far more specifically related to individual tasks, if they are to give appropriate indication of pupil progress which can immediately inform teaching and planning.

To return to the example previously given in English (imaginative story writing), the objectives of the lesson are for children to incorporate four objects into a story; to structure the beginning of the story so that location and characters are described and the atmosphere portrayed. To move from these lesson objectives to achievement criteria demands another level of specification. For example, how will the children demonstrate their level of skill in relation to each of these objectives?

In order to account for varying pupil needs, it may be that for some pupils the objectives set will be different: perhaps only two objects are to be incorporated into the story. Accordingly, the criteria for success will reflect such differences.

But additional and crucial factors need to be probed in this example – what is meant by 'imaginatively' or (in relation to the other stated objectives) how do you successfully describe location, atmosphere and characters? These areas should form part of the initial discussion with the children about the task. Illustration, example and comparison are important tools for communicating to pupils what they should be aiming for.

For example:

Teacher: Listen very carefully to this example:

It was Wednesday. Mum was late for work. She picked up her key and ran along the road to catch the bus. Mrs Thomas was taking me to school. She had a red jumper with a rose on it. Wednesday mornings we always have hymn practice which is not much fun when you have a sore throat . . .

Tell me what you think about the way I have used the two objects key and rose?

Child: *I don't think you have used them very well.*
Teacher: *Why is that, why do you think they are not used very imaginatively?*
Child: *Well, you have only just said the word in the sentence and not said anything else about what it was like.*
Teacher: *Good, thank you. What do other people think?*
Child 2:   *I don't think it is imaginative because you have not said what will happen to them – it's just boring.*
Teacher: *Good. Who agrees that it is not imaginative? What would we have to do to make it a bit more imaginative?*
Child 3:   *You could say that the key fell out of Mum's pocket as she ran for the bus and someone found it.*

At the end of the initial task discussion, specific highlighted points, which have been elicited, can usefully be written up and left in a prominent place during the activity. For example:

Using the four objects imaginatively

- Make sure something happens in the story and the four objects play a part in this.
- Include something surprising or unexpected for each object.

Beginnings

- Where is your story set?
- How does this place make you feel?
- What are the people in your story like?
- Use adjectives (describing words) for each of these parts of your beginning.
- Make the beginning interesting so you will want to find out what happens next.

If children are to be given an opportunity to consider their work in relation to the criteria for the task, then an appropriate framework must be constructed. This prepares the way for pupil self-assessment. The assessment process required pupils to judge their work. In the context of criterion-referenced pupil self-assessment a variety of skills are needed. Fundamentally, pupils are required to think critically about their work and to relate it to the stated criteria. This assessment process demands the complex skills of comparing, examining evidence, interpreting, reasoning and decision-making. These skills are important dimensions of learning and may be supported through other curriculum areas. They are skills which need to be developed throughout a child's education. Their use within pupil self-assessment is therefore a means of developing learning as well as judging it.

What becomes crucial in the self-assessment process is the support and guidance given at appropriate stages. Children need to understand the conventions of assessment judgements which relate to different aspects of their work. For example, it may be appropriate to say, 'That is a good picture because I like it', but not 'the answer is three because I like its shape.' Some decisions will require recognition of precise rules, whereas others will require judgements which draw on creative process. Guidance is needed to direct the children towards the framework most appropriate for the given task.

With adequate support, children in Key Stage 2 show remarkable skill in relating their work to criteria. However, the extent to which their assessments are exclusively criterion-referenced must be further probed.

The influence of personal and social development

Children's learning cannot be developed or assessed in a vacuum which excludes personal and social influences. Although attempts may be made to minimise these influences, they cannot be eliminated. Children have a keen sense of 'fairness' in the assessment process. In a research study carried out to examine the role of criteria in pupil self-assessment (Dann 1991) pupils stated that they used the criteria given but also added their own priorities. Without this additional dimension pupils felt that their views were not fairly represented in the assessment process. For example, pupils considered their work in relation to what they had previously achieved, in relation to how much effort they put into it, as well as how much enjoyment they gained from it.

In self-assessment schemes, in which pupils were invited to assess their work only in relation to stated criteria, the pupils said that they included these additional issues themselves before reaching their final judgement. Thus pupils were not willing to dwell exclusively on curriculum-related criteria for their assessments. They would draw on other influences whether these were made explicit or not. Hence any attempt to develop pupil self-assessment must recognise the important role which pupils give to the social context of their learning and their personal priorities and expectations.

It is only through communication of this nature that teachers and teaching assistants can recognise the range of issues which influence learning and which enable further teaching to be effectively planned and taught.

The future

Effective teaching demands an understanding of pupil learning. A range of evidence is required for this to represent the variety of experiences and opportunities encountered and the way in which they are interpreted by both teacher and pupils. Actively engaging pupils in the assessment process is an aspect of formative assessment which can yield valuable information for teachers as they seek to develop and understand pupils' learning. For pupils, it can provide a useful vehicle for developing critical thinking skills, for expressing concerns and priorities about learning, and for fostering a sense of trust and communication with the teacher. Pupils must be at the centre of teaching, learning and assessment in the primary classroom.

References

Dann R. (1991) *Pupils' assessment in the primary school.* Unpublished PhD dissertation, University of Southampton.

Gipps C. (1994) *Beyond testing.* Lewes: Falmer Press.

Holt J. (1974) 'The tyranny of testing', in: G. Davis and T. Warren (eds), *Psychology of Education.* Lexington, MA: D.C. Heath & Co.

Torrance H. (1993) 'Formative Assessment: Some theoretical problems and empirical questions'. *Cambridge Journal of Education,* **23** (3), 333–43.

Section 4
Perspectives and voices

Carrie Cable and Ian Eyres

The chapters in this final section cover a range of perspectives, and a wide range of voices including those of children, teaching assistants, teachers, advisors and a writer. We felt they all had something important to say about how children learn, what and how they should learn and how they can best be supported in their learning. The chapters encourage us to stand back from our practice and to reflect on different views and approaches – an essential element in continuing professional development.

In Chapter 26 Ian Eyres and his colleagues describe the findings of a research project in which children were invited to describe the role of their teaching assistants. Although the official roles of teaching assistants and teachers are quite distinct, at classroom level there appear be more similarities than differences, at least in the opinion of the children interviewed. In Chapter 27 we continue with the theme of children's perceptions, this time of assessment practices. In her research, Patricia Atkinson found that children valued being consulted about their views of their own learning and appreciated the variety of approaches and techniques used in their school for assessment purposes.

In Chapter 28 Chris Scrivener describes an environmental project in which children were provided with the opportunity to work with a complex problem, debate their ideas, make decisions, present their ideas to powerful people and experience an outcome which meant their voices had been listened to. In Chapter 29 we look again at parental involvement, this time in terms of children's literacy development. In his study of Bangladeshi families, Adrian Blackledge found that parents' willingness to engage in their children's literacy development was frustrated by the gap between home and school concepts of literacy and the lack of understanding of home literacy practices.

Even experienced teachers and teaching assistants meet challenges in their relationships with children and children who feel alienated by what they are offered. In Chapter 30 Gary Trainor reflects on his own learning as he sought to develop an approach that would enable a child to integrate socially in his classroom. In Chapter 31, Philip Pullman reminds us that learning should be fun and that we learn more about language when we are in situations where we can play around with it and realise its power and potential through story, poems and songs. Pullman has vigorously opposed the National Literacy Strategy, and some schools have shared his reservations, preferring to preserve and enhance approaches they feel are effective alternatives. In Chapter 32 Thelma Hall describes some of these approaches to literacy practice in schools in the north of England.

The responsibility for co-ordinating the work of additional adults involved in children's learning varies from school to school. Sometimes this role is carried out by deputy headteachers, a phase co-ordinator or a senior teaching assistant. In Chapter 33 Liz Gerschel explores the ways in which Special Educational Needs Co-ordinators (SENCOs) in one authority manage teaching assistants and support for children's learning. Chapter 34, the final chapter in this book, returns to the themes of Chapter 1: play and the curriculum. Dympna Meikleham describes and reflects on the Enriched Curriculum, an initiative in Northern Ireland to reintroduce a play-based curriculum, and the impact this has had on learners and on support for children's learning in her school.

Chapter 26

'Whoops, I forgot David': children's perceptions of the adults who work in their classrooms

Ian Eyres, Carrie Cable, Roger Hancock and Janet Turner

Despite their unique perspective and the profound importance of many local and national initiatives to their everyday lives, the views of children are rarely the focus of educational research. This chapter features the voices of children in several English primary schools articulating their idea of the role of teaching assistants. It would appear that the clear distinction between the roles of teachers and teaching assistants conceptualised at the levels of management and policy breaks down somewhat in the context of real classrooms.

Over the past 20 years, teaching assistants have made up an increasing proportion of the primary school workforce. Children are the group most significantly affected by such educational innovations, but they rarely have the opportunity to comment on them (Norris 1998). This study, therefore, set out to explore children's perceptions and experiences of teaching assistants. Seventy-three children between the ages of five and eleven years were interviewed in six primary schools. For younger children the interview began with a task in which they were invited to draw the adults in their classroom, and this proved a useful starter for discussion. The main findings of the study are set out below.

Children are happy to work with many different adults in the classroom

The 73 children reported working with a total of 66 teachers, 71 assistants and 2 adult volunteers: a total of 129 adults, of whom fewer than half were qualified teachers and fewer than a third were their class teacher. The 'Teachers and headteachers' category were senior staff who occasionally work in classrooms, supply teachers who work regularly or occasionally with classes, and teachers who have specific responsibilities for supporting children learning English as an additional language or particular children with a learning difficulty or impairment.

Assistants outnumber teachers by a factor of nearly three in most of the schools, and while many are employed part-time, the number of children with whom they have contact is increased by their working in more than one classroom in a week; some have other roles, for example midday supervisors.

As she drew them, Samantha, a five-year-old, named adults in the following roles (Figure 26.1, left to right): teaching assistant, deputy head, teaching assistant, teaching assistant, teaching assistant. David, the class teacher, is included only after the sudden realization: 'Whoops, I forgot David!'. She also includes a computer in the background—evidence of a perceived 'virtual teaching assistant'?

Figure 26.1 'Adults in my classroom' (Samantha, Year 1)

In his classroom, Alan similarly gave an impression that a number of adults were involved:

> There's Miss Ball, my teacher, Miss Audley, Miss Monroe and Miss Wells and sometimes Miss Morgan. (Alan, Year 3)

The number of adults mentioned by children tended to be greater towards the end of Key Stage 1 (Year 2) and at the beginning of Key Stage 2 (Years 3 and 4). In some instances adults were working with specific children. More frequently the adults mentioned were working with groups, either inside or outside the classroom, on literacy 'catch-up' programmes such as Additional Literacy Support (ALS) (DfES 1999). Children also mentioned 'going out of the classroom' or being taken in groups by teaching assistants for a range of activities, including reading, maths and science.

Some of the adults mentioned by children were qualified teachers, many engaged to support children with EAL or special educational needs. Some children encountered supply teachers on a regular basis and a few experienced a climate of constant change (one pair reporting that they had had 6 changes of supply teacher that year!). For some children the teaching assistant provided a sense of continuity they would not otherwise have experienced.

The overwhelming impression gained from this study is that children are comfortable with the number of adults they encounter and with their comings and goings, so long as there is some degree of stability and continuity. Many cited their class teacher as meeting this need, while a few others saw a particular teaching assistant as a more or less constant presence.

Children notice the different working patterns in the classroom and how they are managed

Apart from the class teacher, children appear largely to perceive the adults in their classrooms as being attached either to individual children:

Rebecca only works with Kelly. (Billy and Sushi, Year 2)

Or to a particular group:

I work with Miss Morris because I'm in the phoneme group. (Philippa, Year 3)

The link between teaching assistant and group appears to be strong in the minds of some children and a number of those interviewed identified the 'ideal' classroom as having one teaching assistant per group. With the arrival of the National Literacy Strategy (DfEE, 1998), much has been made of the new emphasis on whole-class teaching; at the same time, patterns of group-based working, with groups often adult-led rather than collaborative, have also become well-established and this organisational structure is certainly significant in the eyes of the children in this study.

As in the study carried out by Doddington *et al.* (2002), our data suggests that children are well aware of which group they and other children have been assigned to, and welcome and rely on the additional support they receive from teaching assistants in group work activities.

We're in this little group and we usually just do what others do – but just easier because in our group we don't do . . . we can't do some of the hard stuff. (Robin, Year 6)

It isn't that easy to get help because if you're the bestest group, they think you can't have help. (Naseem, Year 2)

Assignment to groups was largely perceived in terms of 'ability' and there was a sense in which 'higher' groups enjoyed higher status – Naseem's words, above, convey a sense of self-esteem.

It appeared that the children perceived differences in status between adults, especially between the class teacher ('our real teacher'):

> Mrs Wilson is my teacher. (Shamila, Reception)
>
> Miss McAngel is the actual teacher teacher teacher. (Laila, Year 6)

and others who may be 'just' assistants:

> Barbara isn't a proper teacher: she helps us, she doesn't actually teach us. (Mark, Year 6)
>
> He used to normally work in the lowest group because he just helps. (Sadia, Year 4)

The second quotation suggests the intertwined low status of both adult and children.

Without the overall responsibility of the class teacher, qualified teachers in supporting roles did not appear to be perceived any differently from teaching assistants:

> He [Mr Burke, EMTAG support teacher] works with us on Wednesdays . . . (Ewan, Year 6)

Class teachers are not simply seen as 'more important' per se but also to have a management role, which sets them above the other adults in the class.

> [. . .] Helen and Chris [. . .] sort of sit and talk and Barbara sits and listens and then she, um you know, they would say, 'Oh, could you do this for us Barbara, could you do that? Or could you help these children please' and like, she would do that, you know. (Jane, Year 6)

These examples illustrate the way in which children see teaching assistants as *assistants*, lending support to the teacher's teaching role. The children didn't simply notice this relationship in respect of ad hoc support; the perception that teachers have higher status is reflected in the perception that they have overall responsibility for the management of classroom activity:

> She tells us what groups are doing and she tells us which group is doing group reading. (Joshua, Reception)

It would seem also that in at least some cases the class teacher's authority has some practical benefits:

> Melissa [class teacher] . . . sorts it [social problem] out quick . . . she would like really sort the problem out. (Jade, Year 3)

There are other instances of teachers being seen as the ultimate authority over behaviour, but there are examples where teaching assistants are seen as powerful disciplinary figures too.

Teachers and teaching assistants are different, but it's difficult to say how

This question was at the heart of much of our discussion with the children. On the face of it, teachers and assistants are very different. Teachers have usually followed at least four years of higher education before qualifying. Teaching assistants need no formal qualifications and provision of training opportunities is variable. The two groups have different conditions of employment, patterns of working inside and outside the classroom and very different salary structures. According to recent government guidance, teaching assistants should undertake a range of non-teaching tasks, thereby freeing teachers to teach (DfES 2002, 2003). Our interviews probed the extent to which children perceived teachers and assistants as carrying out different roles. Analysis of what children told us (Table 26.1), suggests an apparently clear distinction between the two groups' activities.

Table 26.1: Children's views of what teachers and teaching assistants do

A teacher:	An assistant:
• helps children write things	• does group reading
• tells stories	• helps with reading
• tells groups what they are doing	• hears people read
• tells which group is on the carpet	• helps children find reading books
• tells what assistants should do	• helps children write things
• tells us the work	• rubs things out and corrects writing
• tells us stuff	• watches children when they write
• tells us what to do	• watches what the teacher's doing
• reads a book on the (group) tables	• takes childrens outside the classroom
• gives children work (D)	• helps on the computer
• makes us sit on the floor (D)	• does children's 'files'
• seems to mostly teach childen	• helps with work
• teaches the class	• helps with sums
• teaches you different things	• helps with art work
• teaches all the stuff	• explains things
• teaches what we have to do	• translates things
• does much harder work	• works with children on the computer
• does more stuff	• tells children about the computer
• stays in the classroom	• tells you off if you're really being naughty
• has lots of jobs to do	• does literacy
	• does PE
	• helps the literature people
	• takes people out of the classroom to read with them
	• takes people out when they are less good
	• prepares things
	• talks to children
	• writes things on paper
	• shows children homework

At the very least, this table does help to illustrate the variety of activities that adults were seen to be engaged in, both directly in working with children and, in the case of teaching assistants, in supporting the teacher's work. As the interviews focused on the role of teaching assistants it is not surprising that the right hand list is longer than the left. However, readers familiar with primary classrooms would doubtless identify many items which could appear in both columns and, of course, if a child says that teachers do a particular thing, that does not mean they think that teaching assistants don't do it and vice versa.

Overall the lists give an impression of teachers who 'tell' and teaching assistants who 'help'. However, despite these apparent differences, many children seemed to have great difficulty in explaining how the activities of people whose standing in the classroom they obviously saw as different, differed in practice.

> Interviewer: *How is what Jean does different from what Anna does?*
> Heather: *It isn't really. (Heather, Year 2)*

> Well the helpers seem to help out and do what the teacher does and the teacher seems to mostly teach children. But sometimes the helpers teach children. (Sarah, Year 3)

Statements like these were often the result of much prompting and reached via a great deal of speculation on the child's part. One girl speculated about the different roles as though she were carefully unravelling the clues to a mystery:

> Well, there's something very, very, very, very strange about the teacher. The teacher does more maths than the other teachers and Miss Rose [teacher] is quite – is more active than all the other teachers . . . Er, let's see – Mr Burke [EMAG support teacher] really does more stories than Miss Rose and about questions about stories about 'wish you were here' stuff. Let me think – there's something fishy . . . Mrs Dell [helper] does more reading than Miss Rose. They all do more reading than Miss Rose. (Asma, Year 2)

It seems easier to identify the teaching assistant role when it involves more menial tasks:

> Daniel like tells you what to do on your work. Daniel tells us the maths on the board. Tammi is like at the back of the class, like sharpening the pencils, and she sets out the things on the tables, the sheets we are going to write on. (Fraser and Jane, Year 1)

In the main we concluded that these children regarded teachers and assistants as doing very similar things. This echoes the findings of Moyles and Suschitzky (1997) that Key Stage 1 children were not very questioning about the two roles, although the children in this study were often willing to attempt to explain the differences. In fact they often saw the task as a stimulating riddle: they knew there was a difference but they just couldn't put their finger on what it was.

> Well Miss McAngel is the actual teacher, teacher, teacher. She actually teaches us everything because she's just a teacher and she teaches us everything. But, if you like, you've got another teacher, they teach us – pretty much they'd teach us everything

but Miss McAngel would do different things with us – d'you know what I mean? – sort of, I can't put it into words really – but [looking towards Tim, her friend] can you help? (Lisette, Year 6)

Omar, a Year 2 boy, said he had to write more intensely when with his teacher, which perhaps is a token of the higher esteem in which the teacher is held, or perhaps of her superior motivational skills.

Overall our impression was of children racking their brains for evidence to support the view that people with different job titles must be doing different things, rather than articulating a difference they found obvious or even particularly visible within their everyday experience. Perhaps we should not be surprised at this. Hancock *et al.* (2002) found many assistants were taking on teaching-related activities with children, and the literacy and numeracy strategies have led to a considerable blurring of the teacher/teaching assistant boundary. Reports from Open University Specialist Teacher Assistant (STA) students suggest that even some OfSTED inspectors find it hard to distinguish between trained assistants and teachers.

The notion that teaching assistants 'help' may be less helpful than it appears

We have noted above the possible inference that 'teachers tell and teaching assistants help'. Certainly 'help' and 'helper' were words used often when explaining the teaching assistant role.

> *Raymond:*   *I'm drawing Mrs Monroe.*
> *Interviewer:*   *Is she your teacher?*
> *Dushanti:*   *No, she just helps.*
> (Raymond and Dushanti, Year 2)

In many of the schools, teaching assistants and other adults who were not teachers were referred to by other staff and by some of the children as 'helpers'.

> [Imogen]'s our helper in our class. (Rebecca, Year 1)

In fact the word 'help' occurred so frequently in the extracts we had selected for this paper that we felt the need to return to the full transcripts to see if some explanation could be found there. One thing we found was the frequent use of that word in the questions about teaching assistants. Questions of the type: 'How does Mrs X help you?' abound. Three of the questions in the schedule which guided the interviews also emphasised the notion of 'helping':

- How does this [support for groups] help you with your work?
- Can you tell me more – (give an example) of how Mrs/Mr X has helped you?
- If you had a problem with your work, would you ask for help from anyone (any adult)?

This is not to suggest that the interviewer was leading the children's responses. However, given the interview schedule and the field of enquiry, 'help' was a word difficult to avoid. In the light of this we feel we should be very careful in drawing any conclusions from children's statements to the effect that they see teaching assistants as 'helping'.

As we have seen, some of the children articulated this relationship in terms of helping the teacher and others in terms of helping them or specific children in the class.

One boy emphasised the teacher-support role of an assistant and brought out the teacher's lead responsibility:

> Well I think it's different because the helpers, they come in and they help with things that the teacher needs help with and stuff like that ... the teachers, they have to prepare most of the stuff and the helpers just help the children with their reading and writing when they need help. (William, Year 4)

Some older children in the study appeared quite clear in their minds about the differences.

> Mary doesn't teach, she helps. She just helps us out with our work.
>   Rachel [teacher] teaches what we have to do. And if we find difficulties, Rachel sometimes helps but Mary [assistant] is the main person to help. (Sasha, Year 6)

Perhaps, however, Sasha is not using the words 'teach' and 'help' in the way education professionals would. Is 'teaching us what we have to do' a matter of advancing knowledge and understanding or simply the setting of tasks? Certainly the examples of 'tell' more often relate to giving instructions than to fostering learning. On the other hand, when Mary 'helps', is it the same kind of help as in, say, 'helping with the washing up' where the helper reduces the task by doing some of it, or, as seems more likely, does Mary give the kind of support which enables Sasha to do the task for himself? What Sasha identifies as 'just' helping could well be the kind of 'assisted performance' that Tharp and Gallimore (1988: 21) see as virtually synonymous with teaching. Further research into classroom interactions would help illuminate these questions.

References

DfEE (1998) *The National Literacy Strategy: A framework for teaching.* London: DfEE.

DfES (1999) *Additional Literacy Support.* London: DfES.

DfES (2002) *Time for Standards: Reforming the school workforce.* London: DfES.

DfES (2003) *Raising Standards and Tackling Workload: A national agreement.* London: DfES.

Doddington, C., Bearne, E., Demetriou, H. and Flutter, J. (2002) *Sustaining Children's Progress in Learning at Year 3.* Cambridge: Homerton College.

Hancock, R., Swann, W., Marr, A., Turner, J. & Cable, C. (2002) *Classroom Assistants in Primary Schools: Employment and deployment, project dissemination report.* The Open University, Faculty of Education and Language Studies. Available from: w.r.hancock@open.ac.uk.

Moyles, J., with Suschitzky, W. (1997) *Jills of all Trades? Classroom assistants in KS1 classes.* London: Association of Teachers and Lecturers.

Tharp, R.G. and Gallimore, R. (1988) *Rousing Minds to Life.* Cambridge: Cambridge University Press.

Chapter 27

What do pupils and parents think?

Patricia Atkinson

Children and parents don't often get asked what they think about the assessment of their own learning. Patricia Atkinson, a headteacher in Stirling, decided to research the views of pupils and parents in her school and found that pupils appreciated a variety of approaches and techniques, the opportunity to help others and the chance to talk about assessment as part of the process of learning. However, she found that parents didn't always agree with their children's views.

Why study assessment?

For several years I was involved in staff development in a Scottish Region. I wished to evaluate how pupils and, to a lesser extent, parents viewed assessment as an aid to effective learning. I was keen to see whether the advice given in the Scottish National Guidelines for Assessment 5–14 (SOED 1991) was adequate. The guidelines stress the need for assessment to be informative, practical and positive, but my feelings were that recording of assessment was taking over the curriculum at the expense of teaching and learning.

I decided, within the classroom setting, to concentrate on what I saw as the most useful forms of assessment for improving learning, namely formative (to inform the learning process), and diagnostic (to enable appropriate action to be taken). However, I did not ignore a third form, summative (summarising a child's progress).

What kind of investigation?

I had been involved in action research for 15 years, carrying out small-scale studies in language, thinking, and equal opportunities, all based around two central themes – personal development for children and staff, and empowered participation by children, sometimes now called 'children's voices'. I believe teachers should be building their own knowledge-base from practice, and making it public. My strongly held belief is that teaching should be a research-based career, contributing to the overall knowledge of effective education.

Action research is eminently suitable for professionals studying their own situation – the teacher can be a participant, but also a researcher. It is appropriate for studying a dynamic situation in depth. In general, action research involves at least one cycle of Planning, Action, Observation and Reflection as part of the process of improvement. When children's views are also taken into account, action research becomes democratic and empowering.

In this study I used an approach suggested by Whitehead (1985), based on a number of practical questions:

- What is my concern?
- Why am I concerned?
- What do I think I could do about it?
- What kind of evidence will I collect to help me make judgements?
- How will I collect the evidence?
- How will I check that my judgement is reasonably fair and accurate?

Assessment strategies and techniques used in class

The study was planned to look in depth at whatever assessment I happened to have undertaken in the previous weeks.

A whole repertoire of assessment strategies was used, such as any teacher might fit into his/her programme. These varied from very informal and positive formative styles (for example a brief word of encouragement) to diagnostic (through observation and discussion) and summative (written grades or final comments on actual performance). Assessments were practical, oral and written, and included marks, single words, comments and suggestions for improvement. I included considerably more self- and peer-assessment than is implied in the Assessment 5–14 document.

All routine work in folders or jotters was marked in pencil, to allow for change. Only blue or black pen was ever used for summative assessment, no red. Children normally marked their own work in maths, made judgements about quality and were not required to do corrections if they realised what they had done wrong. Children often swapped work for comment by peers. I checked jotters regularly and held discussions about learning (curricular) from self- and peer-assessment, and learning (personal and social) from being given this responsibility.

I allocated time in class to what I call 'meta-assessment', or talking about the interlinked processes of learning and assessment, plus reflection. In time this talking about targets, criteria for assessment and processes of assessment was taken for granted by children and reflection became a feature of their effective learning.

Shortly after the research was carried out, HMI praised the effect this had in school. Pupils were able to tell the Inspector very clearly, exactly what they were learning and why, and how they were being assessed, or assessing themselves, and why.

Research design

The research was designed around four different enquiries in order to provide for triangulation, or cross-checking of evidence:

- Informal observation (first term): Brief written notes
- Pupils' questionnaire (mid-session): Assessment in general
- Pupils' questionnaire (June): Assessment of specific work
- Parents' questionnaire (end of session): Assessment strategies in general

Informal observation and questionnaires are both methods which classroom teachers find manageable. Questionnaires in particular are useful in that they can be analysed in different ways, and at home after work! They have their limitations, but the main purpose of this research was to find what children thought of their assessment activities as an aid to learning.

What children's voices revealed

Informal observation

During the first term, children found a number of aspects of assessment helpful for their learning, all of which I refer to later in this chapter.

Mid-session questionnaire

A questionnaire was designed to focus in on most of these. It contained 18 questions on general aspects of assessment, all based on the children's positive comments in October, namely:

- who actually assessed the work
- whether grades, comments or suggestions for improvement were helpful
- self- and peer-assessment
- keeping personal records of assessment
- thinking of others' feelings when assessing their work.

All pupils valued almost all forms of assessment in the repertoire. They valued the range of assessment strategies, the range of purposes, and the discussion about assessment. They believed these aspects of assessment helped them to learn more effectively.

Pupils also responded positively to the involvement of different people (themselves, adults and children) in their assessment. They wanted to do well and hoped for general advice that would further help them. They were keen to know what could be improved and to be given suggestions for ways to do so. But of particular interest was the confirmation that they liked to help other people with their schoolwork, either while actually working and learning, or in terms of assessment. Interestingly, the children appreciated the value of assessment, and all our talk about it, as a part of the process of learning. In particular, they appreciated those assessment techniques which were based on self and peer-assessment. They also welcomed other strategies which focused on reflection. Embedding talk about assessment into the normal day not only motivated children, but also helped increase self-esteem in some.

Teachers now accept it matters how children regard themselves. If children see themselves as competent learners, then they want to learn and are willing to find ways to do so. When children see learning as a desirable process they learn more effectively and efficiently.

The teacher is a key person in the development of reflective ability. She/he may help children to look into themselves, to question themselves, to develop an ability to be fair to themselves, to judge their performance adequately. And children value respect from their teachers. They thrive on opportunities for autonomy, responsibility and power. They can be independent learners when they know not only the purpose of each activity but also the assessment criteria, in advance. When they are clear about these, children achieve more, through paying attention to the key aspects required. The affective (feelings) and cognitive (intellectual thinking) spheres must be developed together.

End-of-session questionnaire

The second pupil questionnaire was designed as a further form of triangulation, revisiting aspects of assessment already evaluated by children, but based on 20 specific pieces of work that had been assessed during the year. These ranged from one page to a whole book, and included: a class test on punctuation; assessment with grades, comments, suggestions and criticisms; and self-, peer- and parent-assessment.

Once again it was clear that all children valued most forms of assessment.

Pupils felt that responsibility for self-assessment and evaluation was useful even though it might be hard. They particularly liked the feeling of doing well when they had found something difficult. They enjoyed the satisfaction in being required to think, not only about curriculum knowledge and skills, but also about their approaches to work, their ways of working and their reflection on how they were progressing as they journeyed through their last year at primary school.

Analysis of the original, informal observations and both questionnaires demonstrated that children especially valued:

- knowing that assessment was on-going, including routine oral work and activities
- knowing in advance what would be assessed (out of all the learning taking place)
- a mix of informal and formal assessment
- variety
- reference to official documents (SEED guidelines) as targets for learning

- grades (5, 3, G, G+, VG, Excellent) for completed pieces of work (summative assessment)
- asking parents for comment
- self-assessment
- peer-assessment.

What parents' views revealed

The parents' questionnaire was about assessment in general. I asked parents to comment on all aspects of assessment, in discussion with their child. Parents were asked about self-assessment, oral and written, marks and judgement, record-keeping, tags with grades and comments, positive and negative ('next steps'), written remarks and peer assessment.

Interestingly, though parents' views generally confirmed the value of different forms of assessment, some parents had views completely at odds with the children. Some parents were unsure of self-assessment, and some were very uncomfortable with the idea of written peer-assessment. This was not what the children thought.

Two parents were not happy with children marking their own work. I have great sympathy with the parents who gave these views, because it is conventional for teachers to mark children's work themselves. I can understand their concerns. However, the present research confirms the value of other forms of assessment in the child's wider, personal and social development.

My long-term experience is that when pupils mark or, even better, evaluate work for themselves, it benefits both teacher and child. It gives the teacher time for more detailed analysis of children's progress or problems, or for generally more useful preparation for future lessons in other subjects. Also, marking at the time, or immediately after finishing, is known to be beneficial to learning, but many teachers find this too difficult to do in class, so mark after work.

The children themselves found that it was useful for them in a whole variety of ways, including the speed at which their work was self-marked, and corrected, if required.

Self-assessment and self-evaluation helped children to become better learners, being more aware of themselves and their ways of working, all of which are known to produce better thinkers. In addition, self-assessment enhanced motivation for many, and thereby self-esteem.

Research now shows that working out all 'corrections' in maths can be counterproductive (Haigh 1997). This confirms my own experience that a little give-and-take is extremely valuable in motivating children. When children are given responsibility for their own learning, correction or evaluation, they feel respected.

Just as a few parents were uncomfortable with self-assessment, a few also expressed opinions against peer-assessment, such as pupils evaluating each other's work. I was surprised about the strength of the reaction to this form of assessment from a minority of parents, as the children had so strongly valued peer-assessment. Not one child that year ever commented that negatively about another child's work.

Children openly spoke of taking account of others' feelings when assessing their work. I already had plenty of evidence from previous years that children would normally do so, but I thought they might be shy about admitting it in writing. An approach that takes account of others' feelings is awarded Level E Language (Talking), the level expected for most children, not in primary school, but when they reach second year in secondary school (S2 in Scotland, Year 9 in England and Wales).

Nevertheless, the fact that this was the least popular aspect of assessment for parents requires further reflection. While many of the fears about children being negative to others, and about children being too immature to cope with the responsibility of this, are unfounded, aspects to do with sensitivity and tact need further consideration. We could think that children should perhaps only choose their own partners for written peer-assessment, but we might also wonder whether children would recommend improvements to a friend. On the other hand, it may be that primary children work and learn better with a close friend.

The questionnaire demonstrated that the parents wanted useful information about their child's progress (especially regarding their achievements or what they might need help with), and not simply summative assessment.

Recommendations for classroom practice

Taking all four parts of the research together, the aspects of assessment that were particularly valued by parents and children for improving the children's learning were:

- knowing in advance what would be assessed (out of all the learning taking place)
- a mix of informal and formal assessment
- variety
- grades (5, 3, G, G+, VG, Excellent) for completed pieces of work
- asking parents for comment
- self- and peer-assessment

What matters most to children is to have assessment as a part of the process of learning, and of the process of thinking about learning and talking about learning. As a result of my study I recommend that teachers:

- develop a repertoire of procedures and techniques
- match learning to assessment, and let children know in advance what will be assessed
- ask children their views

- cut down on routine marking to gain time for taking a closer look at specifics
- keep parents informed regularly, simply sending home children's assessed work for comments, if convenient
- do not confuse assessment for learning with record keeping
- develop self- and peer-assessment, as well as reflection on achievement to aid children's critical thinking and self-esteem.

A wider research context

It is perhaps useful to compare my hands-on experience of children's views of the usefulness of assessment to those of Black and William in their 1998 review of the literature. I agree with their view that formative assessment is what matters:

- The principal purpose of assessment is to support learning rather than accountability.
- The purpose is to enable pupils to understand the ways in which they can contribute and become responsible for aspects of their own progress.

My research also confirms that children agree with the findings of the Review of Assessment 5–14 (Hayward *et al.* 2000) that assessment should:

- support learning, provide feedback and identify next steps in learning to result in significant learning gains
- involve pupils meaningfully in their own learning
- help pupils understand the ways in which they can contribute and become responsible for aspects of their own progress
- help the learner to perceive a gap between present and desired knowledge
- help identify the action necessary to close the gap
- take account of the impact of attitude and motivation on students' learning
- reflect the central importance of self-assessment
- stimulate the correction of errors through a reflective approach to them
- improve deep rather than surface learning (such as strategies to pass tests).

References

Black, P., and William, D. (1998) 'Assessment in classroom learning'. *Assessment in Education,* **5** (1), 7–75.

Haigh, G. (1997) 'Ten out of ten'. *Times Educational Supplement Scotland,* 13 June, 'Primary' supplement.

Hayward L., Kane, J., and Cogan, N. (2000) *Improving Assessment in Scotland: Report of the consultation on the Review of Assessment Pre-school and 5– 1.* Glasgow: University of Glasgow/SEED.

Scottish Office Education Department (SOED) (1991) *Assessment 5–14*, Edinburgh: HMSO.

Whitehead, J. (1985) 'An analysis of an individual's educational development: The basis for personally-oriented action research', in: M. Shipman (ed), *Educational Research: Principals, policies and practice.* Lewes: Falmer Press.

Chapter 28

Getting your voice heard and making a difference

Chris Scrivener

In this chapter, Chris Scrivener describes an environmental project carried out in a school in a highly deprived area of Oxford. Although the curriculum focus of this chapter might be seen as geography, or citizenship, it contains important lessons about English too. The project (which is explained at greater length in Scrivener's original article) gave pupils the opportunity to work with a complex problem, debate their ideas and present them to a powerful external audience; they learnt that through language and literacy they could make a significant difference to the world they live in.

The 2002 Earth Summit: a context for engaging learning

The Johannesburg Earth Summit in September 2002 provided an excellent opportunity to raise teachers' and pupils' awareness about global citizenship and to engage them in in-depth studies of local environmental issues that make explicit the link between local and global issues. The creation of a curriculum development project based around the Earth Summit also provided a tangible exemplification to enhance teachers' understanding of education for sustainable development (ESD).

As the world's leaders prepared to meet in South Africa pupils in the 15 schools in the Hamilton Oxford Schools Partnership (HOSP: an Education Action Zone (EAZ) serving an area of socio-economic deprivation in East Oxford) investigated environmental issues in their local area during the second half of the summer term. A celebration event – the Oxford Earth Summit – was planned for the start of the autumn term. The pupils brought their projects to the debating chamber of the county council where, before an invited audience of city and county councillors and the local MP and government minister, they described how their actions made a difference by 'thinking globally, acting locally'.

The planning principles that guided the development of the work of all schools in preparing for the Earth Summit were adapted from the Geographical Association's publication: *Geography and the New Agenda: Citizenship, PSHE and Sustainable Development in the Primary Curriculum* (Grimwade, Jackson, Reid and Smith 2000). They are that:

1. The issues selected for study would exemplify the concept of sustainable development, and in particular the idea of 'think globally, act locally'.
2. The selection of the specific issue would be decided through discussion by the teacher with the young people, so that it would represent a genuine concern felt and expressed by them.
3. The young people would be encouraged to gather information and knowledge on the issue so that they could make informed decisions which take account of reliable data and of a range of viewpoints.
4. The young people would be listened to and their views taken seriously.
5. The young people should be taught to express their own point of view, to challenge the views of others, to negotiate and compromise, and to make individual and group decisions in light of discussion.
6. The young people would be taught the value of weighing up evidence before making any decision.
7. The young people would be aware that actions are appropriate to circumstances, that some actions are more likely to succeed than others, and that there are limitations to what individuals and groups can achieve.
8. The young people would be aware that change can happen at different levels: individual, local, national and global.

The Oxfordshire Advisory Service's curriculum vision statement (Advisory and Improvement Service 2002) encourages schools to provide a balance between the academic, physical and creative areas of the curriculum. The statement articulates a series of principles that underpin a dynamic and relevant inclusive curriculum, including that of 'enabling developing minds to think and work creatively, critically and reflectively'. It is this goal that the partners in the project wished to achieve by means of a high-profile major event to celebrate the work undertaken by the pupils. All of the schools received external support, but the greatest credit must go to the class teachers who initiated, enthused and supported their pupils to research and report upon their investigations.

Officers of the LEA (Local Education Authority) and EAZ officers took responsibility for creating the links with external agencies, and to undertake the organisation and management of the summit event.

The excellent report *Rescue Mission: Planet Earth 2002*, and the *Junior Indicators Pack* (Peace Child International 2002a, 2002b), were used to develop teachers' knowledge and understanding of the key issues and how young people could take action to make a difference. Each teacher agreed to identify issues in consultation with the targeted year group to ensure that the topics were selected by the pupils themselves. The teachers agreed to meet again a month later to confirm the selected topics, and to begin planning the learning activities. It was at this stage that each school was connected with an 'expert' adult – in the country or city councils, a non-governmental organisation (NGO) or voluntary group, e.g. the country's sustainability project officer, local wildlife trusts.

The opportunity for participation in a young people's Earth Summit gave important and essential meaning to the work:

- It provided a forum in which pupils' beliefs and opinions would be valued because they were being heard by adults other than teachers.
- It required that the investigation stage of the work would be sufficiently rigorous to withstand scrutiny by people whose decisions and actions might be called into question.
- It demonstrated a process of debating, based on the power of evidence and the skills of presentation.
- There was a possibility that something might happen as a consequence of the work undertaken by the pupils.

The Earth Summit contained a number of elements designed to ensure a high-profile event and to ensure that young people's voices would be listened to and acted upon. Holding the event in the main county council chamber gave the event status in the eyes of the young people, and at the same time helped to secure the support of the local councillors. The local MP, Andrew Smith (also a government minister), gave the keynote introduction making the event newsworthy to the local media (whose usual reporting of local activities is about crime, drugs and vandalism). Key officers of the local councils, local environmental groups and individuals were invited. All of these adults were the audience with whom the young people needed to communicate and engage.

The opportunity to hold a live video conference with young people from a school in Johannesburg provided a clear demonstration of global citizenship in action. The fact that South Africa is on a similar time zone to the UK (only one hour difference) makes it feasible to have school-to-school real-time contact. The Sir Edmund Hillary School (a clue of former times!) serves the predominantly black families who live in the inner-city district of Kensington and so represented a 'typical' South African urban school – an important consideration when trying to challenge many young people's stereotypical images of Africa. There was much about recycling and reuse that the Johannesburg youngsters were able to tell their peers in Oxford!

Creating and implementing the principles for learning

The Windale School project was led by Mary Whitlock, the headteacher, who identified the Earth Summit event as an opportunity to contribute to an important element of the principles and values of the school: developing children's skills in making choices and being able to reflect upon the consequences of their actions. A characteristic of the community that the school serves is that many people – both adults and children – believe themselves to be disenfranchised. The Earth

Summit forum provided the teachers with the context to develop both cognitive and affective skills: to create new local knowledge and to use this knowledge to engage in a debate with adult decision-makers. The pupils had the opportunity to develop dynamic elements of learning: to identify, plan and resource a project; to consider how to present their ideas in order to persuade the adults of the value of their arguments and the consequences of their actions. If it were to be successful then it would challenge the perception of disenfranchisement, and demonstrate to the pupils how they could get their voices heard and, most importantly, make a difference to their own lives.

The original plan had been to involve all of the classes, but the scale of activity and support that would have been required contributed to the decision to work with a single class. The target class was a Year 4 that became a Year 5 class in the autumn term. The project was undertaken with the class by the headteacher working with a newly qualified teacher (NQT).

The teachers began by explaining the concept of the Earth Summit as a background to a class discussion about issues that affected children in terms of where they live, what they do in the local area, and how it could be improved. They guided the discussion to describe the problems but also identify ideas for possible solutions. An initial brainstorm identified three issues about which the pupils were very concerned: the hazard of crossing roads, the problems of litter, and the fears associated with drug dealing and drug abuse. Discussion of the drugs issue acknowledged its importance to daily lives, but the children understood that many of the solutions were in the hands of adults and there was less potential for them to 'make a difference'. The choice between the traffic safety and the litter was made by the children on the basis that safety was a more important issue: it was a matter of danger rather than being unsightly. The children were outraged when told that the governing body had petitioned the city and county councils unsuccessfully for safety improvements.

When planning the project the teachers identified two distinct strands: carrying out an *investigation* to gather evidence, and using the information to *create a presentation* for the summit.

The investigative work led to the generation of 'local knowledge' – information that is critical to an informed debate but which is not hitherto known (Posch 1993). The pupils devised a questionnaire to find out how children travelled to and from school. They learned about the importance of framing questions so that the results can be collated and displayed accurately. They developed their observation skills when they undertook traffic surveys and asked their friends and family about their views. This stage of the work meets some of the programme of studies in geography (the aspect of geographical enquiry and skills), and in mathematics (using and applying maths: data handling and representation).

The work to create a presentation to the summit illustrates well the challenges of using complex real-world issues as contexts for teaching and learning (as well as providing an excellent context for developing a wide range of literacy skills). Discussion with pupils about the presentation involved the development of many higher-order thinking skills, raising awareness about the importance of audience, about the need for reasoned argument, about identifying and answering counter arguments, and about the importance of being succinct. A key decision for all teachers when handling controversial issues is the level of influence and guidance that they provide. In this example the teachers decided that they needed to help the children at the point when they were looking for solutions by helping them evaluate the feasibility of the ideas that the pupils generated. For the Windale teachers the basis for their judgement about intervention goes back to one of the guiding principles of the work: that pupils would learn how to make a difference. If the pupils' arguments were not rooted in the kinds of language used by adult decision-makers, and did not acknowledge some of the external constraints (for example, financial), then the power to challenge the perception of disenfranchisement would be lost.

The pupils did have some prior experience of working with PowerPoint as a presentation too but were less knowledgeable in using information and communications technology (ICT) as part of an oral presentation. They discussed the purposes of the presentation, and how visual images could be used to support the telling of their story. They took a series of digital images to illustrate the problems caused by traffic.

A small group of pupils, together with a teaching assistant, attended the Earth Summit to present their findings and to persuade the appropriate adults to take action. The action of sharing with adult decision-makers knowledge that the pupils had generated through their investigation had an immediate impact at the summit: the local councillors promised to investigate the pupils' concerns with council officers. They also responded positively to the pupils' invitation to visit the school to discuss their findings – two months after the summit three councillors, four council officers, and a reporter from Radio Oxford arrived at the school to meet the pupils and to take part in a guided tour of the traffic issues. Two weeks later the director of environmental services for the country council also visited the school.

The outcome is that some of the traffic improvements suggested by the pupils are being implemented. The *Oxford Times* (13.12.02) headlined its report: 'Children cause council about-turn on safety', and a similar theme was used in the local radio report. Mary Whitlock reported: 'They have taken on a local issue and presented their case in a clear, snappy form and learned an important lesson that you can make a difference if you are prepared to fight for something.'

Reviewing the learning

The environmental investigation involved teachers in pedagogical practices that are very different to the usual teaching methods. Much of the current approach to curriculum planning involves a specification of the intended learning outcomes in terms of systematically organised knowledge (the objectives-led curriculum). Such an approach makes it difficult to incorporate more dynamic elements of learning, such as exercising initiative and taking responsibility for individual and group actions (Posch 1996). The framework for teaching and learning is specified in terms of principles rather than objectives, a distinction that involves a distinctive pedagogy.

The principles that guided the pupils' learning in all of the schools that took part in the Earth Summit are similar to those first developed by the OECD Environment and Schools Initiative project (described in Elliott 1998):

- Pupils should experience the environment as a sphere of personal influence, through the identification of problems and issues in the local environment.
- Pupils should have the opportunity to shape their environment, through participation in the decision-making processes.
- Pupils should accept the environment as a challenge for personal and group initiative, and responsible action.

The Windale pupils were involved in exploring an issue that they had identified as of importance to them as young people, but whose resolution depended upon the action of adults. Their investigation provided the evidence (the 'local knowledge') with which to persuade local councillors to take practical steps. They used the forum of the Earth Summit to publicise their knowledge and to engage with the decision-makers.

There are similarities in this approach to learning to the accelerated learning cycle model developed by Alistair Smith (1996) and now widely used by teachers in order to raise levels of achievement. Content is accessed through a series of sequential processes. The initial activities to explore environmental issues of concern to pupils represent a method of connecting the learning and of creating the 'big picture' (what the pupils hope to achieve), which in turn leads to the activity of 'describing the outcomes' (in this example, of identifying possible courses of action for the pupils' investigations).

The outcomes of the pupils' efforts to secure environmental improvements are already visible outside the school. The pupils who participated in the project have learned how to influence the decision-making process and demonstrated to themselves and the wider community how to 'make a difference' to their lives. In a community that doesn't often celebrate achievement and empowerment, they have demonstrated how to overcome feelings of disenfranchisement. The hope is that they will continue to develop these dynamic qualities of learning, and be able to take greater control over their lives than is the case for many families in the school catchment. That at least is the aspiration of Mary Whitlock and her staff.

References

Advisory and Improvement Service (2002) *Education in Oxfordshire: A Vision for the Future.* Oxford: Oxfordshire County Council.

Elliott, J. (1998) *The Curriculum Experiment: Meeting the Challenge of Social Change.* Buckingham: Open University Press.

Grimwade, K., Jackson, E., Reid, A. and Smith, M. (2000) *Geography and the New Agenda: Citizenship, PSHE and Sustainable Development in the Primary Curriculum*. Sheffield: Geographical Association.

Oxford Times (2002) 'Children cause council about-turn on safety' 13.12.2002.

Peace Child International (2002a) *Rescue Mission Planet Earth 2002*. Buntingford: The White House. Available from The White House, Buntingford, Herts, SG9 9AH (telephone 01763 274459) or online at www.peacechild.org

Peace Child International (2002b) *Rescue Mission Planet Earth: Junior Indicators Pack*. Buntingford: The White House.

Posch, P. (1993) Research Issues in Environmental Education. *Studies in Science Education*, **21**, 21–8.

Posch, P. (1996) 'Curriculum Change and School Development'. *Environmental Education Research*, **2** (3), 347–62.

Smith, A. (1996) *Accelerated Learning in the Classroom*. Stafford: Network Education Press.

Chapter 29

Bangladeshi women and their children's reading

Adrian Blackledge

> As Thelma Hall argues later in this section, children can benefit greatly from their parents' involvement in their learning to read. Adrian Blackledge's study of Bangladeshi families found that mothers were very keen to support their children's reading at home, but were frustrated by the gap between home and school literacy and by schools' lack of understanding of home literacy practices. Blackledge concludes the chapter with six recommendations to help bridge this cultural divide.

This study initially developed from questions about what happens when young, minority-language schoolchildren take home reading books which they are expected to read with their parents. Interviews with the mothers of young Bangladeshi children in Birmingham revealed that the home–school reading process reflected structural relations of power between minority and majority groups in society. In Bangladeshi families home and community literacies were associated with cultural identity, cultural transmission and symbolic power. School literacy, on the other hand, was a source of frustration and disempowerment.

Literacy as a social process

Different families and communities have different literacies (Street 1993). Cultural groups may differ in what they consider to be their 'texts' and in the values they attach to these, and may also differ in what they regard as literate behaviour. The same person may be regarded as 'illiterate' in one culture, while appearing to be quite literate in another. Often, 'school literacy' tends to define what counts as literacy, and this may construct the lack of school literacy in deficit terms (Street and Street 1991). That is, those who are not literate in the terms prescribed by the school may be seen as illiterate and therefore lacking essential skills.

When literacy is transferred from a dominant culture to a minority culture which has not historically been literate, majority culture values may be transmitted as part of the 'package' of literacy. In order to acquire literacy in the majority language it may be necessary for the learner to adopt some of the cultural behaviours and values of the majority, and risk sacrificing cultural group identity (Ferdman 1990). It was in the context of this theoretical framework that literacies in a Bangladeshi community in Birmingham made visible relations of power between the dominant and minority group.

Method

The initial stage of data collection was to record on audio-cassette reading interactions between 18 six-year-old Bangladeshi children and family members as they attempted to read school books at home. The same children were recorded reading in school with their teachers. These data, reported elsewhere (Blackledge 1999), revealed that the children usually read with their siblings, who used a narrower range of support strategies than did the teachers. Several days after each recording was made, I interviewed the children's mothers, and their teachers. A bilingual/bicultural interpreter who lived in the local community assisted with the interviews, which were conducted in Sylheti (a spoken, but not literate, language of north-east Bangladesh). The interviews took place in the women's homes.

The women had migrated to Britain between seven and seventeen years earlier. Most of them had attended school for five or six years in Bangladesh, although three had never been to school. All of the women were able to read and write Bengali (the standard language of Bangladesh), except the three who had not attended school. None of the 18 reported that she was a confident reader or writer of English, or a confident speaker of English. All of the women reported that Sylheti was the only language used by them in the home. They said that their children spoke English to each other, and Sylheti when speaking to parents and other adults at home.

The 18 Bangladeshi women were interviewed about their children's reading, and their attempts to support their children's literacy learning. In addition to questions about their children's home reading practices, the women were asked about their interactions with the school as they attempted to find out about their children's academic progress. The children's teachers were interviewed about the process of teaching literacy, and their attempts to involve Bangladeshi parents in their children's school-related learning.

The women's attitudes to their children's English learning

The 18 women were asked about their attitudes to their children's language learning. All of them were positive about their children learning English at school. A common response was the following: 'It is very important that the children learn English, because this is where they live. They need to learn English to do well at school.'

The women's aspirations for their children's educational attainment were high, and they wished to do everything possible to support their progress. However, they found difficulties in contributing to this process.

Almost all of the women said that siblings were the main providers of English reading support. One of the women said that she did attempt to help her child to read English, and two said that their husbands sometimes helped. There was no evidence that the women's lack of reading support for their children was due to lack of interest. Rather, it seemed to be due to a feeling of powerlessness: 'It's very hard to teach the children at home because I don't speak English. I am trying my very best.'

Some of the women indicated that the reason they were unable to support their children's reading was not a deficiency in them, but the fact that the reading resources sent from school were in a language in which they were not literate: 'I would like the story books to be in English and Bengali, because I could explain the stories to the children. I can't read the English books.'

Some of the women said that nursery-age children brought home dual-text books, in Bengali and English. They welcomed these books, and read them to their young children. For the most part, however, books taken home by children were in English only.

School support for home literacy learning

The women were asked whether they had ever received explicit advice from the school about how to support their child's reading at home. Seven of them replied that they had received such advice, while eleven said that they had not. The women typically described the advice they had been given as follows: 'The teacher has told me that if I can't understand a book, I can talk about the pictures. But if the book was in Bengali and English I could read the story myself.'

The teachers had given advice to these women which correctly assumed that they were unable to read English. However, the women's responses clearly demonstrated that although they could not read English, they were literate in Bengali, and they could have used this literacy to support their children's reading.

Most of the women said they would like more advice about how to support their child's reading, but they found it difficult to approach the teachers at the school: 'I did ask the teacher for advice about how to help Shanaz to read, but because I didn't know the language, or read and write, I felt embarrassed and couldn't understand. I don't really say anything to the teachers now.'

Although the problem of approaching teachers about children's reading is not confined to minority-language speakers, these mothers clearly identified the home–school language divide as the main reason that they had difficulties communicating with their children's teachers. The teachers had responded to this need by planning a strategy for educating the parents in home reading support: 'There are a lot of parents, particularly younger parents who have been educated in this country, they have some understanding of the system, and they do ask a lot of questions . . . we think they might be quite a captive audience.'

This positive step may not have solved the difficulties of the group in this study, however, as none of them had been educated in Britain. In fact, in targeting those parents who already had some understanding of the education system in Britain, the school potentially increased inequality (Toomey 1989), as those parents in most need of support were excluded. Those who were already relatively able to relate to the school had the opportunity to become further empowered if they could play by the rules of the school and 'understand the system', while also using and comprehending the language of the school. Those who either were unable, or refused, to adopt the cultural and linguistic norms of the school remained outsiders.

The women's attitudes to the cultural value of Sylheti

All of the women believed that maintenance of Sylheti was important for their children. Their main reason for this was that they wanted to be able to communicate with the children. However, the home language also seemed to have a symbolic importance for the women, as they indicated that Sylheti transmitted aspects of their cultural identity. This positive attitude to the cultural role of Sylheti was evident in responses to questions about storytelling in the home. Fifteen of the women said that they told stories to their children in the home language. These stories were told regularly, and were in a variety of traditions: 'I tell the children stories in Sylheti, traditional stories, Islamic stories, and stories I make up myself. I do this two or three times a week.' 'I make up stories for my three boys, like "there were once three princes who became kings", and so on.'

These responses make it clear that home-language storytelling was thriving in the homes of these families. This 'oral literacy' (Delgado-Gaitan 1990) activity was used to reinforce religious and cultural traditions. Teachers were aware of home-language storytelling as a valuable learning opportunity, but they had been unable to realise its potential in the classroom. The cultural and linguistic resources of the families remained in the private domain of the home, as the women were reluctant to enter the public domain of the school.

The women's attitudes to their children's Bengali literacy learning

The women were also asked about their attitude to their children's Bengali literacy learning. Bengali was the standard language of community literacy for these families, and different from Sylheti, the spoken language of the home. The women's responses made explicit the links between the community language and cultural identity. Most of the women either taught their children to read and write Bengali, or sent them to a local community class to learn. Although they spoke of the importance of Bengali for reading letters from the home country, the language had a significance beyond its function as a means of communication. It represented the group's identification as Bengalis, and their difference from the majority culture, and from other minority cultures: 'It is very important to me that he learns the language because we are Bengali. It is good that he has English as a second language.'

Twelve of the eighteen women took steps to directly support their children's Bengali literacy learning: 'As often as I can I will spend twenty minutes teaching them Bengali. I sit with the children for two hours on Saturdays and Sundays, and I teach them Bengali and Arabic.'

Those women who did not offer support at home for the children to read Bengali said that they would send their children to a tutor for this purpose when they were eight years old. The women's active support for the children's Bengali literacy learning made visible the symbolic association between language and cultural identity. They were able to offer Bengali literacy support to their children without having to acquire a new language, and without having to adopt aspects of the majority culture. Bengali literacy had a symbolic significance beyond its use as a means of communication.

For these women, to learn to read and write Bengali was to be Bengali. Teaching their children to be literate in Bengali represented a symbol of solidarity with their cultural group. Economic power was not likely to accrue from their children learning to be literate in Bengali. Yet the women invested considerable resources in Bengali literacy instruction. Far from being 'illiterate', the women organised their homes so that they actively taught their children to become literate in the community language.

Communication with their children's teachers

The Bangladeshi women had opportunities to talk to their children's teachers in formal and informal settings, including parents' evenings, parents' workshops and day-to-day contact when bringing children to, or collecting children from school. However, despite these opportunities, the women largely said that they found communication with teachers difficult because they were unable to speak English. There were rarely bilingual Sylheti-English school staff available on a day-to-day basis, and at parents' evenings interpreters were spread so thinly that young children often took on the role. For this reason some of the women had stopped going to parents' evenings.

The school had recently developed an initiative to involve parents in the school curriculum by inviting them to come into school to share in parents' workshops, which demonstrated aspects of the curriculum. Although a Sylheti interpreter was present, some of the women said that she was inappropriate for the role, as she was too young. Some of the women found these workshops useful, while others spoke of their 'embarrassment' at going to the school site, as they could not speak English. So although this school was doing more than most to communicate with this marginalised group of parents, the Bangladeshi women were still frustrated in their attempts to support their children's school work, and in their efforts to find out information about their children's progress.

Summary

These Bangladeshi women had a clear sense of the value of their languages and literacies. They operated successfully in their home and community linguistic domains, where their languages were accepted and valued. Both the spoken Sylheti language and the literate language of Bengali were important features of their cultural identity, and had a symbolic significance beyond their functional use. The women's languages represented solidarity with their cultural group.

The school seemed to consider that they were unable to contribute to their children's literacy learning, because their home and community literacies did not fit with the literacy of the school. The teachers did not incorporate the families' languages in the education of their children, or provide advice or resources to enable the women to become involved in their children's schooling. In dictating that the language of interaction in, and with, the school was solely English, the teachers demanded that the Bangladeshi mothers play by the cultural and linguistic rules of the dominant majority, or put at risk their children's academic progress. If they were willing and able to acquire the language and literacy of the school, they were able to gain access to information about their children's education. If not, they remained disempowered in their attempts to support their children's education.

Implications for policy and practice

Each time people are required to learn another language in order to participate in society, an act of injustice occurs (Tollefson 1991). In the study presented here, a group of women was effectively prevented from finding out about, or contributing to, their children's education. The main reason for this was that the school required that the women become proficient readers, writers and speakers of English in order to participate in the educational process. Schools in similar contexts can take steps to redress the balance of injustice by:

- sending reading books home with children; these should be high-quality, dual-language texts. Where possible, these should be texts which originate in the heritage country of the family.
- talking to parents about their literacies, including 'oral literacies' such as storytelling. Plan for the parents' languages and literacies to be authentically incorporated in the curriculum. All children will benefit from seeing that teachers give high status to minority languages.

- offering parents practical, comprehensible advice about how to use school reading books at home. If parents will not come into the school (many parents perceive the school as the domain of the teachers), other sites can be used – libraries, community centres, etc. There is much evidence (Toomey 1993) that home visits to parents can make a significant difference to their confidence and competence as home literacy tutors.
- ensuring that appropriate, trained interpreters are available at all times, including the beginning and end of the school day, parents' evenings, parents' workshops, women's groups, coffee morning, etc. Ask parents' permission to use individual interpreters for particular situations, and try to offer alternatives – for example, should a neighbour be involved in a sensitive conversation about a child's behaviour or attainment?
- recruiting teachers who speak the language(s) of the community served by the school, and encouraging them to use their languages where appropriate. Of course this does not mean simply helping young children until they are able to speak English, but is about valuing the languages of the school community at all levels. The study presented here makes it clear that languages are very much associated with cultural identity.
- involving minority parents in policy-making and planning. Schools may have the best intentions in developing policy for all children, but they may be unaware of the needs and resources of the community. Only a local community can really know what is necessary for its children (Corson 1994).

At a time when the management of learning in English primary schools is becoming increasingly controlled from the centre, it is important to develop language and literacy policy and practice at the local level, to meet the needs of local communities. In this way the teaching of literacy in minority communities can become the site of renegotiation rather than reproduction of power, and the balance of injustice can be redressed.

References

Blackledge, A. (1999) *Literacy, Power and Social Justice.* Stoke-on-Trent: Trentham Books.

Corson, D. (1994) 'Bilingual education policy and social justice', in: A. Blackledge (ed), *Teaching Bilingual Children.* Stoke-on-Trent: Trentham Books.

Delgado-Gaitan, C. (1990) *Literacy for Empowerment.* London: Falmer Press.

Ferdman, B.M. (1990) 'Literacy and cultural identity'. *Harvard Educational Review,* **60**, 181–204.

Street, B. (1993) 'Introduction: The new literacy studies', in: B. Street (ed), *Cross-Cultural Approaches to Literacy.* Cambridge: Cambridge University Press.

Street, B. and Street, J. (1991) 'The schooling of literacy', in: D. Barton and R. Ivanic (eds), *Writing in the Community.* London: Sage.

Tollefson, J. (1991) *Planning Language, Planning Inequality.* Harlow: Longman.

Toomey, D. (1989) 'How home–school relations policies can increase educational inequality'. *Australian Journal of Education*, **33** (3), 284–98.

Toomey, D. (1993) 'Parents hearing their children read: a review. Rethinking the lessons of the Haringey Project'. *Educational Research*, **35**, 223–6.

Chapter 30

Social outcasts

Times Educational Supplement, Friday Forum

'Deal with the behaviour, not the child', has long been an axiom of positive behaviour strategies, but in his account of how he helped one pupil, Mary, to integrate socially, primary teacher Gary Trainor explains how he found that more than a 'one size fits all' approach was needed. By working within a newly established whole-school positive behaviour policy, which stressed the quality of adult–pupil interaction, Gary learnt what it would take to draw Mary into the activities of the class.

How do you get behaviour right? It depends on your character, the character of your pupils, the nature of your school and the nature of the incident. But there are common threads, ideas and solutions. In the Friday forum we're asking you to share your experiences. We're not telling you how to do it: you're telling us how you've managed a particular child's behaviour on a particular day. This week, a problem that took longer than a day to sort out: Belfast primary teacher Gary Trainor describes how he encouraged Mary, the child who didn't fit in.

Corrosive relationships between pupils can spoil a class. Pupils like to feel part of a group, and if there's one child who can't or won't play to group rules, if there's one who becomes the butt of humour and ill-humour, classroom management can be sorely tested. For the ten-year-olds at St Kevin's, a Roman Catholic primary on the Falls Road, Belfast, that butt was Mary, and Mary wasn't helping matters. Class teacher Gary Trainor had to face the fallout almost every day.

Mary was often late for school; she was overweight, truculent, unsmiling and unco-operative, and nobody ever wanted to be her partner, sit next to her or play with her at break time. She became the butt of jokes and name-calling and such playground discord would come back into the classroom on every occasion. Mary would complain about her peers' behaviour towards her; they would always deny her allegations and Mr Trainor would have to disentangle the mess.

She would constantly complain that so-and-so had taken her pencil, or pushed her, and it was no good saying to the others, 'Did you take her pencil?', 'Did you push her?' We were all getting bogged down with it. At first I tried to talk to Mary about it.

I told her to ignore it, to walk away, but she didn't respond. She had a leave-me-alone attitude, and we got nowhere. I tried talking to groups of pupils about it, but that didn't work either.

It was a quagmire, one of those repetitive discipline issues that is so frustrating. I would find myself talking to my wife about it, would find myself thinking, 'Oh my God, what am I going to do now?' on the way into school.

When I asked children to work with partners I would hear them bickering about who was going to pair up with Mary. She would hear them too. It was cruel, and it bothered me to see a child so isolated. There were others in the class who were quiet and overweight, but they weren't being picked on and isolated in the same way. It was as if her refusal to co-operate, to interact, to respond in any way, was attention-seeking, even if the attention was negative. She was forlorn; her whole body language said, 'I am not happy.'

As a teacher with a no-nonsense approach to discipline, Mr Trainor was dismayed that his usual 'firm but fair' method of managing pupil behaviour was making few inroads into this seemingly intractable problem. He tried talking to the girl's mother, who confirmed that Mary didn't mix with friends at home either, and who was also at a loss as to what to do about it. In the event, his realisation that he would have to adopt a very different approach coincided with a whole-school change in the culture of behaviour management.

Mr Trainor, 35, a Primary 6 teacher, has always regarded himself as direct and lively, but also as someone who leads from the front. 'My approach was, "Right kids, come in, sit down, this is the way we are doing it." I dealt with the issue, not the person. If a child had done something wrong, no matter whom, I would deal with it in a set way; there would be no room for manoeuvre.'

But, over time, Mr Trainor found his 'black and white' approach to teaching was becoming increasingly ineffective, especially in an area where children were coming into school carrying the burden of significant social deprivation and with increasingly complex needs.

St Kevin's draws from the Whiterock and St James districts of West Belfast, the city's poorest wards, and former recruiting grounds of the IRA; drugs and crime rates are soaring and family cohesion is suffering. Half of the school's pupils are on the special needs register and half are entitled to free school meals. The school itself, a maze of sprawling, crumbling brick extensions and boarded-up windows, looks like a building under siege. At times it has been.

When Mr Trainor started teaching at St Kevin's, ten years ago, there were more than 700 children in the school. Depopulation and falling birth rates have cut that number to just 480. But a new state-of-the-art school, which opened last month, has emerged beside it, evidence of the commitment from the Northern Ireland Assembly to reinvigorate the education system.

The headteacher, Kay McGuinness, was determined to fashion a building that would meet the needs of the wider community, and help to raise self-esteem. She was also adamant that with a new school would come a new approach to teaching and learning. She introduced training to help staff and pupils move towards a positive behaviour policy; everything that happens in school, she says, has to be for the benefit of the children.

Mr Trainor has taken this to heart and believes this positive approach has helped him tackle pupils' more complex behavioural problems and, in particular, to find a way to help Mary.

> One of the things we've realised as a staff is that how well children learn depends on their interaction with their teacher. If you are intimidating, pupils tend to shut down, they don't learn effectively. They still know where they cannot cross the line with me – the one kind of behaviour I cannot tolerate is disrespect – but I have shifted my line into their domain. I try to give them more credence for what they are and what they already know; for their feelings and aspirations. Before, I wouldn't have wanted to know, but now I try to connect with what they are doing at home, their families, their interests.

With Mary, he latched on to the fact that she was a good listener and could be astute. He began to praise her for it, and made sure other pupils heard him. Instead of making an issue of her being late every morning (for reasons he knew were outside her control), he let it go.

'Interrogating Mary about why she was late was always our first interaction of the day,' he says. 'But as I began to see things from her point of view, I made little of it.'

He also introduced circle time, when 'we could focus on bullying'. After a while Mary would be one of the first with her hand up to make a contribution. Again, he made a point of commending her. He also introduced 'brain breaks', carving up lessons with five-minute breathers involving fun activities.

> I started to get the kids to do things like massage the shoulders of the person next to them, or make a human sculpture; Mary had to get involved, no question. She was reluctant at first, but a year down the line she was more accepting and accepted for being involved.
>
> I began to show more that I accepted her, and the other pupils followed my example. I began to see myself as a role model. I made a point of putting time aside to chat to each pupil each week, getting to know what they were up to, how they were feeling. I became aware that a positive comment to a child might be the only positive thing that had happened to them all week.
>
> It paid off, especially with Mary. Her manners improved and I praised her for it. She started being helpful and was one of the first to get our pupil of the week award. She began to take part regularly in PE, whereas before she would have 'forgotten' her clothes. She was still not the most popular girl in class, but she communicated. More importantly, she was no longer a catalyst for disruption.

Mr Trainor says he has never been the kind of teacher to read up on behaviour management but admits that the whole-school focus on the issue has changed his entire philosophy.

> Children are coming to school not knowing how to behave and you have to teach them, just as you need to teach them how to read and write. Whereas before we would have dealt with poor behaviour by sending a child to a senior teacher, or shouting, now we work on it creatively, through drama and music, through empathy and an emphasis on collaboration.
>
> I look closely at how children learn; not how I teach. That's where I'm starting from.

Chapter 31

Common sense has much to learn from moonshine

Philip Pullman

Philip Pullman is able to write about learning to read and write from the perspective both of a former middle school teacher and of a highly respected author. Rather than teaching children about grammar rules, he argues that the main concern of schools should be with the picture books, stories, poems and songs which are the full realisation of the powers of language. The confidence children need to become readers and writers comes from playing, speculating, and 'fooling about' rather than 'drilling and testing . . . and correcting'.

The report published this week by the University of York on its research into the teaching of grammar will hardly surprise anyone who has thought about the subject. The question being examined was whether instruction in grammar had any effect on pupils' writing. It included the largest systematic review yet of research on this topic; and the conclusion the authors came to was that there was no evidence at all that the teaching of grammar had any beneficial effect on the quality of writing done by pupils.

Needless to say, this goes against common sense. That particular quality of mind, the exclusive property of those on the political right, enables its possessors to know without the trouble of thinking that of course teaching children about syntax and the parts of speech will result in better writing, as well as making them politer, more patriotic and less likely to become pregnant.

For once, however, common sense seems to have been routed by the facts. If we want children to write well, giving them formal instruction in grammar turns out not to be any use; getting them actually writing seems to help a great deal more. Teaching techniques that do work well, the study discovered, are those that include combining short sentences into longer ones, and embedding elements into simple sentences to make them more complex: in other words, using the language to say something.

A word often flourished in this context by the common sense brigade is 'basics'. It's always seemed curious to me that commentators and journalists – people who write every day and who presumably know something about the practice of putting words on paper – should make such an elementary error as to think that spelling and punctuation and other such surface elements of language are 'the basics'. These, and deeper features of language such as grammar, are things you can correct at proof stage, at the very last minute, and we all do that very thing, every day. But how can something you can alter or correct at that late point possibly be basic? What's truly basic is something that has to be in place much earlier on: an attitude to the language, to work, to the world itself.

And there are many possible attitudes to take up. There are some that are confident and generous and fruitful, and others that are marked by fear and suspicion and hostility. We instil these attitudes in children by the way we talk to them, or the fact that we don't, and by means of the activities we give them to do, and the environments we create to surround them, and the games and TV programmes and stories we provide them with. The most valuable attitude we can help children adopt – the one that, among other things, helps them to write and read with most fluency and effectiveness and enjoyment – I can best characterise by the word playful.

It begins with nursery rhymes and nonsense poems, with clapping games and finger play and simple songs and picture books. It goes on to consist of fooling about with the stuff the world is made of: with sounds, and with shapes and colours, and with clay and paper and wood and metal, and with language. Fooling about, playing with it, pushing it this way and that, turning it sideways, painting it different colours, looking at it from the back, putting one thing on top of another, asking silly questions, mixing things up, making absurd comparisons, discovering unexpected similarities, making pretty patterns, and all the time saying 'Supposing . . . I wonder . . . What if . . .'

The confidence to do this, the happy and open curiosity about the world that results from it, can develop only in an atmosphere free from the drilling and testing and examining and correcting and measuring and ranking in tables that characterises so much of the government's approach, the 'common sense' attitude to education.

And the crazy thing is that the common sense brigade think that they're the practical ones, and that approaches like the one I'm advocating here are sentimental moonshine. They could hardly be more wrong. It's when we do this foolish, time-consuming, romantic, quixotic, childlike thing called play that we are most practical, most useful, and most firmly grounded in reality, because the world itself is the most unlikely of places, and it works in the oddest of ways, and we won't make any sense of it by doing what everybody else has done before us. It's when we fool about with the stuff the world is made of that we make the most valuable discoveries, we create the most lasting beauty, we discover the most profound truths. The youngest children can do it, and the greatest artists, the greatest scientists do it all the time. Everything else is proofreading.

Take the National Curriculum. The authors of the York study remind us that it lays down that children aged five to seven 'should be taught to consider: a) how word choice and order are crucial to meaning, b) the nature and use of nouns, verbs and pronouns' and so on; that children aged seven to eleven 'should be taught word classes and the grammatical functions of words, including nouns, adjectives, adverbs, pronouns, prepositions, conjunctions, articles', as well as 'the grammar of complex sentences, including clauses, phrases and connectives . . .' Think of the age of those children, and weep. It simply doesn't work.

What does work, the York study maintains, is writing in a meaningful context: writing as a practical hands-on craft activity. One of the implications of this is that teachers have to be confident about writing – about play, about delight. Too many are not, because they haven't had to be; and the result is the dismal misery of the 'creative writing' drills tested in the SATS, where children are instructed to plan, draft, edit, revise, rewrite, always in the same order, always in the same proportions, always in the same way. If teachers knew something about the joy of fooling about with words, their pupils would write with much greater fluency and effectiveness. Teachers and pupils alike would see that the only reason for writing is to produce something true and beautiful; that they were on the same side, with the teacher as mentor, as editor, not as instructor and measurer, critic and judge.

And they'd see when they looked at a piece of work together that some passages were so good already that they didn't need rewriting, that some parts needed clarifying, others needed to be cut down, others would be more effective in a different order, and so on. They'd see the point of the proofreading, at last; and they'd be ready, because they were interested, to know about subordinate clauses and conjunctions and the rest. The study of grammar is intensely fascinating: but only when we're ready for it.

True education flowers at the point when delight falls in love with responsibility. If you love something, you want to look after it. Common sense has much to learn from moonshine.

Chapter 32

Beyond the tests: literacy in successful schools

Thelma Hall with Ian Eyres

Thelma Hall has many years experience as a primary headteacher and has supported many students in initial teacher education and on the Open University's Specialist Teacher Assistant course in schools across the north of England. In this chapter she writes about a number of schools which were determined to preserve what they valued in their approach to teaching literacy, despite the pressures to conform to a rigid national strategy. The first part of the chapter is a useful introduction to the National Literacy Strategy for readers who may not be familiar with it.

The National Literacy Strategy

The National Literacy Strategy set a challenge to primary phase schools in England to raise the achievement in English of all children by the age of 11. The Framework set out the structure of what 'should' be taught from Reception to Year 6 while the Literacy Hour laid down the means by which the strands of the Framework (DfEE 1998) were to be taught. It was intended that a dedicated hour of literacy teaching should be undertaken in all primary schools in England in every age group in Key Stages 1 and 2.

The Government committed over £50 million of funding in the Strategy's first year to ensure that training, support and resources were available to schools and LEAs. A Literacy Task Force provided support for every school, with the aim of ensuring consistency of teaching across the country.

The Framework is explicit and very specific in both content and teaching methods, providing a structure that was built upon a year-by-year format setting out clear expectations for each year group. It gives teachers and teaching assistants a detailed structure of the skills identified as essential to the literate 11-year-old. The training aimed to ensure that all concerned understood basic grammatical terminology regardless of their subject specialism. Many previously exotic terms – morpheme, grapheme, phoneme – became everyday words in the staffroom and this common language empowered many staff, particularly teaching assistants, to participate in discussions and planning for the first time.

The strategy required that literacy be taught for an hour each day and that two thirds of that time should be given to direct teaching involving the whole class, with the remaining time mostly given to group work. Many saw this structure as a straitjacket, and regretted the loss of individual teaching, which the training tended to dismiss as inefficient in terms of the teacher's time. The Framework was seen as a 'practical tool' to help teachers to meet the target of 80 per cent of all 11-year-olds achieving the expected standard (Level 4) for reading and writing. Despite substantial early progress towards this target, to date the target has not been met, and serious shortfalls remain, particularly in the areas of writing, and the overall performance of boys.

Although the strategy had no legal status, the majority of schools and LEAs saw it as a requirement, an impression firmly reinforced by an aggressive inspection regime. The result has been enormous changes in the teaching of English as schools adjusted their curriculum planning to accommodate the Literacy Hour.

Throwing the baby out with the bathwater?

In presenting a particular view of how literacy should be taught, the Strategy chose to exclude many long-established elements of practice. Reading, and particularly writing, had often been taught through work in other curriculum subjects, ensuring that the work had relevance and interest. Many classes had daily 'silent reading' sessions, when the class teacher or a teaching assistant would listen to the children read individually. The child's achievement would be recorded during each session and a home–school diary would support the valuable partnership between parents and school staff. (By contrast, the only reference in the Framework concerning home involvement is that 'Parents may be interested to read the Framework.') Efforts would be made to ensure that children who did not have the support of home were listened to more regularly. Many schools enlisted the voluntary help of parents to help with this enormous task and to be involved in other activities in the classroom. Most school days would end with story-time, which was seen as an essential part of developing children's understanding of the structures of written language while extending their vocabulary and their imaginations and showing that reading is a great source of enjoyment.

Many schools were reluctant to abandon what they saw as successful practice and parents were often very vocal if children were no longer given time to read to an adult in school. Many of those which adopted the strategy devised means of continuing the important element of parental involvement to ensure that a home–school dialogue was maintained. This meant taking time, outside the Literacy Hour, which would otherwise have been given to other subjects.

Alternative approaches

Some schools, confident in the success of their established approach, continued to follow the route they had already found successful. These brave schools had to demonstrate this success to both their local authority and to the national inspectorate (OfSTED) and particularly show success in end of Key Stage assessments. That the schools were able to do this shows that there are other ways of tackling the teaching of reading and writing effectively.

The loss of opportunities for extended writing caused a great deal of concern for many teachers. Schools willing to countenance alternative approaches looked for ways to allow time for children to write by adjusting the structure of the hour or by abandoning it for the purposes of writing. For example, Cullercoats Primary School in North Tyneside sets aside one session of literacy time per week to give children the opportunity to write at length. St Joseph's Primary School, in Loftus, Cleveland, allocated time across the school day for written work to be completed. Badger Hill Primary School in Cleveland planned blocks of two, three and four weeks to develop writing linked to a topic. In this school, I saw a group of Year 6 children working on a piece of writing linked to a visit to the theatre. The results were all very different but what united them was the amazing range of vocabulary and the complex structure of English used. Boys at this school regularly achieve scores above the national average in end of Key Stage assessments. Badger Hill has never adopted the Literacy Hour or the National Literacy Strategy.

Some schools were concerned at the way the Strategy focused on literacy as a set of skills independent of context. At Cullercoats School, I saw a class of Year 2 children writing instructions for making vegetable soup. They had bought the ingredients, prepared them, chopped them and put them in the pan. Photographs of every stage of their work were on display as they discussed the activities that had led to the exciting point of tasting the soup. The children were determined that instructions that were to be given to other classes should be detailed, ordered and exact. The teacher had finely planned the skills to ensure National Literacy Strategy targets were met but she had added two ingredients – time and the motivation that comes from enjoyment and a real purpose. Many teachers have expressed concern at the loss, within the structure of the National Literacy Strategy, of time for extended writing that was a feature of children's work in the past. More recently, OfSTED (2003) in its report on schools where boys achieve well as writers, has acknowledged that writing tasks need to be 'purposeful, through seeking "real" audiences'. In this class, the teacher, Miss Stewart adjusted the Literacy Hour to meet the needs of the children and the context of the activity. This is what good teachers do: they are happy to introduce new ideas, but retain a flexibility that allows them to respond to observed need.

The NLS framework acknowledges the value of writing to support other curriculum subjects, but its insistence that learning objectives should be for literacy rather than the subject did limit schools' scope to follow this path. Where they felt able to, the experience was richly rewarding. I saw work from a school set near Hadrian's Wall which used a visit to develop letter writing after the children marched to a mile castle on a cold and windy day. Adverbs and adjectives were enthusiastically found to illustrate the real feelings they had experienced as they honed their writing in preparation for the letters to be sent home. These points of grammar were contextualised not simply in an isolated extract from a text, but in real meaningful activity. Many of the grammatical skills defined in the Framework were incorporated as a natural part of the work into the topic 'Romans' and motivation was enhanced by the fact that these were real letters to be sent to real people. The children marched as Romans over the unwelcoming and exposed land. In the bitter chill they could imagine the feelings of those strangers isolated in a strange and hostile land. Six years after the publication of the Framework, the Primary National Strategy (which has succeeded both the Literacy and Numeracy Strategies, while leaving the Frameworks in place) advocates just such cross-curricular development of literacy 'where children are engaged by learning that develops and stretches them and excites their imagination' (DfES 2003).

Teachers and teaching assistants can influence a child's progress profoundly by fostering a sense of success. It seems to me that almost any well-structured programme will achieve its short-term aims if the responsible adults are sufficiently knowledgeable and confident that they will do so. Our enthusiasm and belief in a chosen approach and confidence in children's ability will help motivate them to meet our expectations. These are very potent elements in the learning process. However, progress in literacy can be presented to children either as an abstract game, with success counted in the number of correctly placed full stops and adverbs (to be rewarded with stickers), or as an increasing ability to use literacy to meet the learner's purposes and needs, an intrinsic reward often accompanied by satisfaction and enjoyment. I would argue that the latter route, where children are fully engaged with their reading and writing, is much more likely to motivate them. I believe that motivation is the key to learning across the curriculum: all the schools I know that demonstrate high levels of achievement share a belief in the importance of motivation.

Literacy with a purpose

Mrs M. Roberts, Literacy Co-ordinator in St Joseph's, explained how their topics were carefully planned to excite and interest the children. Time is invested at the start of each topic to devise a special event, which starts the work in an atmosphere of excitement. The topic of the Tudors started with the headteacher, Mr M. Atkinson, dressed as Henry VIII and the staff as his wives and courtiers. The children were the commoners invited to the beheading of Ann Boleyn. You can imagine the excited buzz of discussion that followed. The historical information was eagerly researched and both factual and imaginative writing of high quality was produced following this highly emotive introduction. While topics are not chosen specifically with boys in mind, planning always ensures that their interests are catered for. Mrs Roberts commented, 'One of our most successful themes was "Space". It interested both boys and girls, but there is no doubt that the high level of motivation was reflected in the boys' written work.' With the current interest in Harry Potter, The Lord of the Rings and Star Wars she is hoping this term's project on fantasy will again provide a high motivation for learning. She sees this as the critical feature of the inspirational approach. I would agree, but underpinning this is detailed planning of the skills needed to be developed by the children. Planning of all these aspects was shared by all the staff but led by Mrs Roberts, who shared her expertise with all the other staff involved.

Mr Atkinson and Mrs Roberts talked of the pressure children experienced because of national testing. Mr Atkinson emphasised his strong belief in empowering the children to achieve to the best of their ability and pupils at the school now learn to mark their own work according to the standards of each National Curriculum level and then set their own targets. Shirley Clarke gives many examples of marking strategies and prompts in her book Enriching Feedback in the Primary School (Clarke 2003). She says that 'formative assessment is a powerful vehicle for focusing on effective learning' and that 'feedback is the central theme of formative assessment'. She explains how 'shared learning intentions' and 'shared success criteria' are essential elements in marking children's work. Mrs Roberts developed this approach further by 'translating' the marking criteria used in national tests into language children readily understand. From Year 1 the children are gradually trained, with help and support from teachers and teaching assistants, to understand the criteria and develop these skills using their own writing rather than excerpts from other people's work. I observed this in action with Year 6 children working in pairs or supported in groups. The children identified adjectives, adverbs, capitals, phrases, etc. They then gave themselves a grade, thus seeing in real terms what they needed to improve to achieve the targets. This is empowerment in action.

Whether schools follow the Strategy or not, there is no doubt that the ethos of the school with regard to achievement is a critical factor. Mr Atkinson developed his school curriculum secure in the belief that every child can learn and achieve. He sees the goal of education to be helping each child to grow and be enriched through what he or she learns. St Joseph's School Development Plan is inspired by words of Cardinal Hume.

> The pursuit and possession of truth for its own sake are values of inestimable importance. Not all study has to be at the service of some utilitarian purpose, as I have already indicated. Simply to know and to rejoice in knowing is sufficient justification for study. The individual grows and is enriched by what he or she knows. In this way we grow as human beings and achieve maturity. Appreciation of what is good and beautiful, an insatiable thirst for knowledge, a fearless embracing of the truth whatever its consequences, these surely are the characteristics of an educated person. We should also seek to develop an attitude which would understand – for example – that the most beautiful creation of the artist is the artist himself.
>
> (Hume 1990)

Mr Atkinson has been healthily sceptical about the various initiatives, including the National Curriculum, that have come from the education department over the last 20 years. The heavy emphasis on progress and standards, with outputs measured by tests and delivered in league tables, does not sit well with Hume's 'simply to know and rejoice in knowing'. However, he described to me how he too had to learn and adjust his strongly held views to meet the changing demands on today's children. He has changed the organisation of the school to ensure that the national test results reflect the school's successful teaching methods. However, he also insists that the most important outcome is the confidence and positive attitude to learning enjoyed by children throughout their primary schooling and as they move on into High School and into adult life. Mr Atkinson. has followed the progress of his children into the secondary sector and has seen continued success in Key Stage 3 tests and at GCSE. He feels sure that this is a result of the school's child-centred approach to education linked to the principles of 'inspiration and empowerment'.

The introduction of the National Literacy Strategy represented a revolution in English schools. The training undergone in every school gave a high level of technical understanding to all classroom practitioners, not just English co-ordinators and other specialists, and this gave a firm foundation to planning and practice. However, the early emphasis on points of grammar and apparent disregard for context, purpose and enjoyment did little to motivate children and must have contributed to the Strategy's relative lack of success in certain areas, such as boys' writing. Recent developments of national policy towards a more holistic and meaningful approach to learning to read and write owe much to those schools which were prepared, often in the face of official hostility, to stick to their principles and demonstrate practice which could deliver both high standards and continuing enjoyment and motivation.

References

Clarke, S. (2003) *Enriching Feedback in the Primary Classroom*. London: Hodder & Stoughton.

DfEE (1998) *The National Literacy Strategy: A Framework for Teaching*. London: DfEE.

DfES (2003) *Excellence and Enjoyment – A Strategy for Primary Schools*. London: DfES.

Hume, B. (1990) 'Building Bridges' (Speech to the 1990 North of England Education Conference).

OfSTED (2003) *Yes he can – Schools where boys write well*. London: OfSTED.

Chapter 33

Co-ordinating support for learning

Liz Gerschel

The responsibility for co-ordinating the work of additional adults involved in supporting children's learning varies from school to school. Sometimes this role is carried out by a deputy headteacher, a phase co-ordinator or a senior teaching assistant. In this chapter Liz Gerschel explores some of the ways in which Special Educational Needs Co-ordinators (SENCos) in the London Borough of Greenwich are carrying out this role.

Introduction

The role of classroom support staff has changed dramatically. In 2000, the Department for Education and Skills introduced the generic name 'teaching assistant' to capture:

> the essential 'active ingredient' of their work ... the contribution well-trained and well-managed teaching assistants can make to the teaching and learning process and to pupil achievement.
>
> (DfES 2000: 4)

Since 1998, primary and secondary schools have employed more than 35,000 additional full-time equivalent teaching assistants (TAs), mostly engaged in working with pupils who underachieve or have defined special educational needs, with or without statements. Balshaw (1999) describes significant changes in schools' expectations of the skills and activities of TAs, and in TAs' expectations regarding both the professional roles that they will undertake and their training and support. National Occupational Standards have now been developed and a range of professional qualifications for support staff has emerged, from NVQs to foundation degrees (LSC 2004). Since 2000, DfES induction courses for primary and secondary TAs have explored: roles and responsibilities; curriculum and management; inclusion, special educational needs and disabilities; and effective behaviour management. The DfES (2000) defines the TA role as fourfold – supporting pupils, teachers, the school and the curriculum – and acknowledges the need for the school to support the TA. The introduction of performance management throughout schools, gradually including teaching assistants, has further clarified responsibilities, expectations and entitlements.

The SENCO's role

The increased number of TAs, and changes in expectations, have had significant implications for TA management within local education authorities (LEAs) and schools, particularly for SENCos. The management of TAs in schools is often complex and ill-defined. For example, within the classroom, TAs are managed directly by the subject or class teacher. In primary schools, TAs may be managed by the head, deputy or SENCo, who usually directs TAs with specific responsibility for working with children with statements of SEN. In secondary schools, TAs are often employed to support individual students with SEN and managed by the SENCo or head of learning support but, if deployed within specific departments, may be managed by department or faculty heads. This scenario may be further complicated by the management of TAs with English as an Additional Language (EAL) responsibilities by Ethnic Minority Achievement teachers. Lack of coherence or communication across these management posts can result in confusion. Essential to effective management of TAs are:

- a viable organisational structure within the school, with clearly defined roles and responsibilities for TAs, their managers, including the SENCo, and the teaching staff with whom they work, and
- active support, training and direction for schools from the LEA.

The SENCo has specific responsibilities related to the management of TAs delineated in the SEN *Code of Practice* (DfES 2001):

- to manage the team of SEN support staff in the school, implying a leadership role
- to manage the day-to-day organisation of resources for SEN, which includes the deployment of TAs, may have budget implications, and will certainly imply the use of criteria, whether explicit or undefined, for allocating TAs' duties
- to liaise with and advise teachers and TAs on meeting the needs of pupils with SEN
- to take responsibility for induction and training.

The recruitment and appointment of TAs

Greenwich LEA retains a crucial role in staff training, review and monitoring of provision for pupils with SEN. Through local management of schools (LMS) many responsibilities have transferred from LEAs to schools. Nevertheless, other factors have created opportunities for creative thinking within LEAs, in relation to TAs, including:

- the introduction of a career structure, including higher level TA posts
- changes brought about by national workforce remodelling
- the implications of the Government's vision for an exchange of expertise between special schools and the mainstream (DfES 2004c).

Following the devolution of central funds to schools, Greenwich no longer maintains a central pool of approved TAs from which schools can recruit, and has consequently lost the flexibility to move them into schools when required, for long- or short-term support.

Most schools now advertise locally, interview and appoint, without recourse to the LEA. Schools have little difficulty in recruiting but are not always sure how best to do this.

Doreen Cunningham, a secondary SENCo, intends to introduce a more telling interview process, akin to that used to appoint teaching staff, wherein she observes the candidates in a classroom with students who clearly need help to access the lesson. Although this will have to be very carefully managed, she believes it will give a much clearer picture of aptitude than a short interview.

Hazel Burnie, a primary SENCo, insists that job descriptions move away from the language of 'encourage ... assist ... and build a supportive relationship', focusing instead on developing the child's level of independence and sense of empowerment:

> ... a subtle shift in language, an emphasis on the learning needs of children with SEN, and explicit instructions for supporting the child as part of a group within the classroom context rather than in isolation, thus giving opportunities for developing social skills and levels of independence.

Deployment of TAs within the school

TA deployment presents a dilemma for schools: whether to allocate them to individual students, to classes/year groups or within departments/faculties. Some TAs are still employed to fulfil the specifications on statements of special educational needs for x number of hours of additional or individual support.

Among the dangers of the TA being 'attached' to a single student – the 'Velcro' model – is the potential for a dependency culture: the pupil becomes emotionally dependent on the TA, is less likely to make relationships with peers or be fully included in the class. Conversely, the TA may present a physical barrier between the child and teacher, or other children, be possessive of the pupil ('I'm Jack's helper') but also be economically dependent on the child's presence. Many TAs still endure short-term contracts which afford no job (nor income) security: if the child leaves, the TA may no longer be employed.

Some schools take an innovative approach to the deployment of TAs. Hazel has changed the 'cradle to grave' type of support, where a child is attached to a particular TA on entry to the school or when a statement is granted, and stays with that same TA until he or she leaves. Convincing senior management of the educational benefits of change was relatively easy: persuading the TAs was more difficult. Hazel describes how:

> Through weekly INSET sessions I reiterated the importance of keeping in mind a 'lifetime perspective' of children's needs, and being aware of our role in preparing children to take their place in adult society with the tools to cope with any obstacles they might face. I linked this to concepts of active participation in learning, empowerment, and the need for independence wherever possible, no matter what the area under discussion.

Clarification of roles and responsibilities of TAs and of their managers

Hazel was concerned that TA support was 'often very stifling, encouraging the children to be very dependent and also quite passive in their approaches to learning', contrary to the school's Inclusion policy. To 'close the rhetoric–reality gap' she used her direct contact with management to effect changes in policies and practices throughout the school. Essential to effective deployment of TAs is clarification of roles and responsibilities: all staff need to understand what the TA is there for and the TA needs to understand where he or she fits into the culture of the school. Managers, teachers and TAs have to know:

- what planning, recording, feedback, meetings, information sharing, liaison with parents and other professionals, training opportunities and performance management will be in place
- how, when and by whom these will be undertaken
- what to expect from each other in the classroom and in support.

Team meetings help to clarify roles and responsibilities. As SENCo and TA team line manager, Hazel meets them once a week for about 30 minutes, in order to:

- keep support staff informed of current events in the school
- come together in a mutually supportive environment and air any concerns
- give Hazel a chance to deliver some relatively low-key in-service training – increased levels of knowledge and understanding about children with SEN being key to changing everyday practices
- enable the TA team to develop a sense of itself and its own value.

The meetings enable TAs to feel more open about discussing practical work in the classroom, and have increased knowledge, self-assessment and reflection amongst individuals.

Building a collaborative team within the school: teachers and TAs working together

In a few schools, extremely effective staff training sessions have established the ground rules for teachers and TAs working together, and produced clear statements of the expectations they have of each other. Schools need to develop such collaboration policies. Fox (2003) includes a useful questionnaire on professional relationships as a starting point and Balshaw (1999) proffers training ideas for working towards collaboration policies. In Greenwich, joint training sessions for SENCos and TAs have enabled teams to develop such policies but take-up is still low, perhaps because SENCos don't recognise how much these would support their work.

In our experience, TAs frequently complain of being expected to modify and interpret teaching in the lesson, often without prior notice of what will be taught. TAs should support the child's learning but need to be guided, led and managed by a qualified teacher.

At the least, TAs need plans in advance and a clear structure to their classroom work. Ideally, they will discuss plans with the teacher, in the light of their shared experience of the child's needs. Unfortunately, not all teachers plan with their TAs and not all TAs feel confident enough to approach teachers and ask for lesson plans. Some teachers rely on getting a chance to discuss the next lesson over coffee or at lunch-time, for which not all TAs are paid. This is too casual and is an identified area for SENCos to seek improvement: allocated time for planning is necessary. 'At all key stages, the most influential factor in the effectiveness of in-class support is the quality of joint planning of the work between class/subject teacher and the support teacher or . . . assistant' (OfSTED 1996: 5).

[. . .]

Induction and training of TAs and SENCos

Both LEA and school are responsible for induction, training and professional development of TAs and SENCos. Greenwich LEA:

- trains SENCos in carrying out their management roles
- offers joint training to TAs and SENCos in working collaboratively
- provides DfES TA-induction training
- offers a wide variety of long and short courses, some accredited, for TAs, teachers and SENCos, on specific special educational needs
- provides outreach training from expertise within special schools and units
- facilitates customised whole-school training for staff on collaboration policies and other aspects of TA management and deployment
- hosts a SENCo forum and a TA forum.

School-based induction and training are essential. In weekly TA team meetings, Hazel uses various approaches: 'talk and chalk' type sessions, group discussions and individual tasks. She may focus on a particular syndrome or difficulty, or deal with areas relevant to many children such as self-esteem, anger management or dealing with loss.

Monitoring of the work of TAs and performance management

Only relatively recently have schools begun themselves to tackle monitoring and self-evaluation with regard to TAs. Performance management, statutory in policy and practice for headteachers and teaching staff since 2001, has not yet been 'rolled out' in many schools to include TAs. Continuing professional development is an entitlement for all staff and TAs should benefit from supportive appraisal, not least because of the opportunities for training and career progression that it affords. As managers of TAs, SENCos can follow the TA self-review and structured appraisal meeting (DfES 2004a, 2004b) and the indicators for whole-school self-evaluation in monitoring TA work (DfES, 2000). OfSTED expects schools to monitor how TAs contribute to the quality of teaching and learning, and their cost effectiveness. SENCos will need to develop understandings among senior and middle managers of what good support practice looks like, so that lesson observations and monitoring schedules include evaluations of TA work and SEN provision.

So where now for SENCOs?

This is a transition period for TAs, SENCos, schools and LEAs. Expectations of TA roles and responsibilities are developing towards a concept of meeting needs, which is less about the individual exclusively, and more about personalised independent learning within a group. The focus is directed towards the learning needs of children rather than the coping needs of teachers. Some schools are developing innovative support structures and collaborative teams to realise inclusion, through policies and practices that empower adults and children alike. Staff have discovered that some ways of working result in better professional relationships between adults and greater success for pupils, academically, physically, emotionally and socially. TAs expect to be better informed, prepared, trained and supported – and with better pay and career prospects. Teachers are gaining support for planning, teaching, assessment and review, of a quality they have not always previously enjoyed.

The SENCo is central to this change process but, to be effective in managing the TA team, must have a strong voice in senior management and decision-making. Policies, practices and school systems need to be harmonised, to turn intentions into reality. Practice needs reinforcement from clear collaboration policies, appropriate funding and allocation of time to all staff involved, including the SENCo. Functions that could be included within the management remit of the SENCo are:

- leading the development of collaboration policies clarifying explicit roles and responsibilities of teachers, TAs and managers
- devising better TA recruitment strategies
- developing the skills of teachers in working with TAs: planning, leading and guiding
- introducing innovative methods of TA deployment which match skills and needs and make best use of resources
- leading TA teams through regular and useful meetings
- organising the induction and continuing professional development of TAs, including supportive performance management
- developing effective communication systems within TA teams and between teachers and TAs
- developing senior and middle management skills in recognising good SEN support
- developing monitoring and accountability systems for SEN
- monitoring the progress of individual students, including evaluation of TA teaching strategies and grouping arrangements
- developing TA skills to share with other schools, working closely with the LEA.

References

Balshaw, M. (1999) *Help in the Classroom,* 2nd edn. London: David Fulton.

DfES (2000) *Working with Teaching Assistants: A Good Practice Guide.* DfES 0148/2000. London: DfES.

DfES (2001) *Special Educational Needs Code of Practice.* Nottingham: DfES.

DfES (2004a) *Teaching Assistant File: Induction Training for Teaching Assistants.* DfES 0585/2004 (Primary). London: DfES.

DfES (2004b) *Teaching Assistant File: Induction Training for Teaching Assistants.* DfES 0586/2004 (Secondary). London: DfES.

DfES (2004c) *Removing Barriers to Achievement – The Government's Strategy for SEN.* DfES/0117/2004. London: DfES.

Fox, G. (2003) *A Handbook for Learning Support Assistants: Teachers and Assistants Working Together,* revised edn. London: David Fulton.

LSC (2004) *LSC School Support Staff Sector Plan for 2004–5 and Beyond.* London: Learning and Skills Council.

OfSTED (1996) *Promoting High Achievement for Pupils with Special Educational Needs in Mainstream Schools.* London: HMSO.

Chapter 34

Learning through the enriched curriculum

Dympna Meikleham with Roger Hancock

Dympna Meikleham is a learning assistant at Harberton Special School, South Belfast, and Roger Hancock is a lecturer at The Open University. In the account that follows they review the reasons behind the introduction of the 'Enriched Curriculum' in a group of schools in the Belfast area. They explain the main elements of this curriculum, describe the way in which it is being implemented at Harberton School, and discuss the impact upon children and school staff.

The need for the enriched curriculum

The enriched curriculum is a 'play-based' or 'doing-based' curriculum. It arose out of the activities and collaborations between a number of Belfast primary and special schools, the Northern Ireland Council for Curriculum Assessment and Examinations, and members of the Belfast Education and Library Board.

The traditional curriculum is very similar to the English National Curriculum, which expects children to learn through formal teaching quite early in their school careers. A different curriculum, based on a different pedagogy, was seen to be essential given the difficulties that many Key Stage 1 children were experiencing with the formal curriculum, especially rising five-year-old children in Primary 1 classes. An additional consideration is that many children in Northern Ireland start school a little earlier than their English counterparts and had been expected to start formal learning within the first term.

These difficulties have been further compounded by the fact that over the last 30 years there have been considerable social upheavals in the Belfast area. This has impacted upon families, on parenting, and sometimes adversely affected children's everyday learning opportunities. A significant number of children seem to be missing out on a lot of essential early learning experiences which traditionally help prepare them for school learning. The inner-city areas of Belfast lack suitable play facilities and some children live in high flats. Even riding a bicycle can be difficult for some, but this is clearly important for children's motor development and physical confidence. Free-play experiences are essential if children are to acquire the oral language, social abilities and motor skills that enable formal school learning to be of interest to them.

Finally, thinking was influenced by what happens in a number of other European countries (see Walsh 2000; Mills and Mills 1997). In France, Italy, Spain and Greece, for instance, it is not until children are six that formal learning begins.

The pilot of the enriched curriculum began with a group of six schools (nine classes in all) in the Greater Shankill area of Belfast (see Sproule *et al.* 2002). Currently, 84 schools are taking part. Basically, this curriculum involves the creation of play-based classrooms and holding back on formal teaching of writing, reading and number work. These areas of learning, and the Primary 1 curriculum more generally, are introduced, but this is done through free play and structured play. One of the pilot schools was Harberton Special School, a school for children experiencing mild to moderate learning difficulties, which is located in south-west Belfast.

Organisation at Harberton

As with all primary schools in the Belfast area, new children come to Primary 1 in Harberton in September when they are just under five. Hands-on experience and play are now features of everything that is done. In various ways, play can enter all activities that are planned for the children. There is also an emphasis on physical development. The day is split into sessions so that each indoor period is followed by 10–15 minutes of outside play – sometimes this could be just running-about free play. Some project schools have things like beams and tunnels, balls and hockey sticks for outside play. At Harberton there are a lot of bikes, tunnels, bouncing hoppers, and a focus on sand, water, and paint-brushes to paint the windows, for instance. At the moment, there is no covered area but every child is supplied with a set of wellington boots and a raincoat. Everyone can therefore still go outside unless the rain is very heavy.

Currently, the enriched curriculum goes through to Primary 2, and will eventually move through to the end of Key Stage 1. It is possible that the Foundation Stage could encompass the enriched curriculum or it could become a part of the thinking within the Foundation Stage.

Last year, the children still had to do their end-of-Key-Stage assessments but staff were not teaching to these tests so it is difficult to compare how they were performing prior to and since the introduction of the enriched curriculum. Harberton's vice-principal emphasises that Key Stage assessments are knowledge-based tests but the enriched curriculum is a skills-based method of teaching which gives prominence to the processes of learning. So, some areas in the Key Stage assessment, like verbal reasoning, have probably gone up but 'taught knowledge' may have gone down.

At Harberton, children aren't discouraged from reading and writing if they want to do this. This happens with some children in Primary 1 but more so in Primary 2. However, even though some aspects of formal learning will be introduced there is still an overall ethos of learning through doing and through real experiences. Because Harberton is a special school there might be children who struggle with formal learning throughout their school careers. What the enriched curriculum has done for many children is to reduce the feeling of failure or of having learning difficulties.

To implement the enriched curriculum, some staff have had to be retrained. In Primary 1 at Harberton there was not a huge difference from what staff were doing before, however in some surrounding mainstream primary schools there may have been a considerable difference. In fact, at Harberton, what the enriched curriculum did was to confirm that what was already happening was relevant and important. Before this, staff were feeling under some pressure to introduce the formal teaching of reading and writing, which went against the grain of professional experience and intuition.

Meeting physical needs

As already explained, in the course of a day at Harberton there are the usual two playtimes – at break and lunch – but there is now an additional 15 minutes of outside play. So, approximately every hour and a half children are physically active outside. However, physical needs are also a consideration when children are inside. There might, for instance, be a half an hour of literacy or numeracy followed by five minutes of movement where children can exercise their bodies. The latest inside activity is called 'wiggles and shakes'. This might come at the end of a numeracy session. In a way, this is something that everyone needs – adults as well as children – when they have been concentrating for a while. Physical development and intellectual development should work together and should be linked in meaningful and complementary ways. A break from work is important in order to be better at that work. Most adults find they can only concentrate on something for a certain length of time. Schools tend to assume that children can sit and work for quite long periods.

Staff involvement

Staff at Harberton feel they are sharing in the fun element of learning resulting from the introduction of the enriched curriculum. It has led to a greater involvement in children's play and a better understanding of what interests them. There is now a need to get down and do things alongside children in a more collaborative, co-playing way. Some staff were reluctant to engage in role play themselves but since the introduction of the enriched curriculum adults will often play in the house corner first! Some children can be unsure as to what to do when, for example, the corner is changed into a hospital or a veterinary surgery. So staff now act it out themselves, model it for children and then children feel they can do it. There is, therefore, increased enjoyment for staff in whatever they do with the children. The play dough, for instance, is now made with the children's help rather than being brought in ready made.

Relevance for Key Stage 2

One of things about the enriched curriculum is that it encourages children to do things for themselves – to become independent learners. This will benefit learning in Key Stage 2 because if a child has come through the enriched curriculum they are very able to choose a piece of equipment and work away on it independently. They are also not reluctant to say, 'Can you help me with this?' The enriched curriculum has taken away that element of failure, of being wrong, or not being able to do something. This exploratory confidence and curiosity should come through when children are learning in Key Stage 2.

Harberton is involved with the Literacy and Numeracy Strategies and these do require that children can work independently for some of the time. In Primary 1, children are encouraged, right from age four, to work autonomously and this has great benefits for the Strategies and the focus on independent learning. The higher staff–pupil ratio at the school enables literacy and numeracy lessons to be taught in small groups. The whole class session tends to be around ten minutes and then children will be split up into smaller groups – but there will always be a group that does not have an adult with them. There is a rotation system whereby one group will be with the learning assistant, one with the teacher and one group will be working on their own. This enables the literacy and numeracy lessons to be very alive and very active. Children are at Harberton because they are said to have learning difficulties, but they are, nevertheless, able to work with some independence.

Role of the learning assistant

The enriched curriculum has substantially changed the role of learning assistants in the classroom. They are no longer people who mainly set out the resources for the activities and tidy up afterwards. Since the arrival of the enriched curriculum, learning assistants are very involved in what is going on in the classroom in terms of directly contributing to children's learning. In special schools, assistants have long done more than just distribute resources and support organisation, so the change is, perhaps, more noticeable in a mainstream primary classroom. It is now acknowledged that the learning assistant in the classroom is part of the teaching team for the children.

Effect on staff

Staff feel they have had a pressure lifted off them. What is done now is done because the children are going to enjoy it and that means staff enjoy it too. So, when, for example, it is snowing, time will be found for everyone to go out and experience the snow. Last year, the children built snow people and the lids of the toy boxes were turned into toboggans. It was an important learning experience which took account of a wonderful resource.

A lot of the taught curriculum has, to some extent, become spontaneous just like play itself. However, there is planning for much of what goes on. The school uses a topic-based planning method so, for example, recently the topic was colour. Every week a different colour was selected. When it was orange the children made orange goo and painted their toenails and fingernails. They painted their feet and made orange footprints and went out and had an orange walk, which was a treasure hunt where orange things had been previously hidden or buried. The colour orange was also found around them in the environment. Numeracy activities involved a lot of sorting for orange and there was much language learning that arose from such activities.

Last summer term the topic was mini-beasts. This lent itself to a lot of science and geography, for example. The children were really into mini-beasts, looking under stones, digging up the grass, and every time they found some woodlice they would bring them to staff in their hands.

This was planned learning, but it was also fun. The staff feel convinced that if things are fun for children then they are going to get into it, enjoy it and benefit educationally from it.

Conclusion

The enriched curriculum emphasises that young children:

- learn best through play and 'play-like' structured activities
- need to have widely based oral language experiences and conceptual learning before formal reading and writing can be meaningfully introduced
- need to be involved in a great deal of outdoor and indoor physical activities, including the opportunity for physical play
- need to be immersed in creative activities in the areas of art, music, movement and related forms of play
- need opportunities whereby they can take responsibility for their own learning.

Sproule *et al.* (2002), in their evaluation of the second year of the Greater Shanklin Project involving the use of the enriched curriculum, highlight: the dramatic change in classroom practice that had come about; the measured gains in children's oral language skills; and the way the majority of parents were enthusiastic about the new curriculum. However, they point to the need for continued staff training and the need for greater cohesion of the way in which the new curriculum is being interpreted across the group of project schools.

At Harberton, this curriculum has given increased depth and meaning to the work of learning assistants and teachers. For example, there is no longer a need to feel anxious about time spent on developing feeding, toileting and dressing skills. Instead, children's success in these skills can now be celebrated by including them in reasons for awarding a child 'pupil of the week'. Indeed, these areas of achievement are now seen to be as important as any other area of a child's development.

The enriched curriculum has also had particular benefits for the self-esteem of children who may have difficulty writing or counting. They are now benefiting in other ways from the school experiences offered to them. For instance, their language skills are improving, as is their willingness to try a range of new things. Perhaps more importantly, children appear to greatly enjoy learning in a play way and their enthusiasm is both obvious and contagious. This in itself helps staff to become more involved in exploring and experimenting in terms of their role and practice. As a result, there is no doubt that learning assistants and teachers are enjoying their work much more.

Schools are under considerable pressure to find effective ways of raising educational standards as measured by standardised tests. A greater focus on formal teaching, even with very young children, has been a widespread consequence of this throughout the UK. This is based on the questionable belief that an increased amount of direct teaching, even to very young children, will lead to increased amounts of learning. Given the prevailing nature of this belief and the general support that it receives from government and inspection services, it could be said that it is very courageous for the Belfast Education and Library Boards to introduce the enriched curriculum with an emphasis on learning through play and on children and adults learning alongside each other.

References

Mills, C. and Mills, D. (1997) *Britain's Early Years Disaster*. Research paper. London: Mills Productions Ltd.

Sproule, L., Trew, K., Rafferty, H., Walsh, G., McGuinness, C., Sheehy, N. and O'Neill, B. (2002) *The Early Years Enriched Curriculum Evaluation Project:* Second Year Report. Report produced privately for Northern Ireland Council for Curriculum Examinations and Assessment (CCEA).

Walsh, G. (2000) 'The Play versus Formal Debate: A Study of Early Years Provision In Northern Ireland and Denmark'. Unpublished PhD thesis.

Index

Abbreviations used:
ICT: information and communication technology
TAs: teaching assistants